# NURSING QUALITY ASSURANCE

## Contributors

Mary A. Bruskewitz
Nancy Mansheim Formella
Regina M. Maibusch
Michele M. Malin
Robin Reading Mosleth
SueEllen Pinkerton
Patricia S. Schroeder
Margaret A. Skocir
Margaret A. Smerlinski
Peggy L. Wagner
Cathleen K. Wilson

T & A

# NURSING QUALITY ASSURANCE

## A Unit-Based Approach

Edited by
**Patricia S. Schroeder, M.S.N., R.N.**
**Regina M. Maibusch, S.S.S.F., M.S., R.N.**

St. Michael Hospital
Milwaukee, Wisconsin

AN ASPEN PUBLICATION®
Aspen Systems Corporation
Rockville, Maryland
Royal Tunbridge Wells
1984

Library of Congress Cataloging in Publication Data

Main entry under title:
Nursing quality assurance.

"An Aspen publication."
Includes bibliographies and index.
1. Nursing audit. 2. Nursing—Standards. I. Schroeder, Patricia S. II. Maibusch, Regina M.
RT85.5.N866 1984 610.73'0218 84-2784
ISBN: 0-89443-854-9

Publisher: John Marozsan
Associate Publisher: Jack W. Knowles, Jr.
Editorial Director: N. Darlene Como
Executive Managing Editor: Margot G. Raphael
Managing Editor: M. Eileen Higgins
Editorial Services: Martha Sasser
Printing and Manufacturing: Debbie Collins



Library of Congress Catalog Card Number: 84-2784
ISBN: 0-89443-854-9

*Printed in the United States of America*

1 2 3 4 5

# Table of Contents

**Foreword** ........ **ix**

**Preface** ........ **xi**

**Acknowledgments** ........ **xv**

**PART I—NURSING QUALITY ASSURANCE AND THE UNIT-BASED APPROACH** ........ **1**

**Chapter 1—Evolution of Quality Assurance for Nursing in Hospitals** ........ **3**
*Regina M. Maibusch, S.S.S.F., M.S., R.N.*

Evolution of Standards ........ 3
Evolution of Evaluation in the Nursing Process ........ 5
Evaluation Instruments ........ 6
Evolution of Practice Evaluation in Hospitals ........ 16
Conclusion ........ 18

**Chapter 2—The Unit-Based System** ........ **29**
*Nancy Mansheim Formella, M.S.N., R.N.*
*Patricia S. Schroeder, M.S.N., R.N.*

Unit-Based Quality Assurance Model ........ 29
Impetus for the Development of the Unit-Based Model ........ 38
Unit-Based System vs. Centralized System ........ 39
Concept of Quality and Quality Assurance ........ 41

Quality Assurance in Industry ........................ 43
Responsibility for Quality Assurance ................ 45
Conclusion ........................................ 46

**Chapter 3—A Systems Model for Implementation of Unit-Based Quality Assurance .................... 51**
*Peggy L. Wagner, M.S.N., R.N., CCRN*

The Decision to Change ............................ 52
Metamorphosis of the Quality Assurance System ....... 53
Implementation of the Developed System ............. 59
Effective Unit Quality Assurance Committees ......... 62
Obstacles to Success .............................. 65
Ideas That Did Not Work ........................... 67
Feedback Process .................................. 67
Conclusion ........................................ 68

**Chapter 4—Accountability for Quality Care: Perspectives of a Nurse-Administrator ........................ 71**
*Sue-Ellen Pinkerton, Ph.D., R.N.*

Process of Management ............................. 71
Quality Assurance and Management Functions ......... 72
Conclusion ........................................ 74

**PART II—METHODS FOR DATA COLLECTION .............. 77**

**Chapter 5—The Quality Assurance Process ..................... 79**
*Patricia S. Schroeder, M.S.N., R.N.*

First Quality Assurance Models .................... 79
Unit-Based Quality Assurance Model ................ 82
Conclusion ........................................ 92

**Chapter 6—Retrospective Chart Audits ........................ 95**
*Margaret A. Smerlinski, M.S., R.N.*

Definition of Method .............................. 95
Literature Review ................................. 95
Steps in Retrospective Chart Evaluation ............ 97
Clinical Examples ................................. 100

**Chapter 7—Concurrent Document Review** .................... **111**
*Michele M. Malin, M.S.N., R.N.*

Examples of Concurrent Document Review ............ 111
Advantages and Disadvantages ...................... 117

**Chapter 8—Interviewing: A Valuable Quality Assurance Strategy** .................... **121**
*Cathleen K. Wilson, M.S.N., R.N.*
*Regina M. Maibusch, S.S.S.F., M.S., R.N.*

Strengths and Weaknesses of Interviewing ............ 121
Types of Interviews ............ 124
Clinical Examples ............ 124

**Chapter 9—Using a Questionnaire** .................... **137**
*Peggy L. Wagner, M.S.N., R.N., CCRN*

Respondent Impact Questionnaires ............ 137
Nonrespondent Impact Questionnaires ............ 142
Choosing a Questionnaire as a Data Collection Tool ............ 146
Questionnaire Construction ............ 147
Distributing the Questionnaire ............ 152
Analyzing the Data ............ 152

**Chapter 10—Observation as an Evaluation Tool** .................... **157**
*Mary A. Bruskewitz, M.S., R.N.*

Strengths of the Observation Method ............ 157
Limitations of the Observation Method ............ 158
Role of the Observer ............ 159
Examples of Use of the Observation Method ............ 160
Conclusion ............ 167

**Chapter 11—Combining Techniques in Data Collection** .................... **171**
*Margaret A. Skocir, M.S.N., R.N.*

Techniques that May Be Combined ............ 171
Combining Methods ............ 175
Literature Review ............ 176

An Evaluation Study Using Combined Methods of Data Collection ..... 181
Appendix 11-A ..... 188

**Chapter 12—A Practical Guide to Multidisciplinary Auditing ..... 191**
*Robin Reading Mosleth, R.N., M.S.*

Definition ..... 191
Purpose ..... 192
Preliminary Steps ..... 193
Getting Started ..... 194
Writing Criteria ..... 195
Retrieving the Data ..... 198
Critiquing the Process ..... 199

**Chapter 13—Program Evaluation: Theory, Method, and Practice ..... 205**
*Cathleen K. Wilson, M.S.N., R.N.*

Definition of Evaluation ..... 205
Program Evaluation and Quality Assurance ..... 208
Methodology of Program Evaluation ..... 209
Evaluation of Quality Assurance Programs ..... 214
Conclusion ..... 218

**Chapter 14—Trends in Quality Assurance: A Vision for the Future ..... 221**
*Patricia S. Schroeder, M.S.N., R.N.*

Evolution of Standards and Criteria ..... 221
Increased Attention to Research Methodology ..... 222
Changes in Government and Accrediting Body Regulations ..... 224
Increased Need for and Availability of Computers ..... 224
The Evolving Role of the Nurse ..... 225

**APPENDIX A—SELECT EVALUATION STUDIES COMPLETED AT ST. MICHAEL HOSPITAL ..... 229**

**Index ..... 237**

# Foreword

For over a decade, the concept of quality assurance has been of great interest to providers, payers, and recipients of health care. Among the reasons for this interest are the public's concern about the quality of health care services and the payer's concern about the high cost of such services.

Objective and systematic evaluation of nursing care has been and continues to be an urgent priority within the nursing profession. Nurses have made a commitment to direct accountability to the public, to nursing as a scientific discipline, and to involvement in the shaping of public policy as well as individual health care agency policies. Furthermore, the development of standards for nursing care and the implementation of review systems are well under way.

For many years, those implementing quality assurance programs have asked me where to find materials that can be immediately applied to the clinical unit. I found that I regularly referred such persons to St. Michael Hospital. The nursing staff, especially the clinical nurse specialists, have been willing to share their work in the development of an organizational structure for quality assurance, the methodologies, the results of the studies, and philosophical beliefs about the purposes and utility of quality assurance efforts. Therefore, it was with great pleasure that I learned the St. Michael Hospital nursing staff had decided to write this book.

The book contains the quality assurance ideas and strategies that have been tested in practice at St. Michael Hospital. It has been written for nurse-managers, clinical nurse specialists, practicing registered nurses, in-service educators, nursing educators, nursing students, and researchers—in other words, for all professional nurses. The quantity and quality of nursing studies reported is impressive, but much work remains to be done in the areas of clinical effectiveness, cost benefit analysis, and application of the results to public and institutional policy. This book will help nurses with that work.

*Norma M. Lang, R.N., Ph.D., F.A.A.N.*
Dean and Professor
University of Wisconsin-Milwaukee School of Nursing

# Preface

> A study revealed that patients were inconsistently taught postoperative skills. Corrective action was instituted to standardize preoperative teaching classes and to promote patient attendance.
>
> A study of the appearance of patient rooms on various shifts indicated that one shift consistently "cluttered" the environment. Corrective action was implemented on that shift to increase patients' safety and improve environmental appearance.
>
> Staff nurses in the intensive care unit, who purported to be under considerable stress, were able to isolate their most significant stressors through the use of a questionnaire. Corrective action decreased those significant stressors, thus improving the quality of care delivered.

These improvements in nursing care are representative of the exciting results stemming from a unit-based nursing quality assurance program developed at St. Michael Hospital in Milwaukee, Wisconsin. Each nursing unit has a quality assurance committee composed of staff nurses and headed by a clinical nurse specialist. This system allows the staff nurse to identify standards of care, discuss practice-related problems on the unit, select issues for study, assist in the study, and develop corrective action based on results. Although most hospitals have some form of nursing quality assurance, all too often it is present only to meet the requirements of reviewing bodies and focuses primarily on the nurse-manager. The unit-based system has been developed to address problems perceived by those involved in care and focuses on the staff nurse. As a result, evaluation studies are more pertinent, involvement of nursing staff is intensive, and the program is successful.

It is significant that this book emanates from a hospital setting. Although literature is available about quality assurance, little of it focuses on the practical aspects. Nurses at St. Michael Hospital demonstrate that quality assurance commitment to bring the concept alive. We sincerely hope that this book will stimulate others to try this model and will spark enthusiasm for quality assurance programming.

*Patricia S. Schroeder, M.S.N., R.N.*
*Regina M. Maibusch, S.S.S.F., M.S., R.N.*

# Acknowledgments

As with all works of this nature, gratitude must be expressed to many people. The editors wish to acknowledge the support of St. Michael Hospital administrators, particularly John A. Comiskey, President, and Stephen R. Young, Executive Vice President. This book could not have been compiled without the initial and ongoing support of Dr. SueEllen Pinkerton, Vice President of Patient Services. The encouragement of Cathleen K. Wilson, Director of Nursing in Specialty Practice and Evaluation, also helped us complete this book in a timely fashion. To Kathleen McNelly, Office Coordinator, our gratitude for the care with which she typed the manuscript, not once but several times, and for the editorial assistance she provided. We also wish to thank Mary Bechtel for her help with typing. The contributing authors also receive our deep appreciation; without them, this book would not exist. Our thanks also to the large number of staff nurses who, as members of the unit-based quality assurance committee, have given us the substance of this book.

A few individuals, without knowing it, contributed to this book in substantial ways that call for specific acknowledgment. First, we recognize the inspiration of such national quality assurance leaders as Dr. Norma Lang, Ms. Marie Zimmer, and, more recently, Dr. Jacqueline Clinton. It was Dr. Lang's insight about the essential nature of the staff nurse's role in quality assurance that guided us to the unit-based model. To all of these people, as well as to those unnamed, such as our families and friends, we say thank you.

*Patricia S. Schroeder, M.S.N., R.N.*
*Regina M. Maibusch, S.S.S.F., M.S., R.N.*

Part I

# Nursing Quality Assurance and the Unit-Based Approach

## Chapter 1

# Evolution of Quality Assurance for Nursing in Hospitals

*Regina M. Maibusch, S.S.S.F., M.S., R.N.**

For more than 100 years, authors have written about the evaluation of nursing practice as a process with the minimal elements of (1) setting standards, (2) comparing nursing practice to such standards, and (3) instituting changes to increase adherence to the standards. The unit-based system for nursing quality assurance is a concept that has come of age. Although the issue of assuring quality of care is not new to the nursing profession, the structure of a unit-based system greatly affects the process to be carried out.

## EVOLUTION OF STANDARDS

The first to write about nursing standards in the English language was Florence Nightingale, whose *Notes on Nursing: What It Is and What It Is Not* was first published in England in December 1859.[1] In it, she frequently called for change to achieve higher standards. Dunbar viewed Nightingale as a standard setter for nurses, as shown by her statement in the foreword to the reprint edition of Nightingale's book that "these instructions have become precepts for every good nurse."[2] Nightingale developed a multitude of standards for nursing care in the nineteenth century, whether the care was provided by a family member or someone hired for such service. *Notes on Nursing* has standards regarding

- noise and its control around the sick
- consistency of food and when it should be served
- type of bed and mattress to be used, as well as precepts about the bed linens
- position of the bed in relation to the windows so that the patient can look out

*Appreciation to Maxine Sliefert, M.S., R.N., Assistant Professor at the University of Wisconsin-Milwaukee School of Nursing and doctoral candidate at the University of Illinois, Chicago Medical Center, for encouragement, resources, and insights.

- airiness and cleanliness of the room
- personal cleanliness

Today, these are called structure criteria. Some would call them standards. In regard to observations of the sick, Nightingale said, "What you want are facts, not opinions."[3] Nightingale was a pioneer in standard setting.

In *Notes on Nursing,* Nightingale made no comparison between her standards and existing conditions. Lang noted, however, that Nightingale found the care of military personnel in the British Armed Forces during the Crimean War unconscionable in comparison with that of civilian populations in *Notes on Matters Affecting the Health, Efficiency, and Hospital Administration of the British Army.*[4,5] Through Nightingale's efforts, changes were effected that raised the living standards and the health service for those in the armed forces of that day. Dock stated that 50 to 60 percent of the soldiers died in the Crimean War.[6] Flanagan noted that the death rate in Barrack Hospital, Scutari, Turkey, alone was 42 percent when Nightingale was placed in charge.[7] Within six months, she had reduced the mortality to 2 percent or 22/1,000 according to Flanagan and Dock.[8,9] Just as Nightingale founded modern nursing, so she initiated a process in which (1) standards were set for nursing, (2) the care being provided was compared with the standards, and (3) action was taken to bring about change. In other words, a quality assurance or quality control process was used.

Much has been done since that time to isolate the concept of setting standards from the larger process of evaluation. Probably implicit in all standard setting is the concept of comparison for purposes of evaluation or determining excellence or adherence.

The impetus for the establishment of schools of nursing in the United States came from the desire to set rules and standards that would upgrade nursing care. Schools were seen as a means to a desired outcome. In commenting on the opening of the first nursing schools in New York, New Haven, and Boston in 1873, Flanagan said, "The ultimate objective of those individuals who founded these early schools was the improvement of nursing care."[10] Establishing schools of nursing was quite an indirect approach in terms of setting standards for practice and measuring improved compliance.

Almost two decades after schools of nursing had been established, efforts were again made to set standards for them. This, in turn, improved the care of the sick in hospitals, because schools of nursing were intimately associated with hospitals. In the hospitals with schools of nursing, care was provided primarily by students, so standards for the school of nursing were really standards for the care of the sick in these hospitals. One of three resolutions adopted at the inception of the American Society of Superintendents of Training Schools for Nurses was to establish and maintain a universal standard of training so that the quality of nursing care might be more uniform.[11]

Eldredge addressed the quality of nursing care in 1932 predominantly in terms of the quality of care given by students in hospitals. She defined the quality of nursing care in terms of outcomes of nursing practice, although not in the measurable outcomes used today. Eldredge wrote that quality nursing increases the patient's physical and mental comfort during illness, improves the patient's state of health, and helps the patient to avoid recurrence of the same condition.[12] This was a more patient-centered goal orientation for nursing care than had been previously found.

## EVOLUTION OF EVALUATION IN THE NURSING PROCESS

In the years after World War II, attention was again focused on establishing standards and upgrading nursing care. Furthermore, nursing began to view itself as a profession. In the 1950s, as the nursing process emerged as an identifiable entity with specific elements, evaluation of care was almost always included as a step in the nursing process. Although the earliest writer to identify the nursing process, McManus, did not explicitly discuss evaluation, it was implicit in her writing.[13] Orlando identified function, process, and principles of professional nursing.[14] She argued for a more deliberative, thoughtful process on the part of the nurse, as well as consideration of whether the activity of the nurse had helped the patient, i.e., evaluation. Orlando also pointed out that a "deliberative nursing process has elements of continuous reflection," in other words, evaluation.[15]

Since the conceptualization of the nursing process in recent times, evaluation has been an integral element in that process. In 1959, Abdellah and her colleagues described nursing practice as a process of nursing diagnosis and treatment.[16] In further elucidating nursing practice, these authors equated the nursing process with the problem-solving process. Formulating a hypothesis is the nursing care plan, testing the hypothesis is the provision of the nursing care, and revising the hypothesis is the revision of the nursing care plan.[17] Revision assumes evaluation as a basis, since a change cannot be made without a judgment. So, although not explicitly stated, evaluation is implied as an essential element to this process in every model.

Yura and Walsh were the earliest to describe the four elements of the nursing process as they are often spoken of today:

1. assessing the needs of the patient
2. developing a plan of care to meet the patient's needs
3. implementing the plan of care
4. evaluating the extent to which the plan of care has met the needs of the patient[18]

Many other experts have also identified steps in the nursing process. In 1966, Knowles outlined the nursing process as discovering, delving, deciding, doing, and discriminating.[19] She used the term *discriminating* to indicate an assessment or evaluation of the effectiveness of the care. Little and Carnevali in 1969 used six steps to outline the nursing process;[20] they expressed the evaluative component as "revising any or all components of the nursing care plan as necessary in terms of patient response or changes in his situation."[21] Carrieri and Sitzman in 1971 also included evaluation as the final point in the six-step process they prefer.[22] In 1975, Marriner used the four words that have become quite conventional: assessing, planning, implementing, and evaluating.[23]

Griffith and Christensen viewed the publication of the American Nurses' Association (ANA) standards in 1973 as legitimizing the nursing process.[24] The steps for the nursing process form the framework for the standards that have been developed in the subsequent sets. The ANA standards have two steps that relate to evaluation. Standard VII states, "The client's/patient's progress or lack of progress toward goal achievement is determined by the client/patient and the nurse."[25] Standard VIII states, "The client's/patient's progress or lack of progress toward goal achievement directs re-assessment, re-ordering of priorities, new goal setting, and revision of the plan of nursing care."[26]

Common to all these authors is the belief that evaluation of nursing care is an essential component of the nursing process. The nursing process is, in actuality, the application of the scientific method to nursing practice. Each of these authors urged their colleagues in the nursing profession to be more deliberative and more scientific in their approach to interaction with patients, whether providing physical or psychological care.

To a considerable extent, however, there has been more discussion than action on the inclusion of evaluation as an integral part of the nursing process. After more than a decade and a half of clarification, Griffith and Christensen could still state that "evaluation is frequently the neglected part of the nursing process."[27] Published references to the nursing process consistently contain the element of evaluation, but it is difficult to find evidence of evaluation in the day-to-day recording of nursing care given. Weed made the same complaint about medical care and developed the problem-oriented record in which evaluation is built into the recording process,[28] but such evaluation is highly individual and subjective. Little and Carnevali said that evaluation has two aspects, i.e., "appraisal of the total care given to one patient over a period of time and of that given to groups of patients having some common denominator," such as a nursing diagnosis, a medical diagnosis, a procedure, or admission to the same nursing unit.[29]

## EVALUATION INSTRUMENTS

There are two types of evaluation. One follows rigorous research prinicples; the other is empirical, developed for on-the-spot use with limited concern for tested reliability and validity of the criterion measures.[30-32] The research-based evaluation instruments that use a tested tool were developed primarily for nursing practice in the hospital setting, since, until recently, most of nursing practice was hospital-based.

### Reiter-Kakosh Study

In an effort to identify criteria by which quality nursing care could be measured, Reiter and Kakosh conducted a study from 1950 to 1954 "to establish valid, objective, reliable and usable criteria for the appraisal of nursing care."[33] The criteria they worked to develop were for use in hospitals, as they explicitly stated. This was a notable undertaking at that time in light of the prevailing views of nursing leaders. Finer, for example, included a chapter entitled "Non-measurability of Quality of Nursing Care" in his book *Administration and the Nursing Services*.[34]

Abdellah called the Reiter-Kakosh study "the first significant early attempt to measure the quality of nursing care."[35] As a result of their research, Reiter and Kakosh developed an Observation Guide, which was based on critical questions about the execution of specific nursing actions and patient responses. Reiter and Kakosh measured nursing as defined by the four major nursing operations of (1) administration, (2) observing, (3) teaching, and (4) communicating. They stated that the validity of their criteria was substantiated "because the criteria were evolved from actual nursing care situations which were observed and described by nurse practitioners."[36] Their validity was further established through recognition and acceptance by both nurse-practitioners and experts, a rudimentary type of validity.

The criteria developed in the Reiter-Kakosh study are invalid today, however, because the concept of nursing has been refined and developed. When the concept of nursing changes, the criterion measures must change. If they do not change, the criteria are no longer measuring what exists. Even though nursing research was in an embryonic state at the time of the Reiter-Kakosh study, the project made a tremendous contribution to the evaluation process in nursing.

### Iowa Nurse Utilization Study

A three-year project begun in the fall of 1956, the Iowa Nurse Utilization Study was designed to examine the effects of increased nurse staffing on patient welfare and to determine which nursing actions contributed most to desirable patient outcomes.[37] Professional nurses in the 1950s commonly assumed that additional nursing staff would increase the desired outcomes in patients admitted to hospitals, because the patient would receive more nursing care. Such an assumption grew naturally out of the intense shortage of nurses experienced during World War II and the years following the war.

The study was carefully designed and controlled. Although the central focus of the study was the effect of increased staffing on patient welfare, it was also hypothesized that an in-service program on the "principles and techniques of good patient care" might affect the dependent variable, patient welfare.[38] The study of nursing activities resulted in an instrument of nineteen categories, which included activities ranging from intimate patient care to coffee breaks for the nursing staff. This instrument, as well as all the others developed during the investigation, were tested for reliability and validity.

Patient welfare was measured prior to and after the introduction of increased staffing and increased staffing plus in-service education. Patient welfare measures were developed in three groupings: clinical measures, scaled measures, and sampling measures. Clinical measures included the number of days in the hospital, number of days of fever, number of postoperative days, and number of doses of drugs, e.g., narcotics, analgesics, and sedatives used. Seven instruments were developed for the scaled measures:

1. a seven-point mobility scale used twice a day
2. a mental attitude measure
3. a physical independence measure
4. a measure of special aspects of physical independence
5. a measure of skin condition
6. a measure of the patient's opinion of nursing care
7. a physician's evaluation of the patient's condition and progress on admission and every second day until discharge

The patient activity sampling measures were designed for data collection in four areas: percentage of time in bed, percentage of time in a chair, percentage of time up, and percentage of time spent in communication and occupied leisure.[39]

The Iowa Nurse Utilization Study did not substantiate the assumption that an increase in staffing would increase direct patient care; only small portions of the added nurse time were allocated to direct patient care. Furthermore, analysis of the data did not show a positive correlation between direct patient care activities and patient welfare.[40] The negative findings notwithstanding, the study is another early milestone because of the instrumentation developed and because of its focus on patient outcomes as they relate to process.

## Phaneuf Audit

While the Reiter-Kakosh study was being conducted, Phaneuf developed a method for appraising the quality of nursing care rendered to Blue Cross subscribers in a home care program. The Phaneuf Audit, which was not published until some twenty years after it had been developed, is a method of evaluating nursing care through retrospective examination of the patient record.[41,42] Criteria are based on the nursing process as expressed in the seven functions of professional nursing identified by Lesnik and Anderson:

1. application and execution of physicians' legal orders
2. observation of symptoms and reactions
3. supervision of the patient
4. supervision of others, except physicians, who contribute to the care of patients
5. reporting and recording
6. application and execution of nursing procedures and techniques
7. promotion of physical and emotional health by direction and teaching[43]

The Lesnik and Anderson functions were based on the then prevalent Nurse Practice Acts. By the time the Phaneuf Audit was published in 1972, however, those Nurse Practice Acts were changing to include more independent functions of nurses. In 1972, for example, New York adopted a Nurse Practice Act that identified the independent functions of nursing as diagnosing and treating human responses to potential or actual health problems.[44] If the audit items had been weighted in the 70s or 80s, it can be assumed that more weight would have been given to activities that nurses are capable and licensed to carry out independently rather than to application and execution of physicians' legal orders.

The Phaneuf Audit was developed for use in community health agencies, nursing homes, and hospitals. In fact, it was at that time the only audit tool that was available to hospitals and had been tested to some extent for reliability and validity. Instructions are given for establishing and orienting an audit committee, as well as for increasing inter-rater reliability. It is recommended that 35 hours of orientation be provided and that 10 percent of the charts be reviewed. The system for scoring was designed by a biostatistician who had access to five years of audit data. The weighting scale was adapted to the subcomponents and not vice versa.[45]

Questions of reliability and validity have not been satisfactorily answered regarding the Phaneuf Audit. As a structure and process evaluation tool, it does not use outcomes in the sense of measurable changes in the patient's state or behavior. Donabedien has stated that a well-rounded audit system uses all three types of criteria, i.e., structure, process, and outcome.[46] In addition to the dated content of the nursing process around which the tool is structured, other factors can be questioned. Does a score obtained by combining the scores of the seven functions tested produce a valid picture of the quality of nursing care in a given institution, especially when the greatest weight is given to the dependent function? In clinical research, outcomes determine the validity of the process of care, not only the process itself.[47]

### Slater Scale

In the 1960s, the Slater Scale was developed at Wayne State University College of Nursing, the same institution where Phaneuf had refined her audit tool.[48] Consisting of eighty-four items, the Slater Scale uses nurse observation to identify quality of care.[49] In most instances, the scale is used to do ratings in retrospect, but it may sometimes be desirable to conduct on-the-spot ratings by means of a shadowing technique.[50] When the shadowing method is used, the nurse being rated is followed for 2½ to 3 hours. The Slater Scale facilitates the observation of relevant nursing action at the standard of a first-level staff nurse. Cue sheets have been developed to illustrate each criterion. The directions state that cues can be added, deleted, or adapted to the setting. This raises a question of internal validity. Is the same nursing action being addressed?

The Slater Scale has six subsections: (1) psychosocial and individual, (2) psychosocial and group, (3) physical, (4) general, (5) communication, and (6) professional implications. Each subsection has seven to eighteen criteria.

### Quality Patient Care Scale (Qual PACs)

The Slater Scale focuses on the nurse. The companion tool, Qual PACs, focuses on the patient as recipient of that care.

Derived from the Slater Scale, Qual PACs provides a measure of the overall quality of the nursing care received by an individual patient, whether the caregiver is a head nurse, staff nurse, licensed practical nurse, or nursing assistant. The standard of care, as in the Slater Scale, is that expected of a first-level staff nurse; however, all nursing care provided is measured, regardless of the educational preparation, experience, or job classification of the provider. This seems to perpetuate the philosophy that "a nurse is a nurse is a nurse." A question that must be raised is whether all caregivers should be judged at a first-level staff nurse standard. Some caregivers, such as nursing students, nursing assistants, and orderlies, have less preparation; some, such as experienced professional nurses, have more. Wandelt and Ager responded to this question by stating that the results of evaluation indicate whether a patient care unit meets the standard, not what an individual does.[51] The focus is on the level of care a patient receives, not on the caregiver.

Qual PACs contains sixty-eight items arranged under the same six subsections used in the Slater Scale. It has a number of other similarities to the Slater Scale (Table 1–1). Although developed only three years later, Qual PACs reflected the changing values in society and the profession. For example, Item 22 in the Slater Scale reads, "delegates responsibilities to patients according to their capabilities."[52] This has been changed in Qual PACs to read, "the member of the patient group is provided with the opportunity to assume responsibility according to his capabilities" in Item 19.[53]

**Table 1–1** Comparison of Slater Scale and Qual PACs

| *Factors* | *Slater Scale* | *Qual PACs* |
|---|---|---|
| Place of development | Wayne State | Wayne State |
| Year development began | 1965 | 1968 |
| Year of publication | 1975 | 1974 |
| Data-gathering method | Direct observation | Direct observation and indirect |
| Focus | Competency displayed by a nurse | Care received by a patient |
| Subsection title and number of items | | |
| Psychosocial: Individual | 18 | 15 |
| Psychosocial: Group | 13 | 8 |
| Physical | 13 | 15 |
| General | 16 | 15 |
| Communication | 7 | 8 |
| Professional Implications | 17 | 7 |
| Total | 84 | 68 |
| Cue sheets | 22 | 20 |
| Orientation time | 3 days | 4–5 observations or 2 days |
| Time needed for data collection | 2½–3 hours continuous observation | 2 hours direct care observation; 1 hour chart search |
| Consent | Individual nurse knows she is being observed | Anonymity; no need for consent |
| Scaling | 5 points, deferred | 5 points, assigned immediately |
| Standard of performance | First-level staff nurse | First-level staff nurse |

*Source:* Reprinted with permission from Regina M. Maibusch, St. Michael Hospital, Milwaukee, Wisconsin, 1983.

## Selected Attribute Variable Evaluation (SAVE)

SAVE was developed for the Hospital for Sick Children in Toronto, Ontario, because no tool existed for the hospital's purposes. Therefore, SAVE is specific to this hospital, but the methodology is interesting and useful.[54]

Through a literature survey and questionnaires of the nurses working at the Hospital for Sick Children, 200 criterion items of nursing care were collected. The number was reduced to 80 so that the evaluation tool would be reliable, valid, simple, easy and quick to use, and applicable hospitalwide. A six-point scale was selected to avoid too many average ratings. Those items that had no ratings in poorest and best levels were rejected. This reduced the 80 criteria to a set of 22 items of nursing care that could be used to detect extreme values of poorest or best. They were applicable hospitalwide. Because even 22 items were considered too many for this hospital's purpose, 9-item subsets were developed, making it possible to have 6,800 such subsets. Only in those instances where there was a 90 percent chance that the 9-item subset would match the score of the earlier 80-item tool was the 9-item subset retained. A 70 percent achievement on the 9-item subset was acceptable quality.[55]

Ten SAVE evaluations are done on each nursing unit every month, involving both an internal and external observer. This requires ten hours of nursing time. Five hours are spent evaluating the unit in which the observer is working; the other five are spent evaluating another unit. Each patient is observed by two raters, one from the unit on which the child is located and the other from outside the base unit. After the care received by the child has been observed, which takes 20 minutes, the final score is obtained by adding the points and dividing by the number of items observed. When the two raters compare scores, the inter-rater agreement must be 0.7 for the ratings to be valid. Less than 0.2 percent of the ratings are invalid; most scores are within 0.3 of each other.

Like Qual PACs, SAVE focuses on the care the child receives, not on the caregiver. When validity was tested against Qual PACs, however, only after several changes in SAVE was it possible to reach an $r$ of 0.97.[56] The developers stated clearly that they have published information about SAVE to share the methodology used to devlop it, not to broaden use of the tool.[57]

## Horn-Swain Study

Horn and Swain conducted a study at the University of Michigan in Ann Arbor in the 1970s to develop an instrument to address criterion measures of nursing care.[58] They produced an instrument that measures patients' health status in terms of outcomes of care influenced by nursing rather than by the medical process. Orem's theory of self-care was used to generate and test quality measures.[59] The tool included unusual self-care demands resulting from physical health states, self-care knowledge and skills, and motivational components.

The framework of the study was based on Orem's theory that nursing's special concern is a person's "need for self-care action and the provision and management of it on a continuous basis in order to sustain life and health, recover from disease or injury and cope with their effects."[60] Nursing care outcome items were generated from Orem's nine categories of self-care requirements:

1. air
2. water/fluid intake
3. food
4. elimination of body waste
5. rest/activity/sleep
6. solitude, social interaction, and productive work
7. protection from hazards
8. normality
9. health deviation

To specify the domain of nursing further, items in four areas were generated for each of the nine health aspects:

1. evidence that the requirement has been met
2. evidence that the person has the necessary knowledge to meet the requirement
3. evidence that the person has the necessary skills and performance abilities to meet the requirements
4. evidence that the person has the necessary motivation to meet the requirements.[61]

This nine by four matrix was used to generate 539 patient outcome variables affected by nursing care.

Of the 539 criteria generated, 328 are related to the first seven universal demands of Orem. The last two universal demands had not yet been dealt with when the study ended. The remaining 211 measurement items were developed for the health deviation demands of Orem's self-care model. From the perspective of the four areas, distribution of the 539 measurement items is quite even for the first three, 198, 183, and 155, respectively. The fourth area, which is a more difficult area to measure because it involves measurement of the emotions, has only three, however.

Reliability for variables was set at the following by the authors: "(1) a sample reliability index of at least 0.80; (2) an alpha error of 0.05; and (3) the lower bound of the 95 percent confidence interval to exclude the reliability index of 0.60."[62] Content validity was achieved by applying the two criteria of Nunnally and

Durham, namely, "that the measures should be representative of the domain to be covered, and that the design of the measures should use 'sensible methods' of construction."[63] All criteria were reviewed by the research staff, a national advisory panel, and a panel of clinical nurse specialists to determine the appropriateness of the item as a reflection of nursing practice. Because the patient was to be the primary source of data, the most common types of measurement methods developed were direct physical observation and interviews.

The complete instrument has not been used widely, so there is no information other than that from the developers. It is a monumental work, however, and deserves more widespread use—if not in toto, then in carefully chosen sections.

### Rush Medicus Nursing Process Methodology

The Rush Medicus instrument resulted from a three-phased study undertaken jointly by Rush–St. Luke's–Presbyterian of Chicago and Medicus Corporation.[64] Phase I dealt with the development of a methodology for evaluating the quality of nursing for general medical, surgical, and pediatric units, as well as for the corresponding intensive care units. From a search of the literature with the addition of direct patient care items, a master list of 230 criteria was developed. The major findings of this study phase were the following:

1. No existing methodology adequately measures the quality of nursing care.
2. Existing methodologies are not adequately patient centered.
3. The major problem in this study and the obvious weakness of most other studies was the establishment of interobserver reliability.
4. There is an obvious lack of statistical testing in most existing methodologies.
5. It is possible to develop a methodology, as in this study, to focus on nursing care while also encompassing process variables at all levels of the patient care system.
6. It is possible to develop a methodology, as in this study, flexible enough to permit inclusion of variables which are unique to a specific institution.
7. Patient specific criteria differ most in applicability by intensity of illness rather than by age, type of unit or disease entity.
8. Weighting of objectives and subobjectives did not contribute to differentiating between nursing units in terms of quality of nursing care.[65]

Phase II was a trial of the survey instrument at eighteen hospitals of differing sizes, locations, and characteristics throughout the United States. Complexity of services, sophistication, and intensity of the nursing process were taken into consideration in selecting the participating hospitals. Phase II further developed and tested the Phase I methodology, expanding it to cover care provided in the newborn nursery and the recovery room. Phase II focused on the effects of "organizational factors and educational background" on the quality of nursing care—as tested by the Rush Medicus instrument—and it began to "relate nursing process to measures of patient outcomes."[66]

Again, data were extensively studied statistically. The most important findings were as follows:

1. Statistical analyses have shown a greater degree of validity for the instrument than other process instruments can claim.
2. While nursing process relates to patient outcomes, the relationship is not simple and, therefore, it is not enough to assess patient outcomes.
3. Nursing quality is related to a multiplicity of variables. Organizational structure of the nursing care unit, e.g., registered nurse hours for patient day, continuity of care, as reflected in primary nursing, and coordination of the parts of the patient care system, all related positively to quality.
4. Negatively related were the size and patient census of a unit, as well as non-professional staffing.[67]

In Phase III of the project, the feasibility of reviewing the nursing care provided by individual nurses in a framework of medical diagnosis was studied. The goal was to relate the nursing care measurement instrument to a methodology similar to that developed for physician review by the Professional Standards Review Organization (PSRO). This proved to be difficult, however, because much of nursing focuses on psychosocial problems[68] and must be measured indirectly. It is even more difficult to ascribe specific patient outcomes to one nurse. Although this is theoretically possible in primary nursing, it is tenuous, at best; furthermore, primary nursing as a delivery system is not universal.

Another difficulty arose in connection with the fact that the Rush Medicus instrument establishes a performance standard for the experienced registered nurse that differs from that for the beginner. This approach varies from the stand of Wandelt in the Slater Scale and Qual PACs, in which the standard for all nurses is that of the beginning practitioner.

Findings of Phase III were as follows:

1. It may be feasible to assess the quality of nursing care using patient outcomes and nursing process criteria in a primary nursing setting.

2. In a team or functional delivery system, review of outcomes is not a reasonable method.
3. In the testing of outcome criteria, as they relate to nursing process for five patient populations based on a medical diagnosis, difficulty was encountered maintaining validity and reliability as well as defining the characteristics of the population to which the criteria could be applied.[69]

The Rush Medicus study has significantly advanced the process of quality review for nursing through its extensive reliability and validity testing of an instrument that relates process to outcomes. The instrument, which can be used in any institution with computer capabilities, will become more useful as it is more widely implemented. For nursing managers or administrators who have computer capabilities available, the Rush Medicus instrument is a well-tested though complex quality assurance mechanism.

## EVOLUTION OF PRACTICE EVALUATION IN HOSPITALS

In the 1950s, efforts to identify and maintain quality in hospital nursing departments resulted in nursing audits, i.e., chart reviews using what are now called structure criteria.[70,71] By the 1960s, nursing leaders were again urging the profession to regulate itself and control the quality of nursing practice. The ANA Committee on Nursing Service published standards for organized nursing services in 1965.[72] These were supplementary to the standards issued earlier by sections of the ANA for individual nursing practice, such as those of the Educational Administrators, Consultants and Teachers Section. These standards often were not so much standards of practice for the individual nurse as norms for the employer, however.

In 1965, Lambertsen published six criteria for evaluating nursing care.[73] Although the criteria were based on what was considered "good" patient care at the time, they were never developed into a study to test their validity and reliability; they remain untested standards. A few years later, in 1968, McGuire went beyond the patient chart for auditing and described an audit that called for direct observation of the patient.[74] These observations related primarily to physical care of the patient, although items concerning emotional, spiritual, and teaching needs were included.

With the enactment of the PSRO legislation, Public Law 92-603, on October 30, 1972, quality assurance efforts mushroomed, as evidenced in publications and workshops for the nursing profession. Some nursing leaders, such as Marie Zimmer, director of nursing service of the University Hospitals of Madison, Wisconsin, and Norma Lang, now dean of the School of Nursing at the University of Wisconsin in Milwaukee, Wisconsin, had the vision to urge nurses to assume more specific responsibility for monitoring the quality of the portion of health care that society has entrusted to nurses.

Under the auspices of the Wisconsin Regional Medical Program (WRMP), Marie Zimmer and Norma Lang convened nurse experts in Wisconsin in the early 70s to write sets of outcome criteria for six patient populations.[75] Clinical specialists and other contributors of the University Hospitals published their thoughts in a symposium in *Nursing Clinics of North America*.[76] The shift in emphasis was now away from structure and process criteria, as had been used in earlier audits, to outcome criteria.

In 1974, Lang developed her model for quality assurance.[77] The Lang model was subsequently adopted by the ANA as its model for quality assurance.[78] The ANA held workshops throughout 1976 in various locations in the United States to develop the knowledge and skills of nurses regarding professional responsibility for measuring the quality of nursing care in whatever setting it was practiced. Hundreds of nursing administrators and other leaders attended these sessions.

In addition, the Joint Commission on Accreditation of Hospitals (JCAH), the American Hospital Association, and a group called InterQual sponsored workshops. The JCAH and InterQual workshops provided the participants with well-developed workbooks totally oriented to outcome criteria, based on populations with medical diagnoses.[79-81] These were "how to" books with little room for creativity, but nurses were ready for more independence.

Nurses did not confine their evaluations to the nursing care given patients receiving government assistance, even though these patients were the focus of the PSRO law. Audit committees in hospitals proliferated, many switching from the Phaneuf Audit, Qual PACs, and Slater Scale structure and process criteria to outcome criteria. In some institutions, one individual was responsible for initiating and coordinating all evaluation activity; other institutions functioned with a nursing audit committee. In these committees, all the nursing units, or at least a cross section of them, were generally represented. After the first rush of enthusiasm had subsided, this wide representation changed to lack of interest, often because of lack of expertise. Maternity nurses were not concerned about dialysis. Cardiac intensive care nurses had little concern and expertise about the specifics of quality nursing practice in psychiatry. Nursing practice was becoming more specialized as professionalism increased.

Publications began to disseminate information about quality assurance activities. In September of 1974, the JCAH began publication of the *Quality Review Bulletin,* a monthly journal in which evaluation studies from all disciplines are included and JCAH positions on quality assurance standards are discussed. The Congress for Nursing Practice of the ANA initiated a newsletter, *Quality Assurance Update,* in December of 1977, in which brief news items of quality assurance activities, as well as more scholarly writings, could be shared. As a result of a contract with the Department of Health, Education and Welfare, Office of Professional Standards Review, Bureau of Quality Assurance "to develop model sets of criteria for screening quality, appropriateness and necessity of nursing care in settings for which PSROs have responsibility,"[82] the ANA published *Guidelines for Review of Nursing Care at the Local Level* in 1976.

Numerous other influences could probably be cited, but nurses' growing professionalism, their desire for autonomy, and their desire to assume control over their own practice spurred changes in the auditing process. One development was the unit-based nursing quality assurance program. The unit-based system brought responsibility for nursing practice to the practitioners on the nursing units where the practice occurred, which was consistent with the growing philosophy of self-governance of professional nurses. Just as the composition of quality assurance committees changed in the unit-based system, so, too, the focus of the evaluations changed.

The term *audit* often has the connotation of a retrospective chart review. Groups of nurses concerned about the quality of the nursing practice on their nursing unit are now examining other quality issues, however, so that today a more generic term, *evaluation study,* is appropriate. The studies are varied, and the criteria are often a combination of outcome and process items. Problem-oriented studies evolved naturally in a unit-based system, even before the JCAH guidelines changed in 1980. In a little more than ten years, from the PSRO impetus to today, nursing has moved from retrospective structure and process audits to problem-focused evaluation studies.

## CONCLUSION

Evaluation by practitioners must continue if nurses are to serve society well, and evaluation can only be enhanced by the findings of evaluation research.[83] Advances made in the development of standards of practice, the nursing process, and evaluation of care have been considerable. The unit-based system for nursing quality assurance seems to be the next logical step; that is, placing accountability for the quality assurance process in the hands of those who actually deliver the care. It is difficult to determine the exact direction for this process in the future; however, the richness of the past permits great expectation for the future.

---

**NOTES**

1. Florence Nightingale, *Notes on Nursing: What It Is and What It Is Not* (New York: Dover Publication, 1969), p. xviii.
2. Ibid, p. xv.
3. Ibid, p. 105.

4. Norma M. Lang, "Evaluating Health and Nursing Care," *Quality Assurance Update* 111, no. 1 (Spring 1979): 2.

5. Florence Nightingale, *Notes on Matters Affecting the Health, Efficiency, and Hospital Administration of the British Army* (St. Mark's Lane, W.C.: Harrison and Sons, 1858), p. 5.

6. Lavinia L. Dock, *A Short History of Nursing*, 2nd ed. (New York: G.P. Putman's Sons, 1925), p. 121.

7. Lyndia Flanagan, *One Strong Voice* (Kansas City, MO: American Nurses' Association, 1976), p. 13.

8. Ibid.

9. Dock, *A Short History of Nursing*, p. 123.

10. Flanagan, *One Strong Voice*, p. 17.

11. Ibid, p. 29.

12. Adda Eldredge, "What Is Quality Nursing?" *American Journal of Nursing* 32 (November 1932): 1195.

13. R. Louise McManus, "Assumptions of Functions of Nursing," in *Regional Planning for Nursing and Nursing Education* (New York: Columbia University, Teachers' College, Bureau of Publication, 1950), p. 54.

14. Ida Jean Orlando, *The Dynamic Nurse-Patient Relationship* (New York: G.P. Putman's Sons, 1961), p. viii.

15. Ibid, p. 65.

16. Faye G. Abdellah et al., *Patient-Centered Approaches to Nursing* (New York: Macmillan, 1960), p. 26.

17. Ibid, p. 27

18. Helen Yura and Mary B. Walsh, *The Nursing Process* (Washington, DC: The Catholic University of America Press, 1967), p. iv.

19. Lois N. Knowles, "Decision Making in Nursing: A Necessity for Doing," in *American Nurses' Association Clinical Sessions—1966* (New York: Appleton-Century-Crofts, 1967), p. 248.

20. Dolores E. Little and Doris L. Carnevali, *Nursing Care Planning* (Philadelphia: J.B. Lippincott, 1969), p. 18.

21. Ibid, p. 47.

22. Virginia Carrieri and Judith Sitzman, "Components of the Nursing Process," *Nursing Clinics of North America* 6, no. 1 (March 1971): 121.

23. Ann Marriner, *The Nursing Process: A Scientific Approach to Nursing Care* (St. Louis, MO: C.V. Mosby, 1975), p. 1.

24. Janet W. Griffith and Paula J. Christensen, *Nursing Process: Application of Theories, Framework, and Models* (St. Louis, MO: C.V. Mosby, 1982), p. 4.

25. American Nurses' Association, *Standards of Nursing Practice* (Kansas City, MO: American Nurses' Association, 1973), p. 6.

26. Ibid, p. 6.

27. Griffith and Christensen, *Nursing Process: Application of Theories, Framework, and Models*, p. 153.

28. Lawrence L. Weed, *Medical Records, Medical Education, and Patient Care* (Cleveland, OH: The Press of Case Western Reserve University, 1969).

29. Little and Carnevali, *Nursing Care Planning*, p. 11.

30. Subcommittee on Standards, Section on Nursing, American Thoracic Society, "Development of Nursing Standards," *American Thoracic Society News* 4, no. 2 (Spring 1978): 10–11.

31. Duke University Hospital Nursing Service, *Quality Assurance: Guidelines for Nursing Care* (Philadelphia: J.B. Lippincott, 1980).

32. American Association of Critical-Care Nurses Standard Committee, *Standards for Nursing Care of the Critically Ill* (Reston, VA: Reston Publishing Company, A Prentice-Hall Company, 1981).

33. Frances Reiter and Marguerite Kakosh, *Quality of Nursing Care: A Report of a Field Study to Establish Criteria 1950–54* (New York: New York Medical College, Graduate School of Nursing, 1963), p. 122.

34. Herman Finer, "Nonmeasurability of Quality of Nursing Care," in *Administration and the Nursing Services* (New York: Macmillan, 1952), pp. 116–131.

35. Faye G. Abdellah, "Overview of Nursing Research 1955-1968: Part I," *Nursing Research* 19, no. 1 (January/February 1970): 12.

36. Reiter and Kakosh, *Report of a Field Study to Establish Criteria 1950–54*, 1963, p. 124.

37. Myrtle K. Aydelotte and Marie E. Tener, *An Investigation of the Relation Between Nursing Activity and Patient Welfare* (Iowa City, IA: Iowa State University, 1960).

38. Ibid, p. 3.

39. Ibid, p. 106.

40. Ibid, p. 3.

41. Maria C. Phaneuf, *The Nursing Audit: Profile for Excellence* (New York: Appleton-Century-Crofts, 1972).

42. Maria Phaneuf, *The Nursing Audit and Self-Regulation in Nursing Practice* (New York: Appleton-Century-Crofts, 1976).

43. Milton V. Lesnik and Bernice E. Anderson, *Nursing Practice and the Law*, 2nd ed. (Philadelphia: J.B. Lippincott, 1955), pp. 247–293.

44. "Rockefeller Signs NYSNA Nursing Bill Vetoed Last Year," *American Journal of Nursing* 72, no. 4 (April 1972): 615–616.

45. Phaneuf, *The Nursing Audit: Profile for Excellence*, p. 26.

46. Avedis Donabedian, "Some Issues in Evaluating the Quality of Nursing Care," *American Journal of Public Health* 59 (1969): 1834.

47. Ibid, p. 1835.

48. Maria C. Phaneuf and Mabel A. Wandelt, "Three Methods of Nursing Process–Oriented Nursing Evaluation," *Quality Review Bulletin* Special Edition 8 (Spring 1982): 32.

49. Mabel A. Wandelt and Doris Slater Stewart, *Slater Nursing Competencies Rating Scale* (New York: Appleton-Century-Crofts, 1975).

50. Ibid, p. ix.

51. Mabel A. Wandelt and Joel W. Ager, *Quality Patient Care Scale* (New York: Appleton-Century-Crofts, 1974).

52. Wandelt and Stewart, *Slater Nursing Competencies Rating Scale*, p. 4.

53. Wandelt and Ager, *Quality Patient Care Scale*, p. 2.

54. Edwin L. Weinstein, "Developing a Measure of the Quality of Nursing Care," *Journal of Nursing Administration* 6, no. 6 (July/August 1976): 2.

55. Vivien M. Jenkinson, "Monitoring the Quality of Nursing Care in a Paediatric Hospital," in Charles Tilquin (ed.), *Systems Science in Health Care—Montreal '80* (Elmsford, NY: Pergamon Press, 1981), p. 1591.

56. Weinstein, "Developing a Measure of the Quality of Nursing Care," 3.

57. Tilquin, "Monitoring the Quality of Nursing Care in a Paediatric Hospital," p. 1589.

58. Barbara J. Horn and Mary Ann Swain, *Development of Criterion Measures of Nursing Care* (Springfield, VA: National Technical Information Service, 1977).

59. Dorthea E. Orem, *Nursing: Concepts of Practice* (St. Louis, MO: McGraw-Hill, 1971).

60. Ibid, p. 1.

61. Horn and Swain, *Development of Criterion Measures of Nursing Care*, p. 3.

62. Gerald Rosenthal, *Criterion Measures of Nursing Care Quality* (Hyattsville, MD: U.S. Department of Health, Education and Welfare, Public Health Service, National Center for Health Services Research, 1978), p. 6.

63. Ibid, p. 4.

64. Richard C. Jelinek et al., *A Methodology for Monitoring Quality of Nursing Care* (Bethesda, MD: U.S. Department of Health, Education and Welfare, U.S. Public Health Service, Health Resources Administration, Bureau of Health Manpower, Division of Nursing, 1974).

65. Ibid, pp. 78–79.

66. R.K. Dieter Haussmann, Sue T. Hegyvary, and John F. Newman, *Monitoring Quality of Nursing Care: Part II* (Bethesda, MD: U.S. Department of Health, Education and Welfare, U.S. Public Health Service, Health Resources Administration, Bureau of Health Manpower, Division of Nursing, 1976), p. 1.

67. Ibid, p. 64.

68. R.K. Dieter Haussmann and Sue T. Hegyvary, *Monitoring Quality of Nursing Care: Part III* (Hyattsville, MD: U.S. Department of Health, Education and Welfare, U.S. Public Health Service, Health Resources Administration, Bureau of Health Manpower, Division of Nursing, 1977), p. 13.

69. Ibid, p. 37.

70. Sister Blanche, "A Nursing Audit," *Hospital Progress* 37 (August 1955): 67–68.

71. Pearl R. Fisher, "The Nursing Audit," *Nursing Outlook* 5 (October 1957): 590–592.

72. American Nurses' Association, "Standards for Organized Nursing Service," *American Journal of Nursing* 65 (March 1965): 76.

73. Eleanor Lambertsen, "Evaluating the Quality of Nursing Care," *Hospitals* 39 (November 1965): 61–66.

74. Rita L. McGuire, "Bedside Nursing Audit," *American Journal of Nursing* 68, no. 10 (October 1968): 2146–2148.

75. Marie J. Zimmer et al., *Development of Sets of Patient Health Outcome Criteria by Panels of Nurse Experts: Final Report* (Madison, WI: Wisconsin Regional Medical Program, University of Wisconsin Hospitals–Madison, and University of Wisconsin–Milwaukee School of Nursing, 1974).

76. Marie J. Zimmer (guest editor), "Quality Assurance," *Nursing Clinics of North America* 9, no. 2 (January 1974).

77. Norma M. Lang, *A Model for Quality Assurance in Nursing* (Unpublished doctoral dissertation, Marquette University, Milwaukee, Wisconsin, 1974).

78. American Nurses' Association, *A Plan for Implementation of the Standards of Nursing Practice* (Kansas City, MO: American Nurses' Association, 1975).

79. American Nurses' Association, *Quality Assurance for Nursing Care, Proceedings of an Institute Jointly Sponsored by the American Nurses' Association and the American Hospital Association* (Kansas City, MO: American Nurses' Association, 1973).

80. A.P. Smith, ed., *PEP Workbook for Nurses* (Chicago, IL: Joint Commission on Accreditation of Hospitals, Quality Review Center, 1974).

81. InterQual, *Advanced Nursing Audit Seminar Manual* (Chicago, IL: InterQual, 1977).

82. American Nurses' Association, *Guidelines for Review of Nursing Care at the Local Level* (Kansas City, MO: American Nurses' Association, 1976), p. v.

83. Florence S. Downs, ed., *Nursing Research* 29, no. 2 (March/April 1980): 66–136.

---

## REFERENCES

### Books


Abdellah, Faye G.; Beland, Irene L.; Almeda, Martin; and Matheney, Ruth V. *Patient-Centered Approaches to Nursing*. New York: Macmillan, 1960.

Abdellah, Faye G., and Levine, Eugene. *Effect of Nurse Staffing on Satisfaction with Nursing Care*. Chicago: American Hospital Association, 1958.

American Association of Critical-Care Nurses Standard Committee, cochaired by Judith Thierer and Aline M. Holmes. *Standards for Nursing Care of the Critically Ill*. Reston, VA: Reston Publishing Company, a Prentice-Hall Company, 1981.

American Nurses' Association. *The NPSI: A Nursing Performance Simulation Instrument: Eighth Nursing Research Conference, March 15–17, 1972*. Kansas City, MO: American Nurses' Association, 1972.

American Nurses' Association. *Quality Assurance for Nursing Care, Proceedings of an Institute Jointly Sponsored by the American Nurses' Association and the American Hospital Association*. Kansas City, MO: American Nurses' Association, 1973.

American Nurses' Association. *Standards of Nursing Practice*. Kansas City, MO: American Nurses' Association, 1973.

American Nurses' Association. *A Plan for Implementation of the Standards of Nursing Practice*. Kansas City, MO: American Nurses' Association, 1975.

American Nurses' Association. *Guidelines for Review of Nursing Care at the Local Level*. Kansas City, MO: American Nurses' Association, 1976.

Association of Operating Room Nurses. *WICHE Report: The Relationship Between OR Nursing Activities and Patient Outcomes*. Denver, CO: AORN, 1978.

Atwood, Jan R., and Hinshaw, Ada Sue. "Multiple Indicators of Nurse and Patient Outcomes as a Method for Evaluating a Change in Staffing Patterns." In *Optimizing Environments for Health: Nursing's Unique Perspective*, pp. 235–255. Communicating Nursing Research, vol. 10, edited by M.J. Batey. Boulder, CO: WICHE, 1977.

Aydelotte, Myrtle, K., and Tener, Marie E. *An Investigation of the Relation Between Nursing Activity and Patient Welfare*. Iowa City, IA: Iowa State University, 1960.

Cantar, Marjorie Moore. *Achieving Nursing Care Standards: Internal and External*. Wakefield, MA: Nursing Resources, 1978.

Carter, Joan Haselman, and Hilliard, Mildred. *Standards of Nursing Care*. New York: Springer, 1972.

Carter, Joan Haselman; Hilliard, Mildred; Castles, Mary Reardon; Stoll, Leona D.; and Cowan, Anne. *Standards of Nursing Care: A Guide for Evaluation*. New York: Springer, 1976.

Commission for Administrative Services in Hospitals. *A Quality Control Plan for Nursing Service*. Los Angeles, CA: Commission for Administrative Services in Hospitals, 1965.

Davidson, Sharon Van Sell; Clark, Bette; Burleson, Jean Ellen; Scheel, Crawford; and Christofferson, Sue. *Nursing Care Evaluation: Concurrent and Retrospective*. St. Louis, MO: C.V. Mosby, 1977.

Dock, Lavinia L. *A Short History of Nursing*. New York: G.P. Putman's Sons, 1925.

Donabedian, Avedis. *The Definition of Quality and Approaches to Its Assessment*. Ann Arbor, MI: Health Administration Press, 1980.

Donabedian, Avedis. *The Criteria and Standards of Quality*. Ann Arbor, MI: Health Administration Press, 1982.

Doughty, Dorothy Beckley, and Mask, Norma Justus. *Nursing Audit*. Philadelphia: F.A. Davis, 1977.

Duke University Hospital Nursing Services. *Quality Assurance: Guidelines for Nursing Care*. Philadelphia: J.B. Lippincott, 1980.

Finer, Herman. "Nonmeasurability of Quality of Nursing Care." In *Administration and the Nursing Services*. New York: Macmillan, 1952.

Flanagan, Lyndia. *One Strong Voice*. Kansas City, MO: American Nurses' Association, 1976.

Froebe, Doris, J., and Bain, R. Joyce. *Quality Assurance Programs and Controls in Nursing*. St. Louis, MO: C.V. Mosby, 1976.

Graham, Nancy O., ed. *Quality Assurance in Hospitals*. Rockville, MD: Aspen Systems Corporation, 1982.

Grandbois, Mildred, ed. *Cumulative Index to Nursing Literature*. Glendale, CA: The Seventh Day Adventist Hospital Association, 1974.

Grandbois, Mildred, ed. *Cumulative Index to Nursing Literature*. Glendale, CA: The Seventh Day Adventist Hospital Association, 1982.

Griffith, Janet W., and Christensen, Paula J. *Nursing Process: Application of Theories, Frameworks, and Models*. St. Louis, MO: C.V. Mosby, 1982.

Hall, Beverly A.; Horn, Barbara; Mitsaunaga, Betty K.; and Engle, Thomas. "Quality of Care: Selected Influences and Methodological Dilemmas." In *New Approaches to Communicating Nursing Research*. Communicating Nursing Research, Boulder, CO: WICHE, 1978.

Haussmann, R.K. Dieter; Hegyvary, Sue T.; and Newman, John F. *Monitoring Quality of Nursing Care: Part II*. Bethesda, MD: U.S. Department of Health, Education, and Welfare, U.S. Public Health Service, Health Resources Administration, Bureau of Health Manpower, Division of Nursing, 1976.

Haussmann, R.K. Dieter, and Hegyvary, Sue T. *Monitoring Quality of Nursing Care: Part III*. Hyattsville, MD: U.S. Department of Health, Education, and Welfare, Public Health Service, Health Resources Administration, Bureau of Health Manpower, Division of Nursing, 1977.

Hinshaw, Ada Sue, and Oakes, Deborah L. "Theoretical Model-Testing: Patients', Nurses', and Physicians' Expectations for Quality Nursing Care." In *Optimizing Environments for Health: Nursing's Unique Perspective*, pp. 163–189. Communicating Nursing Research, vol. 10, edited by M.J. Batey. Boulder, CO: WICHE, 1977.

Horn, Barbara J., and Swain, Mary Ann. *Development of Criterion Measures of Nursing Care*. Springfield, VA: National Technical Information Service, 1977.

InterQual. *Advanced Nursing Audit Seminar Manual*. Chicago: InterQual, 1977.

Isaac, Stephen, and Michael, William B. *Handbook in Research and Evaluation*. San Diego, CA: Edits Publishers, 1971.

Jelinek, Richard C.; Haussmann, R.K. Dieter; Hegyvary, Sue T.; and Newman, John F. *A Methodology for Monitoring Quality of Nursing Care*. Bethesda, MD: U.S. Department of Health, Education, and Welfare, U.S. Public Health Service, Health Resources Administration, Bureau of Health Manpower, Division of Nursing, 1975.

Jenkinson, Vivien M. "Monitoring the Quality of Nursing Care in a Paediatric Hospital." In *Systems Science in Health Care—Montreal '80*, edited by Charles Tilquin, p. 1591. Elmsford, NY: Pergamon Press, 1981.

Johnson, Brenda Crispell; Dungca, Consuelo Urtula; Hoffmeister, Denise; and Wells, Sara Jeanne. *Standards for Critical Care*. St. Louis, MO: C.V. Mosby, 1981.

Knowles, Lois N. "Decision Making in Nursing: A Necessity for Doing." In *American Nurses' Association Clinical Sessions—1966*, edited by Beverly N. Dunston, pp. 248–272. New York: Appleton-Century-Crofts, 1967.

Krueger, Janelle C.; Nelson, Allen H.; and Wolanin, Mary Opal. *Nursing Research: Development, Collaboration, and Utilization*. Germantown, MD: Aspen Systems Corporation, 1978.

Lesnik, Milton V., and Anderson, Bernice E. *Nursing Practice and the Law*. Philadelphia: J.B. Lippincott, 1955.

Lindeman, Carol A. (Moderator). "An Empirical Approach to Defining Quality of Nursing Care." (Symposium). In *New Approaches to Communicating Nursing Research*, Batey, Marjorie J. (Ed.). Boulder, CO: Western Interstate Commission for Higher Education, Vol. II, September 1978, 33–43.

Lindeman, Carol A., and Hagan, Dan E. "Targeted Research: Measuring Quality of Nursing Care." In *Nursing Research Priorities: Choice or Chance*, pp. 352–356. Communicating Nursing Research, vol. 8, edited by M.J. Batey. Boulder, CO: Western Interstate Commission for Higher Education, 1977.

Little, Dolores E., and Carnevali, Doris L. *Nursing Care Planning*. Philadelphia: J.B. Lippincott, 1969.

Luke, Roice D.; Krueger, Janelle C.; and Modrow, Robert E. *Organization and Change in Health Care Quality Assurance*. Rockville, MD: Aspen Systems Corporation, 1983.

Marriner, Ann. *The Nursing Process: A Scientific Approach to Nursing Care*. St. Louis, MO: C.V. Mosby, 1975.

Mason, Elizabeth. *How to Write Meaningful Nursing Standards*. New York: John Wiley, 1978.

Mayers, Marlene G.; Norby, Ronald B.; and Watson, Annita B. *Quality Assurance for Patient Care*. New York: Appleton-Century-Crofts, 1977.

McManus, Rachel Louise. "Assumptions of Functions of Nursing." In *Regional Planning for Nursing and Nursing Education*. New York: Columbia University, Teachers' College, Bureau of Publication, 1950.

Miller, M. Clinton, III, and Knapp, Rebecca Grant. *Evaluating Quality of Care*. Germantown, MD: Aspen Systems Corporation, 1979.

Nicholls, Marion E., and Wessells, Virginia G., eds. *Nursing Standards and Nursing Process*. Wakefield, MA: Contemporary Publishing, 1977.

Nightingale, Florence. *Notes on Matters Affecting the Health, Efficiency, and Hospital Administration of the British Army*. St. Mark's Lane, W.C.: Harrison and Sons, 1858.

Nightingale, Florence. *Notes on Nursing*. New York: Dover Publications, 1969.

Orem, Dorthea E. *Nursing: Concepts of Practice*. St. Louis, MO: McGraw-Hill, 1971.

Orlando, Ida Jean. *The Dynamic Nurse-Patient Relationship*. New York: G.P. Putman's Sons, 1961.

Phaneuf, Maria C. *The Nursing Audit: Profile for Excellence*. New York: Appleton-Century-Crofts, 1972.

Phaneuf, Maria C. *The Nursing Audit and Self-Regulation in Nursing Practice*. New York: Appleton-Century-Crofts, 1976.

Reiter, Frances, and Kakosh, Marguerite. *Quality of Nursing Care: A Report of a Field Study to Establish Criteria 1950–54*. New York: New York Medical College, Graduate School of Nursing, 1963.

Rosenthal, Gerald. *Criterion Measures of Nursing Care Quality.* Hyattsville, MD: U.S. Department of Health, Education and Welfare, U.S. Public Health Service, National Center for Health Services Research, 1978.

*SCALE: A Quality Control Plan for Nursing Service, Hospital Systems Improvement Program.* Ann Arbor, MI: University of Michigan, 1965.

Smith, Ann P., ed. *PEP Workbook for Nurses.* Chicago; Joint Commission on Accreditation of Hospitals, Quality Review Center, 1974.

Wandelt, Mabel A., and Ager, Joel W. *Quality Patient Care Scale.* New York: Appleton-Century-Crofts, 1974.

Wandelt, Mabel A., and Stewart, Doris Slater. *Slater Nursing Competencies Rating Scale.* New York: Appleton-Century-Crofts, 1975.

Weed, Lawrence L. *Medical Records, Medical Education, and Patient Care.* Cleveland, OH: The Press of Case Western Reserve University, 1969.

Yura, Helen, and Walsh, Mary B. *The Nursing Process.* Washington, DC: Catholic University of America Press, 1967.

Zimmer, Marie J.; Lang, Norma M.; and Miller, Doris I. *Development of Sets of Patient Health Outcome Criteria by Panels of Nurse Experts: Final Report.* Madison, WI: Wisconsin Regional Medical Program, University of Wisconsin Hospitals–Madison, and University of Wisconsin–Milwaukee School of Nursing, 1974.

**Journals**

Abdellah, Faye. "Criterion Measures in Nursing." *Nursing Research* 10 (1961): 21–26.

Abdellah, Faye G. "Overview of Nursing Research 1955–1968: Part I." *Nursing Research* 19 (1970): 6–16.

American Nurses' Association. "Standards for Organized Nursing Service." *American Journal of Nursing* 65 (1965): 76.

Aydelotte, Myrtle Kitchell. "The Use of Patient Welfare as a Criterion Measure." *Nursing Research* 11 (1962): 10–14.

Blair, Eunice M.; Hauf, Barbara; Loveridge, Catherine; Murphy, Juanita; and Roth, Mildred. "Instrument Development: Measuring Quality Outcomes in Ambulatory Maternal-Child Nursing." *Nursing Administration Quarterly* 2 (1978): 81–93.

Blanche, Sister. "A Nursing Audit." *Hospital Progress* 37 (1955): 67–68.

Bloch, Doris. "Evaluation of Nursing Care in Terms of Process and Outcome: Issues in Research and Quality Assurance." *Nursing Research* 24 (1975): 256–263.

Bloch, Doris. "Criteria, Standards, Norms—Crucial Terms in Quality Assurance." *Journal of Nursing Administration* 7 (1977): 20–30.

Blumber, Mark S., and Drew, Jacqueline A. "Methods for Assessing Nursing Care Quality." *Hospitals* 31 (1963).

Brown, Barbara J., ed. "Quality Assurance and Peer Review." *Nursing Administration Quarterly* 1 (1977): 1–145.

Brown, Barbara J., ed. "Quality Assurance Update." *Nursing Administration Quarterly* 7 (1983): 1–93.

Bruce, Glenda L.; Hinds, Peggy; Hudak, Jane; Mucha, Anne; Taylor, Sr. Mary Carol; and Thompson, Charles R. "Implementation of American Nurses' Association Quality Assurance Program for Clients with End-Stage Renal Disease." *Advances in Nursing Science* 2 (1980): 79–95.

Carrieri, Virginia, and Sitzman, Judith. "Components of the Nursing Process." *Nursing Clinics of North America* 6 (1971): 115–124.

Chance, Kathryn S. "The Quest for Quality: An Exploration of Attempts to Define and Measure Quality Nursing Care." *Image* 12 (1980): 41–45.

Clinton, Jacqueline; Denyes, Mary Jean; Goodwin, Judy A.; and Koto, Edwina. "Developing Criterion Measures of Nursing Care: Case Study of a Process." *Journal of Nursing Administration* 7 (1977): 41–45.

Cuddihy, June T. "Clinical Research: Translation into Nursing Practice." *International Journal of Nursing Studies* 16 (1979): 65–72.

Destel, Lori. "More Than Chart Review: A New Problem Oriented Nursing Quality Assurance Program." *Quality Review Bulletin* 7 (1981): 26–29.

Donabedian, Avedis. "Some Issues in Evaluating the Quality of Nursing Care." *American Journal of Public Health* 59 (1969): 1833–1836.

Donabedian, Avedis. "The Quality of Medical Care." *Science* 200 (1978): 856–864.

Downs, Florence S., ed. *Nursing Research* 29 (1980): 66–136.

Dyer, Elaine D.; Monson, Mary A.; and Cope, Maxine J. "Increasing the Quality of Patient Care Through Performance Counseling and Written Goal Setting." *Nursing Research* 24 (1975): 138–144.

Eichhorn, Marsha L., and Frevert, Elaine I. "Evaluation of a Primary Nursing System Using the Quality Patient Care Scale." *Journal of Nursing Administration* 9 (1979): 11–15.

Eldredge, Adda. "What Is Quality Nursing?" *American Journal of Nursing* 32 (1932): 1189–1196.

Felton, Geraldine; Frevert, Elaine; Galligan, Kathleen; Neill, Mary Kathleen; and Williams, Lillian. "Pathway to Accountability: Implementation of a Quality Assurance Program." *Journal of Nursing Administration* 6 (1976): 20–24.

Fisher, Pearl R. "The Nursing Audit." *Nursing Outlook* 5 (1957): 590–592.

French, Kate. "Methodological Considerations in Hospital Patient Opinion Survey." *International Journal of Nursing Studies* 18 (1981): 7–32.

Gallant, Barbara W., and McLane, Audrey M. "Outcome Criteria: A Process for Validation at the Unit Level." *Journal of Nursing Administration* 9 (1979): 14–20.

Gilson, Betty S.; Gilson, John S.; Bergner, Marilyn; Bobbitt, Ruth A.; Kressel, Shirley; Pollard, William E.; and Vesselago, Michael. "The Sickness Impact Profile." *American Journal of Public Health* 65 (1975): 1304–1310.

Given, Barbara; Given, C. William; and Simoni, Lewis C. "Relationship of Processes of Care to Patient Outcomes." *Nursing Research* 28 (1979): 85–93.

Hageman, Paul T., and Ventura, Marlene R. "Utilizing Patient Outcome Criteria to Measure the Effects of a Medication Teaching Regimen." *Western Journal of Nursing Research* 3 (1981): 25–36.

Harmon, Carol A. "Involving Staff in Nursing Quality Assurance." *Quality Review Bulletin* 6 (1980): 26–30.

Haussmann, R.K. Dieter, and Hegyvary, Sue Thomas. "Field Testing the Nursing Quality Monitoring Methodology." *Nursing Research* 25 (1976): 324–331.

Hegedus, Kathryn Stewart. "A Patient Outcome Criterion Measure." *Supervisor Nurse* 10 (1979): 40–45.

Hegyvary, Sue Thomas, and Chamings, Patricia Ann. "The Hospital Setting and Patient Care Outcomes: Part I." *Journal of Nursing Administration* 5 (1975): 29–32.

Hegyvary, Sue Thomas, and Chamings, Patricia Ann. "The Hospital Setting and Patient Care Outcomes: Part II." *Journal of Nursing Administration* 5 (1975): 36–42.

Hegyvary, Sue Thomas, and Haussmann, R.K. Dieter. "Monitoring Nursing Care Quality." *Journal of Nursing Administration* 5 (1975): 17–26.

Hegyvary, Sue Thomas, and Haussmann, R.K. Dieter. "Correlates of the Quality of Nursing Care." *Journal of Nursing Administration* 6 (1976): 22–27.

Lambertsen, Eleanor. "Evaluating the Quality of Nursing Care." *Hospitals* 39 (1965): 61–66.

Lang, Norma M. "Is Continuing Education in Regional Medical Programs Dead?" *Journal of Continuing Education in Nursing* 3 (1972): 11–15.

Lang, Norma M. "Are Professional Nurses Ready for a Quality Assurance Program?" *Journal of New York State Nurses' Association* 5 (1974): 24–32.

Lang, Norma M. "Quality Assurance in Nursing." *AORN Journal* 22 (1975): 180–186.

Lang, Norma M. "Evaluating Health and Nursing Care." *Quality Assurance Update* 111 (1979): 1–6.

Lindeman, Carol A. "Delphi Survey of Priorities in Clinical Nursing Research." *Nursing Research* 24 (1975): 434–448.

Lindeman, Carol A. "Measuring Quality of Nursing Care: Part I." *Journal of Nursing Administration* 6 (1976): 7–9.

Lindeman, Carol A. "Measuring Quality of Nursing Care: Part II." *Journal of Nursing Administration* 6 (1976): 16–19.

Lum, Jean L.V.; Chase, Marybeth; Cole, Sandra M.; Johnson, Alison; Johnson, Jeanette A.; and Link, Marlene. "Nursing Care of Oncology Patients Receiving Chemotherapy." *Nursing Research* 27 (1978): 340–346.

Majesky, Sophie J.; Brester, Mary H.; and Nishia, Karen T. "Development of a Research Tool: Patient Indicators of Nursing Care." *Nursing Research* 27 (1978): 365–371.

Marriner, Ann. "The Research Process in Quality Assurance." *American Journal of Nursing* 79 (1979): 2158–2161.

McGuire, Rita L. "Bedside Nursing Audit." *American Journal of Nursing* 68 (1968): 2146–2148.

Mitsunga, Betty K., and Hall, Beverly A. "Interpersonal Attraction and Perceived Quality of Medical-Surgical Care." *Western Journal of Nursing Research* 1 (1979): 5–21.

Moore, Karen R. "Nurses Learn from Nursing Audit." *Nursing Outlook* 27 (1979): 254–258.

Moore, Karen R. "Quality Assurance and Nursing Audit: Are They Effective?" *Nursing Management* 13 (1982): 18–22.

Padilla, Geraldine V., and Grant, Marcia M. "Quality Assurance Programme for Nursing." *Journal of Advanced Nursing* 7 (1982): 135–145.

Phaneuf, Maria C. "A Nursing Audit Method." *Nursing Outlook* 12 (1964): 42–45.

Phaneuf, Maria C. "The Nursing Audit Method for the Evaluation of Patient Care." *Nursing Outlook* 14 (1966): 51–54.

Phaneuf, Maria C., and Wandelt, Mabel A. "Quality Assurance in Nursing." *Nursing Forum* 13 (1974): 328–345.

Phaneuf, Maria C., and Wandelt, Mabel A. "Obstacles to and Potentials for Nursing Quality Appraisal." *Quality Review Bulletin* 7 (1981): 2–5.

Phaneuf, Maria C., and Wandelt, Mabel A. "Letters." *Quality Review Bulletin* 7 (1981): 8.

Phaneuf, Maria C., and Wandelt, Mabel A. "Three Methods of Nursing Process–Oriented Nursing Evaluation." *Quality Review Bulletin* Special Edition 8 (1982): 32–38.

Poland, Marilyn; English, Nellie; Thornton, Nancy; and Owens, Doris. "PETO—A System for Assessing and Meeting Patient Care Needs." *American Journal of Nursing* 70 (1970): 1479.

Prescott, Patricia. "Evaluation Research: Issues in Evaluation of Nursing Programs." *Nursing Administration Quarterly* 2 (1978): 63–80.

"Rockefeller Signs NYSNA Nursing Bill Vetoed Last Year." *American Journal of Nursing* 72 (1972): 615–616.

Schlotfedt, Rosella M. "Problems in the Development of Adequate Criteria." *Nursing Research* 11 (1962): 208–211.

Schmied, Elsie. "Living with Cost Containment." *Journal of Nursing Administration* 10 (1980): 1147.

Stevens, Barbara. "Analysis of Trends in Nursing Care Management." *Journal of Nursing Administration* (November-December 1972), 2(6): 12–17.

Subcommittee on Standards, Section on Nursing, American Thoracic Society. "Development of Nursing Standards." *American Thoracic Society News* 4 (1978): 10–11.

Ventura, Marlene R. "Correlation Between the Quality Patient Care Scale and Phaneuf Audit." *International Journal of Nursing Studies* 17 (1980): 155–162.

Ventura, Marlene R., and Crosby, F. "Preparing the Nurse Observer to Use the Quality Patient Care Scale: A Modular Approach." *Journal of Continuing Education in Nursing* 9 (6) (Nov.-Dec. 1973): 37–40.

Ventura, Marlene R.; Fox, Richard N.; Corley, Mary C.; and Mercurio, Stephen M. "A Patient Satisfaction Measure as a Criterion to Evaluate Primary Nursing." *Nursing Research* 31 (1982): 226–230.

Ventura, Marlene R.; Hageman, Paul T.; Slakter, Malcolm J.; and Fox, Richard N. "Interrater Reliabilities for Two Measures of Nursing Care Quality." *Research in Nursing and Health* 3 (1980): 25–32.

Ventura, Marlene; Hageman, Paul T.; Slakter, Malcolm J.; and Fox, Richard N. "Correlations of Two Quality of Nursing Care Measures." *Research in Nursing and Health* 5 (1982): 37–43.

Watson, Annita, and Mayers, Marlene. "Evaluating the Quality of Patient Care Through Retrospective Chart Review." *Journal of Nursing Administration,* 6(2) (1976): 17–21.

Weinstein, Edwin L. "Developing a Measure of the Quality of Nursing Care." *Journal of Nursing Administration* 6 (1976): 1–3.

Williams, Margaret A.; Holloway, Janet R.; Winn, Mary C.; Wolanin, Mary Opal; Lawler, Mariea L.; Westwick, Carmen R.; and Chin, Marguerite H. "Nursing Activities and Acute Confusional States." *Nursing Research* 28 (1979): 25–35.

Zimmer, Marie J. "A Model for Evaluating Nursing Care." Hospitals 48 (1974): 91–95, 131.

Zimmer, Marie J., guest ed. "Quality Assurance." *Nursing Clinics of North America* 9 (1974).

**Unpublished Works**

Lang, Norma M. "A Model for Quality Assurance in Nursing." (Doctoral dissertation, Marquette University, Milwaukee, Wisconsin), 1974.

# Chapter 2

# The Unit-Based System

*Nancy Mansheim Formella, M.S.N., R.N.*
*Patricia S. Schroeder, M.S.N., R.N.*

The quality assurance process has been accepted as a very important component of professional nursing in any setting, but making quality assurance relevant to clinical practice has long been seen as a challenge for nursing. Frequently, staff nurses view quality assurance as something that does not directly relate to caring for patients, but is imposed upon them by administrators. At St. Michael Hospital in Milwaukee, Wisconsin, in the late 1970s, the nursing department decided to make the quality assurance process come alive for staff nurses. The method developed to do that was a unit-based quality assurance program.

As the title suggests, a unit-based quality assurance program is carried out at the individual nursing unit level. Clinical nurse specialists who are skilled in the quality assurance process serve as facilitators, but the program is implemented by the people closest to the activities of patient care, i.e., the staff nurses.

## UNIT-BASED QUALITY ASSURANCE MODEL

The unit-based quality assurance system can best be described through the use of the model adopted by St. Michael Hospital (Figure 2–1).

Encompassing the entire model is the model for quality assurance developed by the American Nurses' Association (ANA).[1] This model has seven commonly identified steps used in the process and provides direction for action in the system. Each nursing unit at St. Michael Hospital has its own Quality Assurance Committee (QAC), responsible for all phases in the quality assurance process. These committees are overseen by the Quality Assurance Coordinating Committee (QACC), which is made up of facilitators or chairpersons of each group, directors of nursing, and the vice president of patient services. Recommendations of the QACC are acted upon by the Nursing Practice Council, composed of four staff nurses and one head nurse, a clinical coordinator, an assistant head nurse, a clinical nurse specialist, an administrative supervisor, and a director.

**Figure 2–1** Model of Unit-Based Quality Assurance Program Used at St. Michael Hospital, Milwaukee, Wisconsin

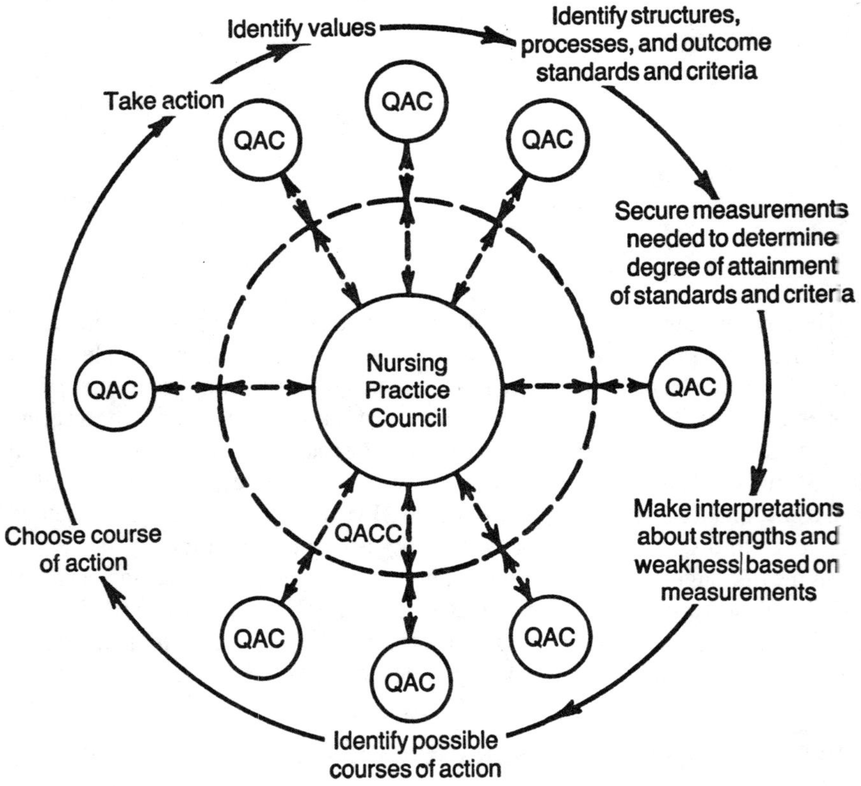


QACC = Quality Assurance Coordinating Committee

QAC = Quality Assurance Committee (on each unit)

*Sources:* Outside ring reprinted with permission from American Nurses' Association Congress for Nursing Practice, *A Plan for the Implementation of the Standards for Nursing Practice,* p. 15. Kansas City, MO: American Nurses' Association, 1975. Remainder of model from St. Michael Hospital, Milwaukee, Wisconsin.

## Unit QACs

The QAC membership on each nursing unit is similar, though not identical. The number of members varies from unit to unit, but the majority of participants are interested staff nurses. The head nurse and clinical coordinator (unit-based instructor) are also members of each committee. In an effort to maintain a professional thrust, only registered nurses are committee members. Most of the QACs are chaired by a clinical nurse specialist who has expertise in both the quality assurance process and the specialty practice of the unit. If the practice of the unit is outside the clinical nurse specialist's area of expertise, a staff nurse is identified to act in a leadership role for the QAC, and the responsibilities of the chairperson are shared.

In general, unit QACs meet on a monthly basis to carry out activities chosen according to the priorities for that individual unit. The structure varies, however. Several large nursing units found that QAC membership was reaching twenty to twenty-five members. Obviously, a group so large cannot function effectively. One group decided to meet every three months to identify and prioritize practice-related issues, as well as to identify other needed quality assurance activities. Subcommittees would be formed to complete these projects, and results would be reported at the next quarterly meeting. This structure has met a great many needs on those experimental units. It has allowed more nurses to participate in a meaningful way, has increased the productivity of the groups, and has allowed nurses to work on those quality assurance projects in which they have a special interest. Another significant benefit is that small groups of nurses who work on second or third shifts can work independently on quality-related projects without attending monthly meetings.

At any given time, the group may be addressing several activities, perhaps at various points in the quality assurance process. Development and implementation of standards and criteria are major activities of the QAC. Topics are selected by the committee as its members perceive the need. The results are shared centrally to restrict duplication of effort.

Identification of practice-related problems, whether actual or potential, is another major function of the unit committee. Problems may be identified through a variety of sources, such as staff observation, head nurse observation, physician input, incident reports, and patient satisfaction/dissatisfaction reports. It is sometimes difficult for the committees to define a clinical issue and develop it into a question appropriate for evaluative review. For example, a nurse may suggest that the committee study a topic as broadly defined as "the elderly in the hospital." This topic should be narrowed to something more specific, such as a comparison of the number of people over 65 chosen as primary patients within 24 hours of admission with the number of people under 65 chosen as primary patients within 24 hours of admission. It is a major function of the QAC chairperson to facilitate the development of the study questions while being careful to retain the staff's original idea.

*Study Procedure*

When a topic for evaluation has been defined and a study developed by a QAC, the committee chairperson submits a quality assurance study proposal to the director of specialty practice and evaluation, who is a doctorally prepared nurse and can provide valuable feedback in the research process. The proposal is written informally on the evaluation study report form (Exhibit 2–1) in accordance with routine instructions (Exhibit 2–2). Included in the proposal is the estimated amount of time required per data collector and the number and level of staff who will be involved. The purpose of this brief review process is twofold: (1) to give the reviewer an opportunity to suggest ways the committee could improve the study design and (2) to prevent duplication of study topics.

When the proposal has been approved, the unit QAC conducts the study. Data collectors are not always members of the QAC. Nurses who are members of the unit QAC maintain the decision-making role, but other nurses are routinely invited to take part in activities. Following data collection, the QAC analyzes the results, determines appropriate corrective action, and assigns responsibility for carrying out those actions. The unit members must be kept informed of study progress and results so that they do not begin to feel that the study group "spies on practice" without providing feedback.

The chairperson of the QAC is responsible for completing the summary of findings and recommendations on the evaluation study report form, as well as for submitting the data summary sheet (Exhibit 2–3). This form includes data on each specific criterion, as well as analysis, recommended actions, and indications that actions were completed. Completion of the data summary sheet according to instructions (Exhibit 2–4) is very important, because this is the primary documentation of problem identification and resolution.

Study reports are signed by the QAC chairperson, unit head nurse, director of nursing for that department, QACC chairperson, and vice president of patient services. This extensive routing is done not only for communication, but also for reinforcement of accountability of unit personnel. Copies of the reports are kept on file on the nursing unit and in the nursing department. One is then sent to the hospital QAC to keep this committee informed as well.

Development of the unit-based QAC system helped to open the door for relevant multidisciplinary audits. Prior to this, such audits had been done, but the initiation of the unit-based system brought about a major increase in nurses' interest and expertise. Nurses began to view problems broadly and to develop ideas for study that involved other disciplines. Communication with other disciplines about patient care problems increased significantly as nurses continued to develop in the evaluative process.

**Exhibit 2–1** Evaluation Study Report

NURSING DEPARTMENT
EVALUATION STUDY REPORT

DATE: ____________

COMMITTEE: ____________

TOPIC:

OBJECTIVES:

TIME PERIOD:

POPULATION:

CONCEPTUAL MODEL/UNDERLYING PRINCIPLES:

METHODOLOGY:

SUMMARY OF FINDINGS

RECOMMENDATIONS:

| | | | | | |
|---|---|---|---|---|---|
| Unit Chairperson | Date | Head Nurse | Date | Director | Date |

| | | | |
|---|---|---|---|
| Quality Assurance Coordinating Chairperson | Date | Vice President - Patient Services | Date |

*Source:* Reprinted with permission from St. Michael Hospital, Milwaukee, Wisconsin. Copyright 1982.

**Exhibit 2–2** Instructions for Use of Evaluation Study Report

| | |
|---|---|
| DATE: | Date the report is written |
| COMMITTEE: | Unit on which evaluation study was done |
| TOPIC: | What was looked at |
| TIME PERIOD: | Period/date data were collected |
| POPULATION: | Description and number |
| CONCEPTUAL MODEL/UNDERLYING PRINCIPLES: | Principles used, theory being tested, definition of terms being used |
| METHODOLOGY: | Collector's study design, and how sample was selected |
| SUMMARY OF FINDINGS: | |
| RECOMMENDATIONS: | Corrective actions, steps taken to rectify the deficits |
| ROUTING: | To occur in the following order: unit chairperson, head nurse, director, VP, QA coordinating chairperson |

*Source:* Reprinted with permission from St. Michael Hospital, Milwaukee, Wisconsin. Copyright 1982.

Communication about each QAC's activities is very important in order to maintain an orderly departmentwide quality assurance program. The chairperson of each QAC submits a quarterly report to the QACC; this report is collated with other reports and reflected in the QACC minutes. In this way, each QAC remains abreast of what other QACs are doing and of how each committee's activities fit into the hospitalwide program.

### *Role of Chairperson of Unit QAC*

The role of the chairperson of unit QAC's is a very important one. In the majority of instances, this role is held by a clinical nurse specialist (CNS) all of whom have expertise in quality assurance and research. As previously stated, when the CNS does not have expertise in the specialty practice of the nursing unit, a staff nurse assumes a leadership role titled as quality assurance associate, with the CNS acting as a facilitator. Chairperson responsibilities are then negotiated and shared between the two.

Overall, the responsibilities of the chairperson include calling the meeting, setting the agenda, and keeping minutes. Study reports are prepared by this person as well. Responsibilities which are always maintained by the CNS include developing the group's knowledge base regarding quality assurance, facilitating the research process, and critique standards of care and criteria sets developed.

### *Role of Head Nurse in Unit QAC*

Head nurses have defined responsibilities in the quality assurance process. They are always members of their unit's QAC and, as such, attend all unit QAC meetings. Because of their unit management responsibilities, they are also respon-

**Exhibit 2–3** Data Summary Sheet

DATA SUMMARY SHEET

Page _____ of _____

Date: __________

TOPIC:

N=

| CRITERIA | CRITERIA MET | | CRITERIA MET BY EXCEPTION | | FINAL | | ANALYSIS | RECOMMENDED ACTION | ACTION COMPLETED SIGNATURE/DATE |
|---|---|---|---|---|---|---|---|---|---|
| | # | % | # | % | # | % | | | |

*Source:* Reprinted with permission from St. Michael Hospital, Milwaukee, Wisconsin. Copyright 1982.

**Exhibit 2–4** Instructions for Use of Data Summary Sheets

1. On each page, identify page number, date and topic.
2. Under "Criteria" column, number and list each individual criterion and its exceptions.
3. Under "Criteria Met" column, indicate number met and percentage.
4. Under "Criteria Met by Exception" column, indicate number met by exception and percentage.
5. Under "Final" column, indicate total of "Criteria Met" and "Criteria Met by Exception" and percentage.
6. Under "Analysis" column, indicate an explanation of the data, why the committee feels these results occurred and some judgment of its acceptability. There must be an analysis for each criterion.
7. Under "Recommended Action" column, indicate a measurable step to be taken to correct the problem. A deadline and the responsible party should be identified. A "Recommended Action" should be indicated for each criterion. If the actions are the same, one can list 'See Criterion #1, Recommended Actions 1.1–1.4."
8. Under "Action Taken" column, a date and signature are needed when the recommended action has been completed.
9. If for some reason the format of the study does not fit this form, or if other information needs to be included, a special sheet should be used to display the data.
10. Once the data summary sheets are completed, the Nursing Department Evaluation Study Report should be completed.
11. When dictating the reports for typing, please dictate in the following manner: Criterion, number met, exception and final, the analysis for that criterion, the recommended action (if any) for that criterion, and the action taken (if any) for that criterion.

    Please do not dictate all the criteria and then go back to dictate the analysis, recommended action and the action taken.

*Source:* Reprinted with permission from St. Michael Hospital, Milwaukee, Wisconsin. Copyright 1982.

sible for facilitating appointed staff nurses' attendance at the QAC meetings. Head nurses play an important role on the QAC. Their perspective in identifying and validating problems proposed for study or discussion provides a check and balance system in the definition of a quality assurance project by ensuring the project's relevance to the unit. Again in their managerial functions, they facilitate the completion of projects on the unit and incorporate the results of quality assurance work into managerial decisions. This function takes into account the head nurses' responsibility for coordination of all activities on their unit and the crucial role that this coordination plays in the accomplishment of the quality assurance goals.

### *Role of Staff Nurse in Unit QAC*

Staff nurse members of the QAC are volunteers from the unit who have expressed an interest in quality assurance. Each staff nurse representative attends all the QAC meetings and assumes responsibility for projects as assigned by the

QAC. All phases of the quality assurance process, including development of standards and criteria, identification of practice issues for discussion or study, development of the study, data collection, analysis and planning, and implementing corrective action, are carried out by the staff. When no quality assurance associate has been named on a unit, the staff nurses rotate the responsibility for reporting on the unit's QAC activities at the unit meetings.

The staff nurse is by far the most important member of unit QACs. The entire premise of this quality assurance program demands that staff have the responsibility and authority to carry out this process. It is critical that QAC members be prepared and supported in carrying out quality assurance on the unit.

**Quality Assurance Coordinating Committee**

The QACC has the major responsibility for defining and coordinating the quality assurance activity for the entire nursing department. Members identify hospitalwide quality issues and develop appropriate strategies to deal with those issues. The review of each QAC's activities through the QAC's chairperson is helpful in carrying out this function, as well as in planning for hospitalwide nursing quality assurance studies that are then assigned to all QACs. The overall review function of the QACC also enables this committee to promote multidisciplinary quality assurance studies, since they have a perspective of the quality assurance activities.

The QACC plans and provides continuing education on quality assurance topics that pertain to the whole department. This continuing education may be provided by the QACC members or may be delegated to appropriate persons. The QACC members also act as a problem-solving group to help QAC chairpersons with problems pertaining to the unit QACs. Furthermore, in reviewing the activities of each QAC, the QACC has the opportunity to make suggestions for improving the research methodology and, thus, the quality of the evaluation studies being conducted. Consultation with the research committee can also be obtained.

In the model for unit-based quality assurance as seen in Figure 2–1, communication between the unit QACs and the QACC is depicted by two-way arrows to illustrate the flow of information between the QACs and the QACC. Surrounding the QACC is a circle made with a broken line, illustrating the openness of its membership. Depending on the agenda, members of the QACs may be invited to attend the QACC meeting with the QAC chairpersons. Some department employees who are not members of the QAC or the QACC may also be invited to attend. The communication lines between the QACC and the Nursing Practice Council are also two-way arrows, illustrating the easy flow of communication between those two structures.

A clinical nurse specialist chairs the QACC. Although the chairperson has unique responsibilities in coordinating the nursing department's quality assurance activities, the main accountability for quality assurance remains with the unit level nurses and QAC chairpersons. If responsibility for quality assurance rests at a level higher than the unit, staff nurses may abdicate their quality assurance responsibilities.

In the unit-based system, the chairperson of the QACC calls and conducts monthly meetings of the members. In addition, the QACC chairperson assists the unit QAC chairpersons and associates in the quality assurance process as needed. Routing of studies and obtaining appropriate signatures is also a function of the chairperson. The final function is to prepare a quarterly report for the hospital QAC.

### Nursing Practice Council

The final component of the unit-based quality assurance model is the Nursing Practice Council, which serves many functions to facilitate the work of the nursing department as a whole. In relation to quality assurance, however, the Nursing Practice Council reviews reports from the QACC in order to monitor its compliance with the nursing department's philosophy, goals, and objectives.

## IMPETUS FOR THE DEVELOPMENT OF THE UNIT-BASED MODEL

Quality assurance activities had been carried out in the nursing department at St. Michael Hospital since the early 1970s, but nursing leaders in the institution realized that the process was not as meaningful as it could be. Nurses were concerned about the direction of nursing as a profession in the institution, about the degree to which their responsibility to society was being met, about ways to examine and measure the impact versus cost of nursing care, and—the most disturbing of all—the achievement of nurses' autonomy and accountability. In addition, nursing research findings were being applied to the hospital setting. Initially, the nursing research program was open only to nurses who had earned a master's degree. It was felt that staff would feel quite isolated from the activities of the administration, however, unless some of these concepts were used at the grass roots level. When the quality assurance program was used at the unit level, the stage was set for staff nurses to understand that utilization of research studies could greatly enhance their own ability to participate in research activities eventually.

The main impetus for change in the quality assurance program, however, came from dissatisfaction with the quality assurance program that was already in place. That system involved a centralized nursing audit committee with one member representing each unit. A schedule of study topics was determined annually, and the primary methodology for study was the retrospective chart audit. It was found that members of the audit committee had little interest in the topics unless they pertained specifically to their unit. For example, a nurse from the obstetric unit would find a study concerning the nursing care of patients with pacemakers irrelevant. Consequently, little enthusiasm was mustered.

The committee reviewed data and then requested appropriate follow-up action from the head nurses of the units involved. This system was thought to be ineffective because, unless head nurses were on the audit committee, they were learning about the problems secondhand. Furthermore, head nurses saw follow-up action as "busy work" outlined for them by a centralized committee and did not view themselves as instrumental in problem solving. The quality assurance model was not real to them in their work, and they viewed it only in terms of the audit committee. These findings are supported by Langford, who stated, "No system, however valid, can be used effectively if it is imposed upon the agency personnel by someone in administration. . . . It cannot succeed as an effective means for improving nursing without the support of all levels of personnel."[2] It was nursing administration's view that the quality assurance process must be real to the head nurses and staff if high-quality patient care is to be provided.

The belief in the importance of quality assurance, plus some significant discontent with the existing quality assurance system, led to the development of the unit-based quality assurance system in early 1980. The program has evolved significantly since that time and has met with an overwhelming degree of success.

## UNIT-BASED SYSTEM VS. CENTRALIZED SYSTEM

A comparison of the unit-based models and centralized models suggests that, regardless of the unit-based method employed, a unit-based method provides a sound quality assurance system with more advantages and fewer drawbacks than does a centralized model.

### Benefits of a Unit-Based System

The first major benefit in the unit-based system is that nurses feel more committed to solving a problem when they have selected the issue to be studied. When the study focuses on their unit and they have participated in the design, implementation, and analysis of studies, the stage is set for them to become invested in the corrective action that will be proposed or to participate fully in the congratulations for a job well-done.

A unit-based quality assurance system enhances nurses' view of their role. By analyzing the data that are applicable to their own unit, nurses can more quickly learn what constitutes high-quality nursing care and how their personal efforts affect the quality of care delivered. The efforts of each nurse take on new importance.

Instituting any quality assurance system is a clear sign of acceptance of accountability for practice.[3-5] McClure, however, has noted the danger that auditing can become an end in itself. In a unit-based system, auditing is not the end result; the process must be evaluated in terms of its impact on patient care.[6] It is easier for each nurse to determine that impact when the care being evaluated is very close to the nurse's frame of reference. A conflict between nurses' traditional humanitarianism and accountability is manifested in frequently heard comments such as "I spend my time giving care, not documenting it," or "The nursing care I give is more important than whether or not there is a care plan." Gortner said that "until scientific accountability becomes as much a part of our tradition as our humanitarianism, we cannot hope to improve the quality of nursing care."[7] A unit-based system is a positive step toward connecting humanitarianism and scientific accountability.

Cost-effectiveness is a major benefit of a unit-based quality assurance system. For example, because nurses are investigating problems and instituting corrective action, they are reducing liability by solving problems through the quality assurance system. Implementation of this type of program requires no cash outlay, although it does require a major commitment and investment of time to organize the program. This commitment can actually be viewed as a commitment to staff development, a step toward upgrading the professionalism of the staff, which in the long run is also cost-effective. The implementation of a high-level professional program, such as a real and useful quality assurance program, not only helps a health care institution to retain its nurses, but also facilitates recruitment, since a professional atmosphere creates a desirable work environment. A unit-based system is also cost-effective because it does not involve middle-level people; it requires only unit level personnel. Compared with a primarily retrospective system, which most centralized systems are, a unit-based system requires less support from the medical records department. This cost benefit might have a small impact on the overall cost of health care. The greatest cost benefit, the one that most directly affects the patient, is that the nursing department deals with situations before they become problems. The key to the unit-based system is monitoring nursing care, not solving problems that occur in spite of it. Although it is difficult to measure the impact of this benefit exactly, it is well-known that dealing with problems after they occur is more costly than solving existing problems.

## Limitations of a Unit-Based System

The major potential limitation to the implementation of a unit-based quality assurance system is the high level of commitment required from the nursing department as it moves into that system. The administrative group of the department must be willing to work through a very complex change process. Instituting a unit-based system changes not only the quality assurance program itself, but also people's thinking about the quality assurance process. The process will become a very real part of every nurse's practice, which can be viewed as threatening or exciting. Staff members' perspective on the project depends on how it is promoted and directed.

In a unit-based system, it is sometimes difficult to coordinate hospitalwide studies. Technically, the QACC holds responsibility for studying those issues, but it is not feasible for the entire QACC to carry out that responsibility. For this reason, a task force, composed of volunteer members from any nursing unit, is often established to study a hospitalwide issue. The task force, either alone or in conjunction with the applicable unit QAC, studies problems and proposes solutions. Because some infection-related issues arise on all nursing units, for example, this central group can pull together common problems and investigate them systematically. Following problem resolution, that specific task force is dissolved.

Adoption of a philosophy supporting the unit-based quality assurance system is the first step in its implementation. Keeping the system functional through the many changes that nursing departments undergo is a continuing challenge. At St. Michael Hospital, the QACC helps maintain, monitor, and motivate the unit QACs and, thus, keeps the unit-based system operating through the changes in the department that may affect it. The QACC also helps in the evolution of the unit-based quality assurance program and of the nursing department as a whole. For example, the method of review for quality assurance proposals that was planned by the QACC was incorporated into the research department.

## CONCEPT OF QUALITY AND QUALITY ASSURANCE

Nurses have long been committed to delivering high-quality nursing care. The definition of quality, however, can vary from person to person and is not easily conveyed. Pardee and colleagues stated that quality nursing care can be defined only in relation to the goals that are set for the patient according to that patient's problems and needs.[8] Quality, then, would be assessed by measuring how well those goals have been met. A unit-based quality assurance system readily allows the nurses who set goals to measure the achievement of those goals.

Quality can also be thought of as having two aspects: technical competence and the art of care.[9] The technical aspect is certainly the most easily measured. According to the definition of quality given by Pardee and associates, however, that measurement would incompletely assess the level of quality. Most quality assurance programs focus on the technical aspects of care because these are the most concrete. Assigning responsibility for the quality assurance process to the unit staff does not guarantee that anything more than the technical aspect will be measured, but it does provide staff nurses with an opportunity to improve their approach in the art of care. A unit-based system makes evaluation of the technical aspects real for them and thus may move them to focus on the art of care as well.

Donabedian stated that there is an overabundance of definitions of quality. Through empirical studies and research, he investigated quality from two interesting viewpoints: the client's and the provider's. Donabedian found that clients cite competence and personal commitment as the two ingredients vital to high-quality care. He summarized the research by stating that, of the two qualities, personal commitment is more difficult to find.[10] Providers, on the other hand, tend to view quality "not in general terms, but by specifying in detail the clinical activities of patient care, focusing almost exclusively on technical management."[11] Donabedian found it difficult to group the technical skills as described in various studies into a classification of clinical performance. This, however, would identify "elements of technical performance concerning which judgments of quality have to be made; it would not improve our understanding of quality."[12]

In studies comparing clients' and providers' viewpoints, an indirect method almost always has been used to assess those views; that is, to answer the study question "What is quality?" subjects were asked to define the services of health care personnel that constitute quality care. Although this is one way to answer the study question, it emphasizes attributes and competencies rather than outcomes of care, which would probably more accurately answer the question.[13] Interestingly, this is true of both clients' and providers' viewpoints.

In summary, Donabedian proposed that the essential core of a definition of quality be the balance of health benefits and harm, and the avoidance of useless care. The role of cost remains unsettled, since it is very difficult to weigh the role of cost against the net profits to health. Nursing quality assurance personnel must seriously consider the definition of quality, always keeping in mind society's charge to the profession.

The term *quality assurance* has been widely accepted as the operationalization of the concept of quality. Quality assurance must be differentiated from quality assessment. Quality assessment reveals the strengths and weaknesses of the practice in terms of established criteria, but it involves no effort to change or improve that care.[14] Schmadl stated that, in order to define quality assurance, five questions must be answered:

1. What are we assuring?
2. For whom are we assuring it?
3. How do we assure it?
4. What measurements can we utilize?
5. What variables is it important for us to scrutinize?[15]

Schmadl went on to propose the following definition:

> Quality assurance involves assuring the consumer a specific degree of excellence through continuous measurement and evaluation of struc-

> tural components, goal-directed nursing process, and/or consumer outcome, using pre-established criteria and standards and available norms, and followed by appropriate alteration with the purpose of improvement.[16]

As Lang stated, quality assurance has as its goal the improvement of practice, not the proving of practice.[17] Assessment of practice, therefore, can be a first step in quality assurance, but unless improvement is made; the process does not constitute assurance of quality.

Partly because of the elusive nature of the definition of quality, it is possible for quality assurance programs to be focused on a goal that does not necessarily improve care. The unit-based quality assurance program prevents the achievement of an unimportant goal because it incorporates the responsibility for quality assurance into staff nurses' jobs. The concept of quality and the use of the quality assurance process are real to these nurses and affect their practice greatly.

A unit-based system for quality assurance has been described at El Camino Hospital in San Francisco.[18] The nursing department has a quality assurance coordinator who assists each unit, but the primary responsibility for quality assurance rests at the unit level. Administrators at Stanford transferred the nursing quality assurance program to the department of nursing research in September of 1981, demonstrating their belief that the concepts of research and quality assurance are closely aligned. The nursing quality assurance coordinator submitted a proposal for a unit-based quality assurance program to nursing service administration. Thirty-one nursing units are involved in the program, which has only begun to be implemented. The goals of this program are similar to the goals established when the nursing department at St. Michael Hospital developed the unit-based system. The primary assumption is that "the professional nurse at the bedside is in the best position to monitor patient care, to identify problems related to the provision of quality care, and to implement change to improve care."[19]

## QUALITY ASSURANCE IN INDUSTRY

Those in industry have recently become more interested in measuring quality and have developed quality circles as one means of measurement. The use of quality circles began in Japan about ten years ago, but the underlying principles were adopted from American statistical control engineers and behavioral scientists who took the ideas to Japan in the 1950s and 1960s in an effort to help the Japanese rebuild their industry following World War II.[20] Participative management and motivational factor theory form the basis for the development of quality circles.[21]

A quality circle is "a small group of people from the same work group who meet regularly to identify, analyze, and solve work-related problems."[22] Because the emphasis is on data collection and analysis, this process is quite closely aligned to the model for quality assurance adopted by the American Nurses' Association. In the use of the work group as the problem-solving forum, quality circles are closely related to a unit-based quality assurance system.

Quality circles have three fundamental purposes:

1. contribution to the improvement and development of the enterprise
2. sustaining a respect for humanity and building a happy bright workshop which is meaningful to work in
3. displaying human capabilities fully and eventually drawing out infinite possibilities[23]

The quality assurance process focuses on patient care and its improvement, which is, in industrial terms, a focus on improvement of the product. Quality circles, on the other hand, focus only indirectly on improvement of the product; they focus on the work environment and its improvement.

Effective implementation of quality circles is a major organizational undertaking. Changes in power, authority, employer, and employee roles are some of the issues that must be faced.[24] Members of the quality circle are the facilitator, a leader, and volunteer members of the individual work groups. It is important for the leader to be the supervisor of the work group and for the facilitator to take responsibility for introducing the concept into the organization and training the leaders. Preparation of supervisors is a commonly overlooked part of the process, even though such preparation may determine the success or failure of a quality circle. The process of implementation is easily cut short or altered by a failure to recognize the impact that the formation of quality circles has on the organization. Such an unforeseen alteration is very often the reason for demise of the circles.

Quality circles and unit-based quality assurance systems have a similar impact on the participants. The opportunity to identify unit-based problems and participate in their solution is a very positive one for workers. Regardless of the success or failure of the process, it greatly reduces the workers' sense of powerlessness, which so often contributes to staff morale problems. In addition, these two models have a similar impact on the power and authority of the organization. The return of some decision-making ability to the unit may be perceived positively or negatively by the members of the management structure, and that perception will uncover the strengths and weaknesses of the organization's management style.

There are some important differences between the quality circle and the unit-based quality assurance system. The topics that are explored vary greatly, for example. A quality circle focuses on any type of problem or situation, ranging from staff abuse of an illness policy to the difficulty of dealing with another department. The purpose of the unit-based quality assurance system, on the other hand, is to examine the practice on the unit in an attempt to improve the quality of care delivered. The sole intent of the quality assurance system is to improve patient care, whereas the quality circle system has other purposes as well.

The success of the quality circle appears to be totally dependent on the degree to which the process for implementation of the concept is completed. The implementation process for a quality assurance system is also important, but the outcome of the process is the main goal; accomplishment of the process itself will not necessarily improve nursing care.

Although the same issues are raised by the implementation of these systems, it appears that a quality circle can be started on a single unit; it is not necessary to start one on every unit. The success achieved by a single unit's quality circle relates only to that unit. A unit-based quality assurance system, however, is only one piece of the department's system for ensuring high-quality nursing care. The purpose of the system is to make a statement about the quality of care delivered by the entire nursing department.

The incentive for quality circle implementation most often comes from the organization itself. The incentive for examining quality in a health care setting most often comes from outside agencies that accredit health care institutions and uphold the quality assurance process as one form of measurement. As nurses continue to grow as a professional group, the value they place on evaluating their own profession's practice through the quality assurance process will increase.

## RESPONSIBILITY FOR QUALITY ASSURANCE

Given the premise of a model for unit-based quality assurance, the answer to the question "Whose responsibility should quality assurance be?" lies in several different perspectives. In order to meet the definition of professionals, the people engaged in the practice of a discipline must monitor their colleagues' practice of that discipline. Nurses have struggled to gain control of their practice. Historically, nurses have been quick to allow monitoring by others. It has been only since the 1960s that nurses have begun to seize control of their professional responsibility and find workable methods to carry out that responsibility. A sound quality assurance program, in any design, is crucial if nurses are to meet their responsibility as professionals in the role of self-regulation.

All professions gain their authority from society; in turn, they are responsible to society for their actions. Recently, the Congress for Nursing Practice of the American Nurses' Association completed a draft describing for the first time the relationship between nursing and society.[25] The concept of accountability, i.e., from whom does the profession derive its authority and to whom is the profession accountable, is a question that can be dealt with effectively by a sound quality assurance program, because it requires the collection and analysis of objective data about the care that is delivered.

The management of any organization must address the question of the cost of the service it provides. A quality assurance program can provide objective data about the activities of nurses and their effectiveness, and these data serve as a baseline for examining the cost-effectiveness of nursing care. Cost-effectiveness is increasing in importance as consumers become more sophisticated and demand a quality product at a fair price. In the current economy, it is no longer possible for health care providers to define their own cost parameters.

An effective quality assurance program can set the stage for autonomy and accountability of nurses. By setting standards for the profession and measuring themselves against these standards, nurses clarify the boundaries of nursing practice and, thus, can assert themselves to realize autonomy. Regardless of the program's design, a quality assurance program enhances nurses' accountability. As results of nursing care are quantified, the nurses who gave the care can easily see their impact and their need for improvement.

## CONCLUSION

The unit-based system for nursing quality assurance is a very important professional step. It is not only a successful method of quality assurance, but it clearly delineates the accountability of all professional staff for quality of care. This has not been affirmed and supported in most other quality assurance models. Use of this system, in part, is the key to the advancement of the professionalism of nursing practice. Although that is a future goal, the present reality is that the unit-based quality assurance system works!

---

### NOTES

1. American Nurses' Association Congress for Nursing Practice, *A Plan for Implementation of the Standards of Nursing Practice* (Kansas City, MO: American Nurses' Association, 1975), p. 15.

2. Teddy Langford, "The Evaluation of Nursing: Necessary and Possible," *Supervisor Nurse* 2, no. 11 (November 1971): 71.

3. Enid Jenkins, "Administration—Standards for Care and Their Influence on Nursing," *The Australian Nurses Journal* 11, no. 7 (February 1982): 38.

4. Geraldine Felton et al., "Pathway to Accountability: Implementation of a Quality Assurance Program," *Journal of Nursing Administration* 6, no. 1 (January 1976): 20.

5. Margaret L. McClure, "The Long Road to Accountability," *Nursing Outlook* 26, no. 1 (January 1978): 48.

6. Ibid.

7. Susan R. Gortner, "Scientific Accountability in Nursing," *Nursing Outlook* 22, no. 12 (December 1974): 768.

8. Geraldine Pardee et al., "Patient Care Evaluation," *American Journal of Nursing* 71, no. 10 (October 1971): 1958.

9. Robert Henry Brook, Kathleen Nies Williams, and Allyson Davies Avery, "Quality Assurance Today and Tomorrow: Forecast for the Future," *Annals of Internal Medicine* 85, no. 6 (December 1976): 809.

10. Avedis Donabedian, *The Definition of Quality and Approaches to Its Assessment,* vol. 1 (Ann Arbor, MI: Health Administration Press, 1980), p. 45.

11. Ibid, pp. 48–49.

12. Ibid, p. 60

13. Ibid, p. 73.

14. Robert Henry Brook, Kathleen Nies Williams, and Allyson Davies Avery, "Quality Assurance Today and Tomorrow: Forecast for the Future," *Annals of Internal Medicine* 85 (December 1976): 809.

15. John Charles Schmadl, "Quality Assurance: Examination of the Concept," *Nursing Outlook* 27, no. 7 (July 1979): 462–464.

16. Ibid, p. 465.

17. Norma M. Lang, "Professionally Speaking—Quality Assurance Review in Nursing," *The American Journal of Maternal Child Nursing* 1, no. 2 (March/April 1976): 78.

18. Joan Nietz Althaus et al., *Nursing Decentralization: The El Camino Experience* (Wakefield, MA: Nursing Resources, 1981), pp. 81–101.

19. Marianne Zalar, "Development of a Unit-Based Nursing Quality Assurance Program," *Nursing at Stanford* 4, no. 5 (September/October 1982): 3

20. Patricia L. Geldbach, Walter F. Klein, and Rusti C. Moore, "Quality Control Circles Solving OR Problems," *AORN Journal* 34, no. 6 (December 1981): 1029.

21. Michael H. Cook, "Quality Circles—They Really Work, But . . . ," *Training and Development* 36, no. 1 (January 1982): 4.

22. Marjorie Maser, "Mount Sinai Invests in Quality Circles," *Health Services Manager* 15, no. 2 (February 1982): 12.

23. William G. Ouchi, *Theory Z: How American Business Can Meet the Japanese Challenge* (Reading, MA: Addison-Wesley, 1981): 265.

24. Cook, "Quality Circles—They Really Work, But . . ."

25. American Nurses' Association, *Nursing: A Social Policy Statement* (Kansas City, MO: American Nurses' Association, 1980).

---

## REFERENCES

### Books

Althaus, Joan Nietz; Hardyck, Nancy McDonald; Pierce, Patricia Blair; and Rodgers, Marilyn S. *Nursing Decentralization: The El Camino Experience*. Wakefield, MA: Nursing Resources, 1981, pp. 81–101.

American Nurses' Association. *A Plan for the Implementation of the Standards for Nursing Practice*. Kansas City, MO: American Nurses' Association, 1975.

American Nurses' Association. *Nursing: A Social Policy Statement*. Kansas City, MO: American Nurses' Association, 1980.

Donabedian, Avedis. *The Definition of Quality and Approaches to its Assessment,* vol. 1. Ann Arbor, MI: Health Administration Press, 1980.

Ouchi, William G. *Theory Z: How American Business Can Meet the Japanese Challenge*. Reading, MA: Addison-Wesley, 1981.

**Journals**

Brook, Robert Henry; Williams, Kathleen Nies; and Avery, Allyson Davies. "Quality Assurance Today and Tomorrow: Forecast for the Future." *Annals of Internal Medicine* 85, no. 6 (1976): 809–817.

Cohen, Adrene G., and Tucker, Edith. "Department of Nursing Implementation of JCAH Standards: A Quality Assurance Program Applied." *Hospital Topics* 58, no. 2 (1980): 38–40.

Cook, Michael H. "Quality Circles—They Really Work, But. . ." *Training and Development* 36, no. 1 (1982): 4–6.

Felton, Geraldine; Frevert, Elaine; Galligan, Kathleen; Neill, Mary Kathleen; and Williams, Lillian. "Pathway to Accountability: Implementation of Quality Assurance Program." *Journal of Nursing Administration* 6, no. 1 (1976): 20–24.

Fifer, William R. "Quality Assurance: Debate Persists on Goals, Impact, and Methods of Evaluating Care." *Hospitals* 53, no. 7 (1979): 163–167.

Forquer, Sandra L., and Anderson, Taylor B. "A Concerns-Based Approach to the Implementation of Quality Assurance Systems." *Quality Review Bulletin* 8, no. 4 (1982): 14–19.

Friend, Gail. "Hospital Inservice Education Through the Quality Assurance Program." *Hospital Topics* 56, no. 2: 10–12.

Gallant, Barbara W., and McLane, Audrey M. "Outcome Criteria: A Process for Validation at the Unit Level." *Journal of Nursing Administration* 9, no. 1 (1979): 14–21.

Geldbach, Patricia L.; Klein, Walter F.; and Morre, Rusti C. "Quality Control Circles Solving OR Problems." *AORN Journal* 34 (1981): 1029–1035.

Gortner, Susan R. "Scientific Accountability in Nursing." *Nursing Outlook* 22, no. 2 (1974): 764–768.

Hegyvary, Sue Thomas. "Nursing Process: The Basis for Evaluating the Quality of Nursing Care." *International Nursing Review* 26 (1979): 113–116.

Howe, Marilyn J. "Developing Instruments for Measurement of Criteria: A Clinical Nursing Practice Perspective." *Nursing Research* 29 (1980): 100–103.

Jenkins, Enid. "Administration—Standards for Care and Their Influence on Nursing." *The Australian Nurses Journal* 11 (1982): 38–40.

Klein, Gerald D. "Implementing Quality Circles: A Hard Look at Some of the Realities." *Personnel* 58, no. 6 (1981): 11–20.

Lang, Norma M. "Professionally Speaking—Quality Assurance Review in Nursing." *The American Journal of Maternal Child Nursing* 1, no. 2 (1976): 75–79.

Langford, Teddy. "The Evaluation of Nursing: Necessary and Possible." *Supervisor Nurse* 2, no. 11 (1971): 65–75.

Lazerri, Mary B. "Quality Assurance Comes Alive at the Unit Level: QAC's." *Nursing at Stanford* 4 (1982): 1, 12.

Maser, Marjorie. "Mount Sinai Invests in Quality Circles." *Health Services Manager* 15, no. 2 (1982): 12–13.

McClure, Margaret L. "The Long Road to Accountability." *Nursing Outlook* 26, no. 1 (1978): 47–50.

Pardee, Geraldine; Hoshaw, Dorothy O.; Huber, Cathee J.; and Larson, Barbara A. "Patient Care Evaluation." *American Journal of Nursing* 71, no. 10 (1971): 1958–1960.

Schaffer, Ken L.; Lindenstein, Joan; and Jennings, Thomas. "Successful QA Program Incorporates New JCAH Standard." *Hospitals* 55, no. 16 (1981): 117–120.

Schmadl, John Charles. "Quality Assurance: Examination of the Concept." *Nursing Outlook* 27, no. 7 (1979): 462–465.

Tucker, Edith. "An Alternate Route to Quality Assurance—A Holistic Professionally Autonomous Approach." *Hospital Topics* 59, no. 1 (1981): 22–28.

Walkley, Philip H. "Process Audit: An Integral Component of a Quality Assurance Program." *Medical Record News* 49, no. 3 (1978): 55–56.

Waszak, John J. "Adapting QC's to Health Care: Some Special Challenges." *Hospital Progress* 63, no. 8 (1982): 47–48, 63.

Zalar, Marianne. "Development of a Unit-Based Nursing Quality Assurance Program." *Nursing at Stanford* 4 (1982): 1, 3, 4.

# Chapter 3

# A Systems Model for Implementation of Unit-Based Quality Assurance

*Peggy L. Wagner, M.S.N., R.N., CCRN*

The implementation of the unit-based quality assurance program, like that of any other program, involves making changes in organizational structure and individual roles. One method of facilitating and structuring the change process is the systems approach, in which the task is broken down into manageable components based on defined objectives. The responsibility and time schedule for each component is clearly delineated. The end result should be an organized, well-timed, and collaborative finale to the process of change.

The basic components of any system are (1) input, (2) throughput, (3) output, and (4) feedback (Figure 3–1).[1,2] In terms of program development, the input can be compared to the present state of the system, the throughput to the developmental process, and the output to the finished product. Feedback is an essential component of the system because it maintains and nourishes growth. Negentropy, defined as an evolution toward increasing complexity and organization, is dependent on a process by which the output is evaluated and continuously fed back into the system as input.

The boundaries of the system define its integration into the environment and its responsiveness to the environment, i.e., to the other tasks and goals of the nursing department, to the process of quality assurance in the hospital, to the progress of nursing science in relation to the evaluation of practice. These boundaries must be semipermeable so that they allow necessary information and energy into and out of the change process, but screen superfluous stimulation.[3,4] This type of planned control ensures structure, harmony, and progressive thinking in the development of the system.

Use of the systems approach facilitates the attainment of a common goal from almost any starting point. Therefore, a custom-tailored unit-based quality assurance program can be developed and implemented in any organization. Bailey and Claus offered a ten-step method to problem solving using the systems approach:

**Figure 3–1** Systems Model for the Development of a Unit-Based Quality Assurance Program

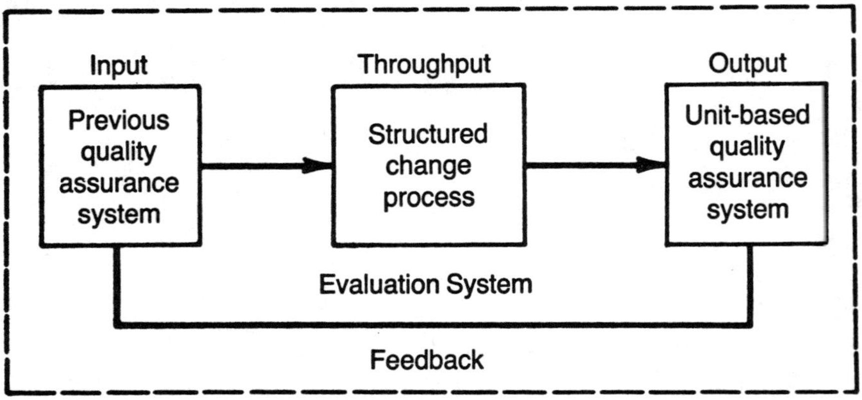


1. Define needs, purposes, goals.
2. Define problem.
3. Specify constraints, capabilities, resources, claimant groups.
4. Specify approach to problem solution.
5. State behavioral objectives and performance criteria.
6. List alternative solutions.
7. Analyze options.
8. Choose the best option.
9. Control and implement decisions.
10. Evaluate effectiveness of action.[5]

This type of structured application of systems theory creates a concrete framework for change.

## THE DECISION TO CHANGE

Before personnel and resources are committed to the development of a unit-based quality assurance program, the following questions must be answered:

1. What are the goals and philosophy of the nursing department for quality assurance? Are they congruent with the goals and philosophy of the unit-based system?

2. How would the concept of the unit-based system fit into the structure of the nursing department? The hospital? What are basic discrepancies, i.e., what pieces do not fit?
3. What resources are available? Are money, time, commitment of both management and grass roots personnel, and qualified leadership adequate for the project?

If and when the answers to these questions indicate readiness in an appropriate climate, system development can begin.

Before the implementation of the unit-based system, the quality assurance structure at St. Michael Hospital was biphasic. It involved (1) the clinical nurse specialist group, which facilitated development of standards, and (2) the nursing audit committee, which assessed compliance with those standards by retrospective chart audit and made recommendations. The impetus for change revolved around frustration with this system. The limited staff nurse involvement with both development of standards and audit resulted in (1) lack of compliance with the standards, (2) scattered knowledge and concern about results of audits, and (3) poor commitment to making changes based on audit results. Also, it seemed that the retrospective audits done by a central audit committee were not always relevant to daily nursing practice and problem solving.

Philosophically, St. Michael Hospital was committed to clinical quality and participative change. Its progressive nursing department often stimulated program development, and change was expected. There were no significant administrative or structural blocks to the redevelopment of the nursing quality assurance program. Resources were plentiful: the managers and professional staff of the nursing department were committed to high-quality patient care; the clinical nurse specialist role had been well developed and provided leadership expertise in quality care and program development; administrative support was inherent.

## METAMORPHOSIS OF THE QUALITY ASSURANCE SYSTEM

Once the commitment to system change has been made, a planned process can be initiated (Exhibit 3–1, Figure 3–2). First, the responsible group must be delineated. This group should include an appointed chairperson, who is responsible for overseeing the process, and representatives from each group that will be involved in the implementation of the finalized plan. Early involvement not only paves the way for future commitment to the plan by all participants, but also provides varying points of view, potentially avoiding basic structural or philosophical loopholes in the completed project.

In the St. Michael Hospital experience, the project development group was chaired by the associate director of nursing, who was at that time the key person

**Exhibit 3–1** Checklist for Implementation of a Unit-Based Quality Assurance Program

| TASK | DATE PROJECTED | DATE COMPLETED |
|---|---|---|
| 1. Form the change group (as applicable) | | |
| _____ Chairperson | | |
| _____ Staff nurses | | |
| _____ Head nurse | | |
| _____ Nursing administration | | |
| _____ Clinical nurse specialists | | |
| 2. Draft the proposed program | | |
| _____ Objectives | | |
| _____ Program description | | |
| _____ Model | | |
| 3. Review the proposed system | | |
| _____ Head nurse | | |
| _____ Staff nurses | | |
| _____ Hospital administration | | |
| _____ Expert | | |
| 4. Finalize the program | | |
| _____ Delineate specific functions of committee and subcommittees and respective chairpersons | | |
| _____ Define membership of committees/subcommittees | | |
| _____ Solidify reporting relationships | | |
| _____ Choose a model | | |
| _____ Appoint chairpersons | | |
| _____ Develop activity review process | | |
| _____ Determine methods of problem solving/evaluation | | |

**Exhibit 3–1** continued

| TASK | DATE PROJECTED | DATE COMPLETED |
|---|---|---|
| 5. Pilot unit (if desired) | | |
| _____ Present to head nurse group | | |
| _____ Determine volunteer unit | | |
| _____ Implement pilot period | | |
| _____ Review of results of evaluation of program | | |
| _____ Revision of plan, if needed | | |
| 6. Implement the system | | |
| _____ Present program to head nurse | | |
| _____ Appoint subcommittee members | | |
| _____ Conduct organizational meetings | | |
| 7. Evaluate the system | | |
| _____ Informal/ongoing | | |
| _____ Formal | | |

responsible for nursing quality assurance. Group members included clinical nurse specialists and assistant directors of nursing. The work of this group was defined by its purpose: to develop a cohesive system of quality assurance for nursing with emphasis on staff nurse involvement and unit problem solving. (Regrettably, because head nurses and staff nurse representatives were not included at the beginning, a complete program reorganization was required before implementation.)

A program description evolved and was consolidated into an organizational flow chart (Figure 3–3). This work was then submitted for review by head nurses, staff nurses, hospital administrators, and an authority in quality assurance, Dr. Norma Lang, who developed the model for quality assurance adapted by the American Nurses' Association Congress for Nursing Practice.[6] The program organization presented to head nurses was passed along to staff nurses at unit meetings for discussion. An interesting discovery was made when staff nurses'

**Figure 3–2** Time Line for Implementing Unit-Based Quality Assurance System

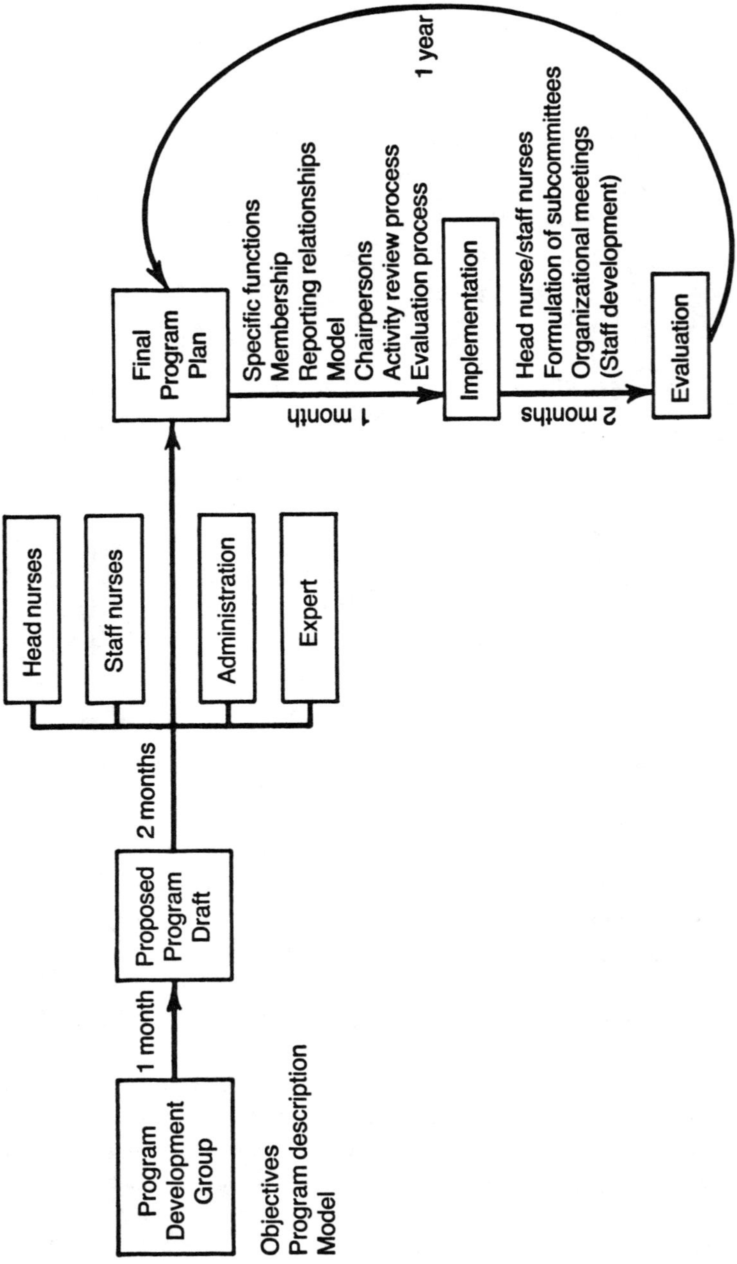

**Figure 3–3** Initial Program Design for Unit-Based Quality Assurance: Administration-Directed Program

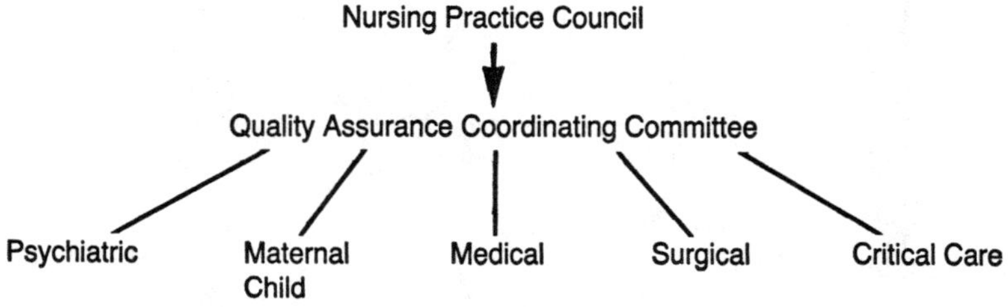


Specialty committees composed of:

- Clinical nurse specialist—chairperson
- Head nurse/assistant head nurse
- Clinical coordinators
- Hospital education
- Directors of nursing
- Supervisors
- Clinical nurse specialists
- Staff nurses

---

reactions were solicited. The program plan remained top-heavy, i.e., most members of the unit committees were clinical nurse specialists, supervisors, hospital education personnel, clinical coordinators, and head nurses. Representation of staff nurses was minimal. Critical evaluation showed that the flow of information, authority, and direction of the program remained with top nursing administration. After a consultation with Lang, the answer appeared to be fairly simple—turn the flow chart upside down, with information from unit committees flowing to a coordinating group and then to nursing administration (Figure 3–4).

It was then that the entire process fell into place. Unit committee membership was redefined so that the majority of members were staff nurses. With continued communication and support from the hospital administration, details of the program were developed. The process of finalizing the program included the following key steps:

1. Delineating specific functions. The basic structural units of the program (i.e., the unit subcommittees, the quality assurance coordinating committee, and the nursing council), the responsibilities of each group, and the duties of participating individuals in achieving program goals were now outlined.

**Figure 3–4** Revised Program Design for Unit-Based Quality Assurance: Staff Nurse-Directed Program

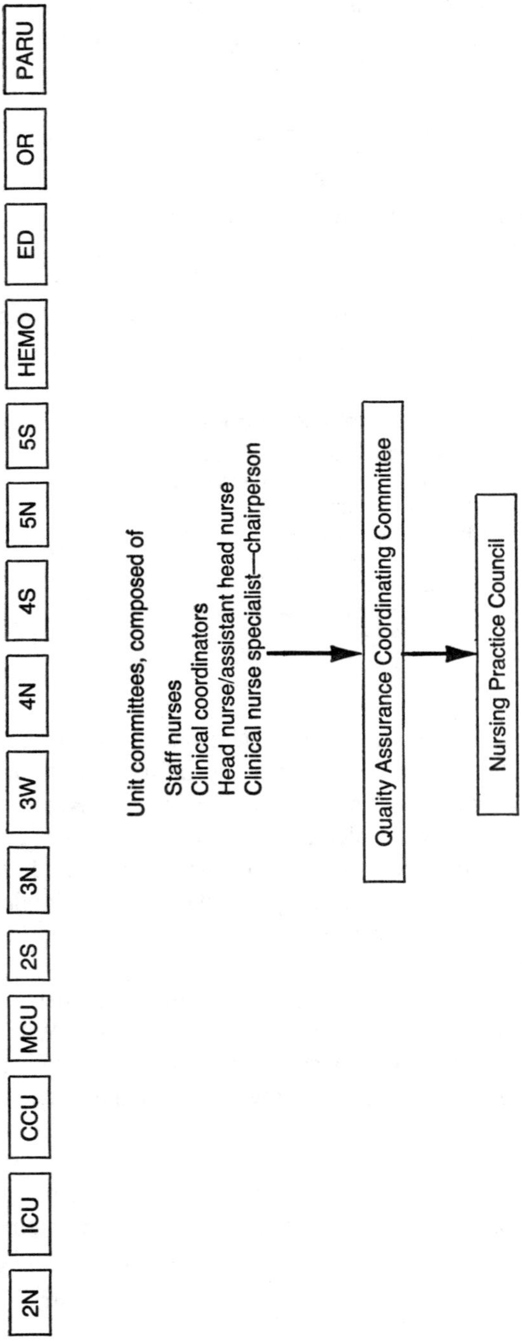

2. Defining membership. The membership of unit committees, as well as that of the quality assurance coordinating committee, was defined in terms of job classifications. Individual members of unit committees were selected later.
3. Solidifying reporting relationships. In the process of delineating specific functions and defining membership, the communication process was reviewed and tested.
4. Choosing a model. Several members of the program development group conceptualized models for graphic representation of the system. All were reviewed, discussed, and put to a vote. The chosen model was then refined.
5. Appointing chairpersons. Clinical nurse specialists became unit committee chairpersons, responsible for implementation of the unit-based system. Nursing units were divided according to the clinical nurse specialists' expertise and the number of hours worked per week. Most clinical nurse specialists assumed responsibility for more than one unit.
6. Developing activity review process. The two key responsibilities of the unit quality assurance committees were defined as developing standards and evaluating nursing practice, and the process for accomplishing each of these was developed (Exhibit 3–2).
7. Determining methods for solving problems and evaluating the system. The feedback loop was immediately put into place. Mechanisms for problem solving within the quality assurance coordinating committee and formal periodic evaluations were delineated.

This process completed the program development stage. The project development group was dissolved and program implementation initiated.

## IMPLEMENTATION OF THE DEVELOPED SYSTEM

At St. Michael Hospital, it was decided to implement the final plan on a hospitalwide basis immediately. (As an alternate strategy, the program might have been tried on one or two units, then reevaluated before wide scale implementation.) Unit committee members were selected at the discretion of the head nurse in consultation with the clinical nurse specialist chairperson. Some committees were composed strictly of volunteers, others of appointees.

The agenda for the organizational meetings on each unit was predetermined by the quality assurance coordinating committee. Items included orientation to the system, discussion of functions of the committee, presentation of the program model, evaluation of the committee's preparedness to perform its functions, development of initial objectives, and scheduling of meetings. Discussion and comparison of these initial meetings revealed that the expertise and motivation varied widely among staff nurses and among nursing units.

**Exhibit 3–2** Process of Developing Quality Assurance Activities

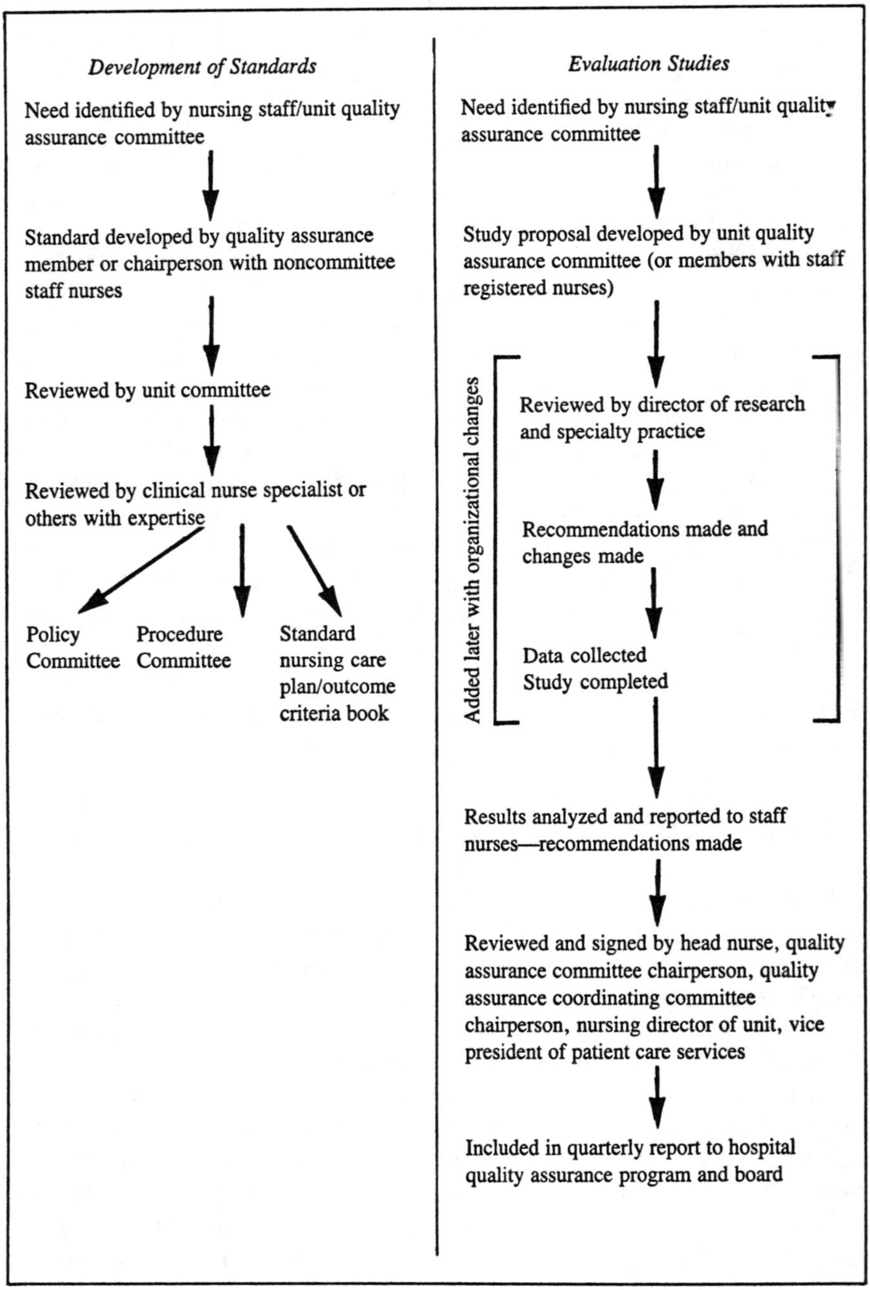

An important part of the implementation process became the education of committee members in four basic areas: (1) definition and concept of quality assurance, (2) identification of problems and formulation of questions for evaluation, (3) familiarity with the research and evaluation process, and (4) identification of solutions to care deficits.

The concept of quality assurance and the requirements of accrediting agencies in their evaluation of care have been in a constant state of growth and development. It was necessary to update staff nurses with varied backgrounds and experience in order to provide a common denominator among the members of each group and among the groups. Since the program was new and unique, its history, especially the fact that it was built on a more traditional quality assurance model, was included in the educational process to give nurses a sense of ownership, motivation, and investment in the program.

Some groups were stymied by the process of problem identification. Nurses were taught how to observe nursing care objectively and to identify deficits within the system, as well as within their own repertoire of skills and knowledge. Strategies used by various groups to identify problems or questions included brainstorming; nominal group process; submitting lists to the quality assurance committee from staff nurses' meetings; consulting the head nurse, director, clinical coordinator, assistant head nurse, or clinical nurse specialists; reviewing incident reports; and comparing perceived level of care against published standards. Generally, once the nurses were psychologically freed to identify problems creatively, the task of the unit committee was to decide on a realistic schedule of activities based on a long list of topics.

To focus on the research process, various chairpersons used three methods at the initial stage of program development: (1) monthly presentation of a research study from the literature, (2) monthly discussion of a research topic, and (3) discussion of relevant research topics with each study. These strategies were most rewarding when they were related directly to patient problems on a given unit. For example, the critique of the methodology and clinical application of a study on how stomach acidity affects drug absorption led staff nurses on modified care to expand their own investigation of nursing strategies to prevent gastrointestinal symptoms in patients taking Quinidine. As the process for review of studies was developed, it was supplemented to include evaluation by a person with expertise in the research process, the Director of Specialty Practice and Evaluation. This was an important addition to the process, because it tightened evaluation study methodology and allowed changes to be based on scientifically credible data.

Once data were collected, results were reviewed either at the quality assurance committee level or at unit meetings to permit greater input from all nursing staff. Compliance and noncompliance with standards were analyzed to determine the factors that were contributing to effective and ineffective nursing practice so that good practice could be reinforced and poor practice changed. Some unit committees could solve problems readily by brainstorming, while other groups began by choosing from options presented to them by the clinical nurse specialist or by the head nurse. Variables in group ability to solve problems effectively appeared to be

1. the communication pattern among nurses
2. the knowledge base of the group (demonstrating the importance of continuing education to make staff nurses aware of the options)
3. the expertise of the clinical nurse specialist chairperson in relation to the unit specialty
4. the motivation and professionalism of the nurses involved

A wide variety of solutions evolved from various studies, such as in-service or continuing education, development of new standards, development of patient teaching materials and programs, revision of nursing forms, and the establishment of hospitalwide committees to assess and correct potential common concerns among units.

## EFFECTIVE UNIT QUALITY ASSURANCE COMMITTEES

Several characteristics emerged as essential for effective unit quality assurance committees. The four most significant factors involved (1) committee membership, (2) specific activities of the committees, (3) relationship of the quality assurance committee to the functioning of the unit, and (4) integration of the unit quality assurance activities into the total nursing department.

### Committee Membership

Soon after the program was implemented, it became apparent that the unit quality assurance committee was less effective if the head nurse (and on some units, the clinical coordinator) was not directly involved with its activities. Head nurse commitment demonstrated the importance given to evaluation of practice on that individual unit and increased the attendance of committee members, as well as the enthusiasm and productivity of the group. These factors, i.e., faithful attendance and motivation, were also independently important as characteristics of members.

Staff nurses who were valuable contributors to the program seemed to have a strong concept of professional nursing and confidence in their own expertise. Previous involvement with quality assurance was sometimes helpful, but only if the nurse was adaptable enough to build upon experience rather than cling to it.

The leadership style of the clinical nurse specialist chairperson either suppressed or facilitated group process and was found to be an important item to evaluate in trouble-shooting the stymied group. Previously established rapport and credibility helped the group to work more productively. Although it was not always feasible for such a person to chair the committee, the work of the group was facilitated if the clinical nurse specialist had expertise in the area. Knowledge of subject matter being studied provided early guidance and consultation and avoided stumbling blocks in the design of studies and the development of standards.

### Activities of the Committee

An early and complete orientation to the concept of quality assurance, to the unit-based program, and to expectations was important in the original group education. New members became more productive in the group earlier if they were given a specific orientation and review of the group's previous work to provide a sense of history and flow of activities.

Tailoring meeting times to group wishes facilitated attendance. Most units preferred a specific monthly meeting date and time, although other units chose to arrange monthly meetings according to the work schedules of members. One unit chose to meet bimonthly; another unit rotated meeting times among shifts; another large unit arranged to meet quarterly with ad hoc work groups meeting more frequently. Any variation acceptable to all members facilitated the process.

A knowledge of studies being done on other units seemed to lead to additional ideas from committee members, participation in joint unit studies, and the use of developed data collection tools, which facilitated the testing of tools for reliability and validity. Review of discussion and conclusions reached at the quality assurance coordinating committee meetings provided staff nurses with a sense of program continuity and cohesiveness, assuring them that their activities were part of a departmentwide emphasis on quality care. Therefore, fixed agenda items regarding quality assurance coordinating activities and quality assurance projects on other units supported successful unit committees.

Interesting study topics and prompt feedback of study results both evolved from and stimulated group motivation. The more stimulating and relevant to daily clinical practice the study topic, the more committed the group to collecting data, analyzing results, and making changes in practice. Furthermore, this led to creativity and urgency in identifying subsequent and significant topics. Excitement related to a study topic could be easily maintained and constructive change made if results were reported as soon as data could be compiled. Structured and continuously moving process was motivating to groups.

### Relationship to Unit

Once quality assurance committee members were educated in the philosophy of quality assurance and trained in the development of studies and standards, they were able to assume responsibility for specific activities assigned by the committee. These project-directed committee members then solicited noncommittee registered nurses from the unit to develop and complete the activity. In this way, all members of the unit participated in and had some investment in the function of their quality assurance committee. Unit members were also involved in reporting quality assurance activities at unit meetings, identifying problems, and developing study recommendations with consensus of the entire professional staff. This total involvement created a feeling of "ownership" among committee members and unit professional nurses that paid benefits in solicitation of topics for study and commitment to change based on standards developed and recommendations from studies. Much less was accomplished if members felt that the group's activities were controlled by either the clinical nurse specialist or the head nurse.

It is important to deal with study results indicating poor compliance with standards in a nonpunitive fashion. If any positive impact or change is to be instituted as a result of studies, areas in which clinical deficits are suspected must be studied. The focus in the presentation of data should be constructive recommendations with a plan for reaudit to show growth. Usually, it is unnecessary and counterproductive to evaluate individuals' skills or practices (depending on the objectives of the study). If a spectrum of practice is presented, most nurses can readily place themselves on the continuum and modify their own practice according to recommendations. If a reaudit shows a continued deficit or a skewed study average because of individuals' poor practices, it may become appropriate to monitor and counsel individuals.

## Integration into the Nursing Department

Just as the involvement of the head nurse is important to committee activities, the commitment of nursing administration to the program and unit activities is essential. Quality assurance may involve financial expenditure for the extra hours required by personnel to work on projects, special scheduling to permit staff nurses' attendance at meetings, and support of recommendations. Without the support of administrators, unit quality assurance activities will be rendered impotent and motivation of members will be dissipated. Furthermore, individual participation in the development of quality assurance projects must be recognized, both informally and formally, and reimbursed financially.

The nursing department must also ensure that there is an adequate number of experienced resource persons within the system to facilitate the program. At St. Michael Hospital, the continuation of the unit-based program is contingent on the number of clinical nurse specialists, their areas of expertise, and their commitment to the quality assurance program. A change in philosophy regarding the staff position of the clinical nurse specialists would necessitate restructure of the quality assurance program. Therefore, nursing administration ensures the continuity and success of the unit-based quality assurance system by its commitment to the clinical nurse specialists.

## OBSTACLES TO SUCCESS

In the implementation process, trial and error revealed several obstacles to successful functioning of the unit-based quality assurance system.

### Obstacles Related to Committee Membership

Members of the unit quality assurance committee should be carefully selected. It was found that nurses who had a questionable concept of themselves as professionals with power to change practice did not contribute positively to group process. Disruptive members undermined efforts of the group and destroyed motivation. Membership on the unit quality assurance committee should, therefore, be held in esteem as a commitment to the development of professional practice and offered as an honor by a head nurse or by colleagues. The members of unit quality assurance committees potentially affect the practice of all other professional nurses on the unit.

### Obstacles Related to Activities of the Committee

Lack of structure at quality assurance committee meetings deterred motivation. A fixed agenda or circulation of a published agenda gave group members a sense of anticipation that improved attendance at meetings. Sometimes, the group determined the agenda for a subsequent meeting based on committee objectives and activities in progress.

Problem identification was stymied without a systematic approach acceptable to committee members. On some units, a yearly schedule of studies to be done was identified and dates for completion projected. This very structured approach provided a perspective in the work to be accomplished, but it did not allow for study of problems or interest areas that evolved. Some groups preferred to develop new studies as a previous activity was completed. Still others kept a running tally of clinical concerns or potential areas for study that was dealt with based on fluctuating priorities. The method used was dependent on the developmental state of the committee and the flexibility and adaptability of its members. The method of problem identification must match the characteristics of the committee. The quality of studies and amount of change generated varied from unit to unit.

Studies without broad applicability to nursing care on the unit decreased the enthusiasm of committee members and could roadblock committee activities. This type of problem was occasionally encountered if the idea for a study originated with the clinical nurse specialist or nursing administrators. With continuing education, however, staff members themselves often ascertained the importance of a practice or standard suggested for study by administrators and requested such a study.

It was important for staff members to identify their own study problems. The imposition of studies to be done by administration belies the objectives of unit-based quality assurance. At St. Michael Hospital, topics of concern regarding quality of the system (primary nursing, documentation, infection control) were delegated to hospitalwide nursing task forces when it appeared that clinical issues were being overlooked at one point during the development of the system. The chairperson of the unit committee must be sure that studies do not serve the interest of individuals, but concentrate on clinical practice issues of interest to the majority of nurses on the unit.

### Obstacles Related to Relationship to the Unit

Because of the dynamic nature of nursing units, there were times when stress prevented productive quality assurance activities. Stressors may occur when the unit is understaffed, when the patient census is high, when an overwhelming number of patients are seriously ill, and when the political climate is tenuous. Although quality assurance is an inherent part of the structure and function of nursing and continues despite such circumstances, the character of activities may change. For example, stress was decreasing clinical problem-solving abilities to such a degree on one unit that the routine quality assurance activities were interrupted to perform a study of specific stressors and ways to reduce stress on the unit and return to a more emotionally controlled climate. Study of practice issues then continued. Concerns of many types, such as stress, are related to the quality of clinical practice and, therefore, are appropriate as topics of study in quality assurance.

### Obstacles Related to Integration into the Nursing Department

The unit-based quality assurance program at St. Michael Hospital proved to be extremely tenacious, despite changes in nursing administrators, including directors of nursing and the vice president of patient care services. It survived budget cuts and staff layoffs in periods of low patient census. The most significant problem seemed to be the turnover of clinical nurse specialists, the identified program facilitators. Although unit quality assurance committees without clinical nurse specialist chairpersons survived, the imbalance of growth and progress stimulated some minor reorganization; the role of staff nurse chairperson supported by a clinical nurse specialist was created.

## IDEAS THAT DID NOT WORK

In the process of implementation, parts of the system proposed initially did not work and were discarded. For example, in the initial design of the unit committees, the evening and night nursing supervisors were included as members of unit committees. As the system evolved, however, it became apparent that supervisors, who have a hospitalwide perspective, did not facilitate unit activities and had more to offer on a different level. Their role in quality assurance presently involves the informal assessment of clinical and systems problems by individual supervisors. Integration of the supervisors into the unit-based system is in process.

At first, an analyst from the medical records department sat on the quality assurance coordinating committee to facilitate communication among departments and retrieval of chart data. As evaluation studies developed, however, not only were fewer retrospective chart audits done, but also committee members began collecting much of their own data from charts. Although medical records department personnel continued to be a valuable asset in the collection of some types of data and in circumstances that required elimination of potential bias in data collection, most activities involving retrospective chart review are now done by committee members. A medical records analyst no longer sits on the quality assurance coordinating committee, but acts as a resource to committee chairpersons as needed.

At the time the unit subcommittees began devising their first studies, there was an attempt to generate an annual audit schedule with the purpose of eliminating repetition, facilitating collaboration between units with similar concerns, and monitoring progress on studies. Since different units function differently—yet effectively—in their planning of quality assurance activities, it was impossible to develop such a schedule. Instead, the chairperson of each unit quality assurance committee submits a quarterly report of activities in progress and activities completed to the quality assurance coordinating committee. The circulation of this report provides the desired communication among units.

## FEEDBACK PROCESS

Feedback is an integral part of any system. It is, in fact, the stimulant to growth of an existing program. Information regarding the program can be reentered into this system both formally, by evaluation, and informally. (See Chapter 13.)

A mechanism is needed to facilitate problem solving, to report progress, and to share successes. At St. Michael Hospital, the quality assurance coordinating committee served this function, acting as an arena for discussion. The system was modified and new concepts integrated at this level. After the initial implementation, the quality assurance coordinating committee focused on motivating quality assurance members during periodic slumps in interest. One strategy that piqued the interest of staff nurses was a poster display of studies from each unit quality assurance committee. This allowed nurses to review the work of colleagues at leisure, stimulating new ideas for study, collaborating on studies, and validation of the data collection tools.

The St. Michael Hospital nursing newsletter, "Notables for Nursing," provides the vehicle for an ongoing report of quality assurance activities. On a rotating basis each month, it highlights one unit's quality assurance work, including evaluation studies, development of standards, and other information regarding quality of practice on that unit.

## CONCLUSION

The implementation of a unit-based quality assurance system is an ongoing process. The use of systems theory as a model for change provides direction in program development and integration within a complex organization. Since each nursing organization has its own unique structure, content of each step will differ; however, use of the basic process can facilitate the integration of unit-based quality assurance within acute care hospitals, long-term care facilities, public health organizations, or industries. The potential for modification of this program is endless.

### NOTES

1. JoAnne E. Hall and Barbara R. Weaver, *Distributive Nursing Practice: A Systems Approach to Community Health* (Philadelphia: J.B. Lippincott, 1977), pp. 19–49.
2. E. Mark Hanson, *Educational Administration and Organizational Behavior* (Boston: Allyn & Bacon, 1979), pp. 152–153.
3. Hall and Weaver, *Distributive Nursing Practice*, pp. 19–49.
4. Hanson, *Educational Administration and Organizational Behavior*, pp. 158–160.
5. June T. Bailey and Karen E. Claus, *Decision Making in Nursing: Tools for Change* (St. Louis, MO: C.V. Mosby, 1975), pp. 18–29.
6. American Nurses' Association Congress on Nursing Practice, *A Plan for the Implementation of Standards on Nursing Practice: A Report by the Congress of Nursing Practice of American Nurses' Association* (Kansas City, MO: American Nurses' Association, 1975).

### REFERENCES

#### Books

American Nurses' Association Congress on Nursing Practice. *A Plan for the Implementation of Standards on Nursing Practice: A Report by the Congress of Nursing Practice of American Nurses' Association*. Kansas City, MO: American Nurses' Association, 1975.

Bailey, June T., and Claus, Karen E. *Decision Making in Nursing: Tools for Change*. St. Louis, MO: C.V. Mosby, 1975.

Hall, JoAnne E., and Weaver, Barbara R. *Distributive Nursing Practice: A Systems Approach to Community Health*. Philadelphia: J.B. Lippincott, 1977.

Hanson, E. Mark. *Educational Administration and Organizational Behavior*. Boston: Allyn & Bacon, 1979.

Katz, Daniel, and Kahn, Robert. *The Social Psychology of Organizations*. New York: John Wiley and Sons, 1966.

von Bertanffy, Ludwig. *General Systems Theory*. New York: Braziller, 1968.

## Chapter 4

# Accountability for Quality Care: Perspectives of a Nurse Administrator

*SueEllen Pinkerton, Ph.D., R.N.*

The responsibility for excellence in nursing practice ultimately falls to the nurse-administrator. In efforts to promote excellence in practice, quality assurance is an essential management tool that can be used in several ways.

## PROCESS OF MANAGEMENT

Gibson, Ivancevich, and Donnelly define the process of management as a series of actions, activities, or operations that lead to some end.[1] The process of management can then be subdivided into three major functions: (1) planning, which is an understanding of what is to be done; (2) organizing, or how it is to be done; and (3) controlling, or whether it was done.

### Planning

Defining the ends to be achieved and determining appropriate means to achieve the defined ends is planning.[2] There are three components in planning: mission, goal, and objectives. The mission involves providing linkages between the environment and the organization. In nursing, the true measure of the value of a nursing service rests in the degree to which it modifies the health behaviors of others.[3] Medical centers commonly have as a mission patient care, research, and teaching. Community hospitals, however, tend to place less emphasis on research and education of members of the health professions.

The goal is the future state or condition that, when realized, contributes to the fulfillment of the mission. Organizations have long-range goals, which may include both general goals for the hospital and specific goals for the department of nursing.

The objectives of the organization are derived from the mission statements and goals, but they are short run, specific, and measurable. Objectives for staff nurses may involve documentation of patient care, which may be monitored by the head nurse and utilized in a quality assurance review. Thus, the objectives may be part of both the long-range goals for the nursing department and the mission of the department of nursing, coming full circle in the planning function.

### Organizing

All managerial activities that are performed to translate the required planned activities into a structure of tasks and authority are included in organizing. The components of the organizing function are (1) defining the nature and content of each job, (2) determining the basis for grouping jobs, (3) deciding the size of the group, and (4) delegating authority.[4]

### Controlling

In the process of management, controlling involves activities managers undertake to ensure that actual outcomes are consistent with planned outcomes.[5] The three components of the controlling function are standards, information systems, and corrective action.

Standards reflect the planning and organizing functions of the management process of the organization. They are the desired levels of achievement specified in criteria of organizational effectiveness. The education of staff nurses and standardization of their skills take place outside the organization, and staff nurses are hired with a basic level of skill assumed. Because of their education and expertise, nurses are autonomous both in regulating their practice through an official board of examiners and in defining an appropriate code of ethics for their practice. Furthermore, their professional association, the American Nurses' Association, is the originator of standards for practice. In this way, the professional collective has control of the practice of staff nurses in the hospital.

Information systems involve comparing planned and actual outcomes. Quality control systems are an important part of this particular component.

Corrective action is taken through the organizing function. As stated earlier, the organizing function includes all managerial activities that are performed to translate the required planned activities into a structure of tasks and authority. Managers must have the authority to take corrective action when planned outcomes differ from actual outcomes.

## QUALITY ASSURANCE AND MANAGEMENT FUNCTIONS

The three components of the planning function (i.e., mission, long-range goals, and objectives) may be closely associated with a quality assurance program. For example, a department of nursing may work toward a goal of increasing research skills through quality assurance activities. Several components of the research process can be used in a quality assurance program:

1. A thorough literature review enhances the knowledge base of the participants in a quality assurance program by providing them with current thinking about an identified nursing problem.
2. Well-developed instrumentation constructed by the nurses participating in the quality assurance program can ultimately lead to better data collection and better information on which to base decisions related to changes in practice.
3. Analytical skills can be strengthened by learning new statistical methods to utilize in analysis of data.

Findings that result from the systematic research process can suggest new theories in nursing and increase the body of nursing knowledge. Thus, a simple research goal that is related to a quality assurance program has many implications for nursing, especially when the goal or objective contributes to the research-theory-practice cycle in promoting the nursing profession.

The quality assurance program may be used to incorporate nursing research findings into practice. For example, nurses may use current research literature reviewed in preparation for quality assurance studies to design corrective action for variances found in their investigations.

A nursing department may have both long range research goals that are derived from the mission statement and short-range objectives that are related to quality assurance plans and variances. Quality assurance plans may be developed quarterly or yearly to monitor objectives set for a department of nursing.

Corrective actions resulting from quality assurance variances may lead to a variety of changes:

- revising procedures within a department
- establishing different lines of authority for the managers in the department
- changing the authority structure of management to increase or decrease the size of the group that is being managed
- changing the basis of job groupings from specialty practice groups to geographical location groups

Corrective action may also lead to an exploration of the role of the clinical nurse specialist to determine if there are specific ways in which the clinical nurse specialist may help the head nurse or other managers to address the particular quality assurance variances. Thus, accountability can be established for the nurse-practitioner, the manager, and the clinical nurse specialist by having them responsible both for monitoring unit objectives through quality assurance programs and for implementing any necessary corrective actions.

Preferably, a department of nursing is self-governing, and the quality assurance reports are submitted to the nurses who comprise the council. The self-governance council, composed of representatives of the nursing staff, may then make suggestions regarding corrective action, standard setting, or accountability, as appropriate. In this way, staff nurses participate in decision making, and the recommended actions are more likely to be incorporated into practice.

One method in which the organizing function can be used in a quality assurance program is in writing job descriptions that identify accountability for standards of practice and thus incorporate responsibility for quality assurance. Job groupings may be designed according to patient classifications so that identified groups of nurses care for patients categorized by the level of care they require. This would affect and be affected by practitioner preparation and position on the career ladder. Therefore, if it becomes necessary to take corrective actions related to various levels of care, such actions may be directed to the appropriate job grouping.

Obviously in administering the quality assurance program, the nurse administrator utilizes the information systems component of the controlling function of the management process. This then becomes the focus of the nurse administrator's use of the management process. In addition to the American Nurses' Association standards that have already been mentioned, other standards may be developed within the department of nursing to promote quality assurance programs and to guide recognized levels of practice. These standards, in turn, give appropriate direction for accountability and responsibility to the different levels of practitioners within the department. The hospital's policies and procedures also offer guides for standards of practice. Documentation systems, such as problem-oriented records, also provide organized approaches for retrieval of data to monitor standards of practice.

## CONCLUSION

Current trends in health care call for increased attention to the expenditure of funds, especially in the area of personnel resources, and nurse administrators will bear a growing burden of accountability in the area of health care costs. In addressing cost containment, nurse administrators will need to bear in mind the importance of educational programs to correct variances discovered in quality assurance programs. There will be a time when educational programs, which traditionally have been first to be cut from the budget, will need to be justified as essential to maintain standards of practice and quality of care.

In this age of budget constraints, nurse administrators must pay increasing attention to the organizational climate, i.e., the properties of the work environment as perceived by employees. Climate exists as a descriptor of the organization and, as such, is not continually influencing the organization to change. It does, however, influence the behavior of people in the organization and is influenced by the behavior, structure, and processes of the organization and its employees. As employees of an organization, staff nurses perform their job while influenced by the organizational climate, and a congruence between nurses and organizational climate has been linked to job satisfaction.[6]

Therefore, as nurse administrators address the important issues of quality assurance and fiscal accountability, it will be important to maintain an organizational climate that promotes job satisfaction. This is an ideal opportunity both for development of the individual professional nurse and for advancement of the nursing profession. The involvement of nurses at all levels in quality assurance will ultimately lead to excellence in practice.

## NOTES

1. James R. Gibson et al., *Organizations: Behavior, Structure, Processes* (Dallas: Business Publications, 1979), p. 40.
2. Ibid.
3. Ruth B. Freeman, cited in Earline L. Bryan, "A Nursing Service Director in an Acute Health Care Center," in *Decision Making in Nursing: Tools for Change,* ed. June T. Bailey and Karen E. Claus (St. Louis, MO: C.V. Mosby, 1975), p. 126.
4. Gibson et al., *Organizations: Behavior, Structure, Processes,* p. 42.
5. Ibid, p. 43.
6. Herbert L. Lyon and John M. Ivancevich, "An Exploratory Investigation of Organizational Climate and Job Satisfaction in a Hospital," *Academy of Management Journal* 17 (1974): 635.

## REFERENCES

### Books

Arndt, Clara, and Huckabay, Loucine M. Daderian. *Nursing Administration: Theory for Practice with a Systems Approach.* St. Louis, MO: C.V. Mosby, 1975, pp. 136–151.

Bernhard, Linda Ann, and Walsh, Michelle. *Leadership: The Key to the Professionalization of Nursing.* New York: McGraw-Hill, 1981, pp. 166–181.

Claus, Karen E., and Bailey, June T. *Power and Influence in Health Care.* St. Louis, MO: C.V. Mosby, 1977, pp. 67–77, 119–134.

Douglass, Laura Mae, and Bevis, Em Olivia. *Nursing Management and Leadership in Action.* St. Louis, MO: C.V. Mosby, 1979, pp. 198–222.

Freeman, Ruth R., cited in Earline L. Bryan, "A Nursing Service Director in an Acute Health Care Center." In *Decision Making in Nursing: Tools for Change,* edited by June T. Bailey and Karen E. Claus, pp. 126–138. St. Louis, MO: C.V. Mosby, 1975.

Gibson, James L., Ivancevich, John M., and Donnelly, James H. *Organizations: Behavior, Structure, Processes.* Dallas, TX: Business Publications, 1979.

Polit, Denise F., and Hungler, Bernadette P. *Nursing Research: Principles and Methods*. Philadelphia: J.B. Lippincott, 1978, pp. 209–223.

Ramey, Irene G. ''Setting Nursing Standards and Evaluating Care.'' In *Management for Nurses*, 2nd ed., edited by Marie Streng Berger, Dorothy Elhart, Sharon Connell Firsich, Shelley Baney Jordan, and Sandra Stone, pp. 63–69. St. Louis, MO: C.V. Mosby, 1980.

Zimmer, Marie J. ''A Model for Evaluating Nursing Care.'' In *Management for Nurses*, 2nd ed., edited by Marie Streng Berger, Dorothy Elhart, Sharon Connell Firsich, Shelley Baney Jordan, and Sandra Stone, pp. 47–53. St. Louis, MO: C.V. Mosby, 1980.

**Journals**

Lyon, Herbert L., and Ivancevich, John M. ''An Exploratory Investigation of Organizational Climate and Job Satisfaction in a Hospital.'' *Academy of Management Journal* 17 (1974): 635–647.

McClellan, Marilyn G. ''Toward Clinical Excellence in Nursing: A Program for Development of Nurses.'' *Nursing Administration Quarterly* 6 (1981): 26–29.

McClure, Margaret L. ''The Long Road to Accountability.'' *Nursing Outlook* 26 (1978): 47–50.

Zimmer, Marie J. ''A Nursing Service Administrator's Perspective.'' *Nursing Research* 29 (1980): 98–99.

Part II

# Methods for Data Collection

## Chapter 5

# The Quality Assurance Process

*Patricia S. Schroeder, M.S.N., R.N.*

Despite the system for monitoring quality of care, the process of quality assurance remains consistent. This process is critical to the maintenance of quality in any quality assurance activity, including both the development of standards of care and evaluation. Data collection methods may vary, but the steps in the process remain the same.

## FIRST QUALITY ASSURANCE MODELS

Many authors have described the quality assurance process as a standard sequence of activities; however, these activities vary slightly in philosophy from author to author and may be correlated with the time the model was developed in relation to the evolution of the quality assurance concept. Two of the most widely accepted models for the quality assurance process are the American Nurses' Association (ANA) model, developed by Lang and adapted by the ANA,[1] and the model developed by Mayers, Norby and Watson.[2]

The ANA model for quality assurance is circular (Figure 5–1). Seven steps in the process are found at various points in the circle. Although the model may be entered at any point because of the unending nature of the process, the first logical step is identification of values. The major sources of these values are the society, the profession, and science, but because all three are dynamic, they must be addressed in an ongoing fashion.[3]

Subsequent steps closely parallel those of other models. After values have been identified, structure, process, and outcome standards and criteria are identified. In this step, values are articulated and placed into a measurable framework. Structure criteria focus on that which is present in the system, whether aspects of the physical environment, the characteristics, or the functions of the system. Process criteria deal with the way in which activities are carried out in the provision of nursing care. Outcome criteria are the goals to be achieved as a result of the

**Figure 5–1** Model for Quality Assurance

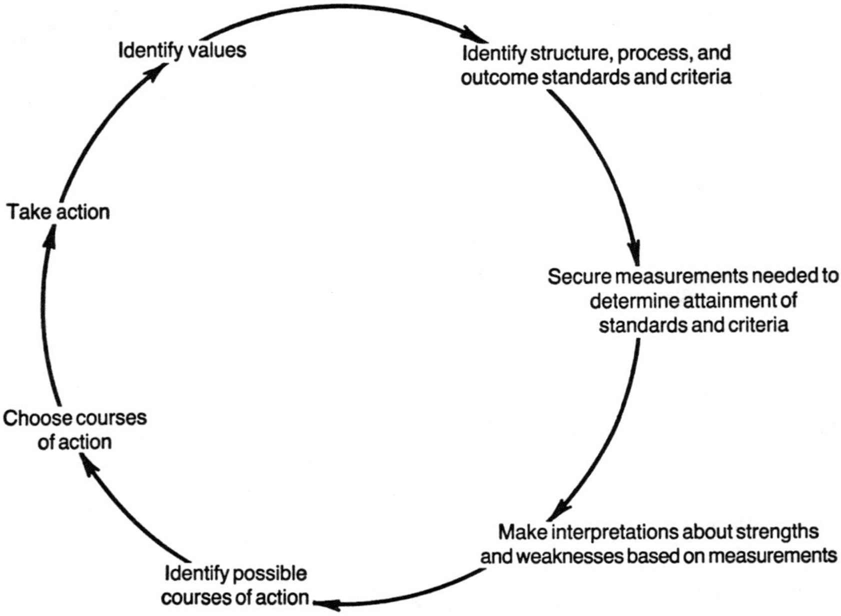


*Source:* Reprinted with permission from American Nurses' Association Congress for Nursing Practice, *A Plan for Implementation of the Standards of Nursing Practice*, p. 15. Kansas City, MO: American Nurses' Association, 1975.

process and perhaps structure. The type of criteria selected is determined by the point in the delivery of care that is to be evaluated.

The study is actually developed and executed when the measurements needed to determine attainment of standards and criteria are secured. Thereafter, interpretations can be made about the strengths and weaknesses of the care, which is the fourth step. The final three steps of the process are to identify possible courses of action, select one, and then take action. These steps provide a logical means to deal with the quality issue and resolve the problem.

The ANA model has been a forerunner in the evolution of quality assurance in nursing. Published in 1975, it paved the way for further conceptualization and development of the process. Undoubtedly, the steps in the process are used in slightly different ways, depending on the user. As a whole, however, this model continues to be viable and well accepted by the nursing profession.

A second model, which is similar and is also considered classic, is that proposed by Mayers and colleagues. The steps of the quality assurance process in this model are somewhat more specific (Figure 5–2). Like the ANA model, the steps flow into each other. Unlike the ANA model, they are not circular, but consecutive.

**Figure 5–2** Steps in Evaluation Process

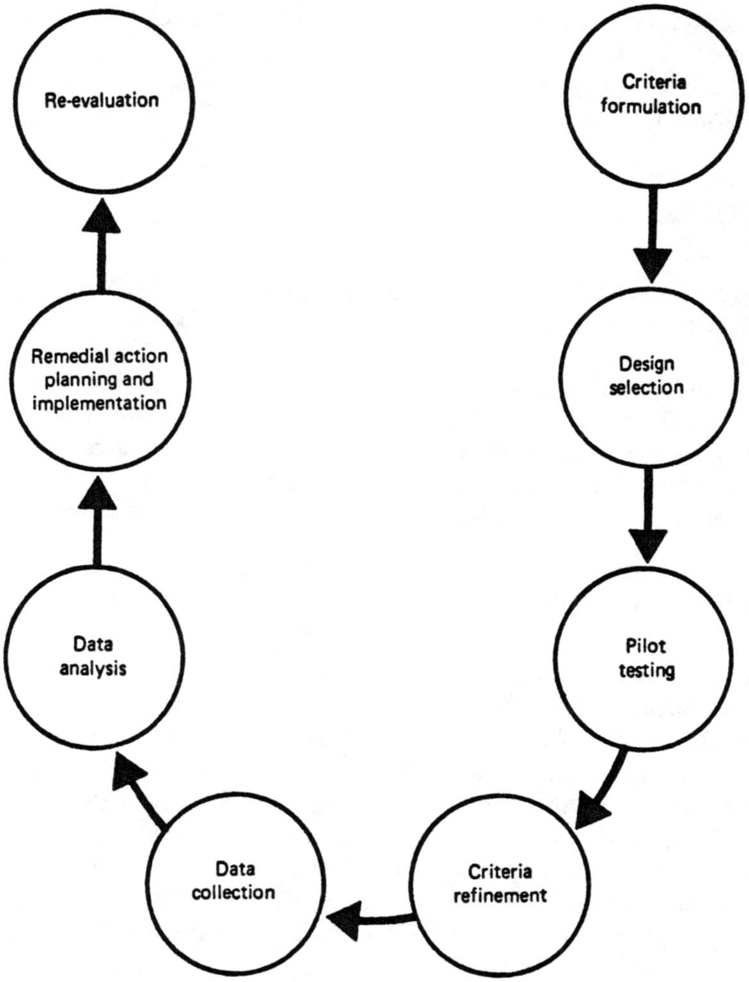


*Source:* Reprinted with permission from Marlene G. Mayers, Ronald B. Norby, and Annita B. Watson, *Quality Assurance for Patient Care: Nursing Perspectives*, p. 1. New York: Appleton-Century-Crofts, 1977.

The first step is the formulation of criteria against which practice can be measured. These criteria can then be developed into a selected study design (step 2) that should be pilot-tested and the criteria subsequently refined (steps 3 and 4). Steps 5 and 6 are data collection and analysis, and the model concludes with the planning and implementation of remedial action, followed by reevaluation.

The final step, reevaluation, is truly a strength in this model. Not only are the evolving standards of accrediting bodies emphasizing reevaluation to a greater extent than ever before, but also those within the profession of nursing expect a demonstration that problems have been resolved as a result of quality assurance activities. The incorporation of the reevaluation step into the model is an important aspect toward achieving this goal.

## UNIT-BASED QUALITY ASSURANCE MODEL

Other authors have developed models for quality assurance, many of which closely resemble the aforementioned two. All too often, however, these models do not provide enough specificity and direction to be used "as is" in a practice setting. For this reason, a third model of the quality assurance process, the unit-based practice model for quality assurance, was developed (Figure 5–3). A comparison of the steps in these three models is found in Table 5–1. The unit-based quality assurance model incorporates aspects of both the ANA model and that developed by Mayers and colleagues, as well as several other steps.

### Step 1: Develop Standards of Practice

All too often agencies institute quality assurance systems that focus immediately on evaluation. Unless high-quality care in that agency has been specifically defined for comparison, however, it is unrealistic to expect that results will be positive. The process must begin with the development of standards and criteria.

According to the ANA definitions, "standards are an agreed upon level of excellence whereas criteria are statements which are measurable and which reflect the intent of the standard."[4] Many standards and criteria can be found throughout the literature; however, agencies must either adopt these or tailor them to the setting, the system, and the client population. Often an agency has standards and criteria, but they may be unavailable to practicing nurses or at least difficult for them to assess quickly. Standards pertinent to clinical nursing practice may also be found in a variety of locations within the institution or in a variety of formats. It is almost meaningless to have standards and criteria unless they are appropriate to the agency and situation, available to the staff, and understandable in format.

Standards and criteria must be based on identified values. In a technologically oriented society, values change at a rapid rate and require ongoing monitoring to remain current and appropriate. Changes in values can have a great impact on health care. For example, prior to the 1970s, the issue of sexuality was frequently avoided, whereas today it is often included as an area that must be addressed with

**Figure 5–3** Unit-Based Practice Model for Nursing Quality Assurance

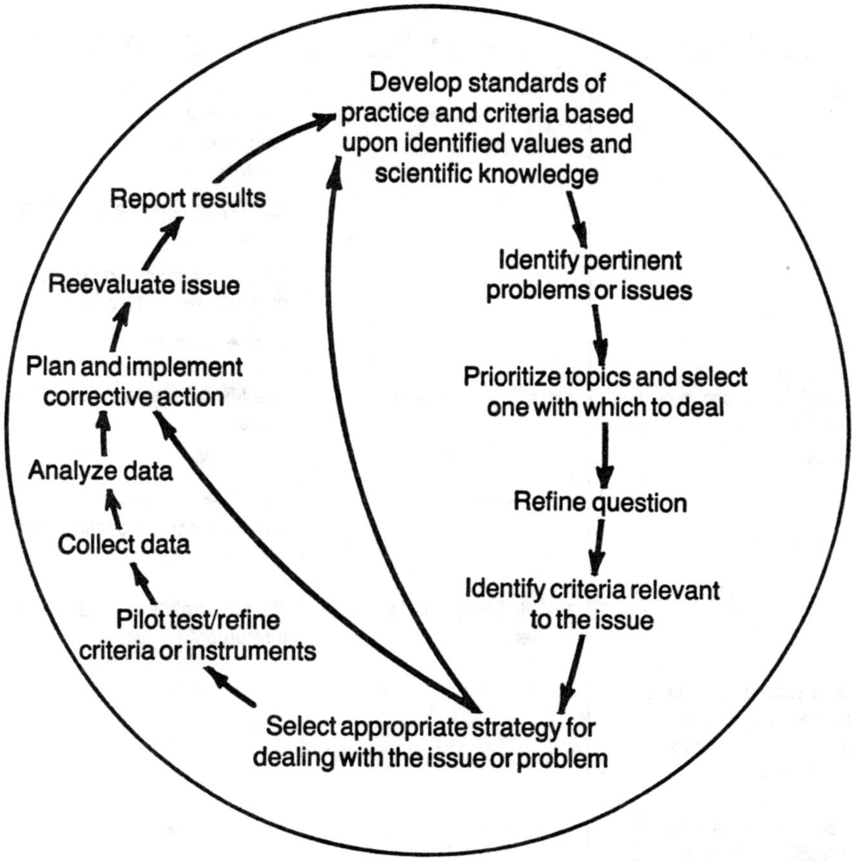


certain client populations. Likewise, professional values change and affect beliefs about quality care. Beliefs about the value of nursing diagnosis may greatly influence the way standards and criteria are developed. Ten years ago, however, this was of little significance to most practicing nurses.

Advances in science and technology also affect health care standards and criteria. An ever-changing knowledge and resource base requires vigilant attention if it is to be used to its greatest potential in achieving quality care. With all of these changes, there is no question that standards and criteria must be constantly updated.

**Table 5–1** Comparison of Three Models of the Quality Assurance Process

| *ANA Model* | *Mayers et al. Model* | *Unit-Based Practice Model* |
|---|---|---|
| Identify values | | Develop standards of practice and criteria based on identified values and scientific knowledge |
| | | Identify pertinent problems or issues |
| | | Prioritize topics and select one with which to deal |
| | | Refine question |
| Identify structure, process, and outcome standards and criteria | Criteria formulation | Identify criteria relevant to the issue |
| | Design selection | Select appropriate methodology for dealing with problem or issue |
| | Pilot testing; criteria refinement | Pilot test/refine criteria or instruments |
| Secure measurements needed to determine attainment of standards and criteria | Data collection | Collect data |
| Make interpretations about strengths and weaknesses based on measurements | Data analysis | Analyze data |
| Identify possible courses of action; choose course of action; take action | Remedial action planning and implementation | Plan and implement corrective action |
| | Reevaluation | Reevaluate issue |
| | | Report results |

## Step 2: Identify Pertinent Problems or Issues

In any attempt to address the issue of quality of care, it is important to focus on pertinent problems or issues. All too often, quality assurance topics have been selected haphazardly. Few people can be enthusiastic about spending time and effort to pursue issues that have little relevance to current concerns, however. Any group of practicing nurses can promptly identify several practice-related problems that require attention. Taking a problem- or issue-oriented focus for quality assurance, as well as having the group itself identify the issue, is a particular strength in the unit-based quality assurance system. The problem-oriented focus is also strongly supported by accrediting bodies such as the Joint Commission on the Accreditation of Hospitals (JCAH).

The identification of pertinent problems or issues in the quality assurance process requires several persons with sufficient overview of the agency (or unit) to provide perspective on the more important issues. It is essential to consider all group functions, such as clinical practice, management, or education. Trust is an important element if the group is to focus on actual problems. Without trust, other methods of problem identification, such as consideration of anonymous written suggestions or ideas of the group leader, may be necessary.

## Step 3: Prioritize Topics and Select One

The identified pertinent problems or issues must be prioritized and a study topic selected. Vanagunas and associates recommended asking the following four questions to help prioritize:

1. Does the problem have definite functional impact, i.e., is it related to quality?
2. Is the problem prevalent enough to require correction?
3. Is the problem solvable?
4. Is the benefit to patient care that would be derived from solving the problem worth the cost of assessing and solving it?[5]

It is also important to address the severity of the consequences if the problem is not pursued. Some problems may not affect the majority of clients, but they may be so potentially harmful that they demand a high priority. On the other hand, some problems may have a limited impact, but they affect the quality of care for many. These, too, may be a priority at some point.

Although the group's interest in a problem should not supersede safety in importance, interest does play a large part in how well and how quickly the problem will be resolved. If the group is committed or can be motivated to make a commitment to the issue, the remaining steps in the quality assurance process will be greatly facilitated. Should the group be unable to agree on the problem of highest priority, it may be wise to take advantage of varying commitments to given issues and split the group into several groups that will pursue their respective topics simultaneously.

### Step 4: Refine the Question

It has been said by many researchers that refining the question may be the most difficult part of any study. This step affects every other step in the process. It is impossible to focus efforts on resolving "a problem with IVs" or "the care of postoperative patients." The group must develop a specific question. Nurses concerned about IV medication errors may choose to study a question such as "Are IVs on the unit labeled according to hospital guidelines?" Nurses interested in the care of postoperative patients may decide to assess whether vital signs are monitored during the first twenty-four hours after surgery as often as required by the standard nursing care plan. In either case, these questions are specific enough to direct the group. If a problem or issue has several important questions pertaining to it, the group must decide whether to address these questions simultaneously or to prioritize these components.

### Step 5: Identify Criteria to Be Evaluated

At a quick glance, it may seem that the identification of criteria to be evaluated overlaps the development of standards of practice (step 1), but this is not necessarily true. Step 5 focuses on which of all the previously developed criteria will be selected for study. Although many criteria may be available regarding the study topic in general, only those criteria that are pertinent to the specific problem being addressed should be selected.

It may be necessary to develop additional criteria, either because present criteria are inadequate or because certain standards did not seem to lend themselves to measurement when considered previously. Newly developed criteria that may be unfamiliar to nurses whose care practices are to be addressed must be made available to them so that they know the standards and criteria against which their care is being evaluated.

### Step 6: Select Appropriate Method

In the unit-based practice model for quality assurance (see Figure 5–3), several possible directions can be taken at this point. It must be decided whether a lack of standards and criteria is the problem, whether there is an obvious corrective action to be taken, or whether the issue should be studied to obtain further data.

### *Lack of Standards and Criteria*

With advancing science, increasing technologies, and changing values, certain standards or criteria may become inappropriate or inadequate. If the problem or issue discussed is really one of inadequate standards, it may be more appropriate to improve those standards than to pursue a study based on criteria that are not consistent with currently accepted levels of excellence. For example, the quality assurance group at one hospital raised the issue of discrepancies between nurses regarding documentation on monitoring strips. It was noted that there were few criteria specifically identifying unit standards for this procedure and that, because they were not measurable, these few were open to different interpretations by different nurses. The group chose to focus its energies on improving standards and developing measurable criteria. Thereafter, the group felt that this problem needed no further study. It may have been studied, however, once the staff was made aware of the standards and criteria and had been given a chance to adopt them.

### *Corrective Action*

There are times when, even without study data, a quality assurance group can identify the necessary corrective action. In such a case, the time, effort, and expense of executing a study would be wasted. For example, one quality assurance group was concerned about inadequate preoperative teaching. Because of the large number of patients having surgery, the group knew it was impossible to provide adequate general information on an individual basis. The group decided that the only feasible alternative was to develop a group class for preoperative teaching with the nurse to reinforce individualized information thereafter. A study would only have confirmed what the group already knew, that preoperative teaching was not being done. The empirical literature, which contains a significant number of studies about preoperative teaching, provided the group with the direction to proceed in examining specific problems related to its own program or population. By carrying out the corrective action without studying the issue per se, the group saved considerable time and effort, avoided duplication, and achieved the same end.

### *Study Development*

In perhaps the majority of instances, a study must be developed to provide concrete data and to describe the problem in a way that suggests an adequate solution. Many considerations go into the selection of the appropriate method for data collection:

1. source of information
2. retrospective or concurrent data
3. timeliness of topic

4. number in sample
5. number of data collectors
6. cost-effectiveness of study

The first step is to identify who or what has the information needed. All too often, quality assurance studies are based on data obtained from charts when documentation may not be the primary source. If documentation is the appropriate source and is inadequate, this problem itself should be investigated. It may be, however, that not all the information required is appropriate for documentation; this must be determined before the study is designed. To use a simple example, if the study is to focus on self-care ability at the time of discharge, the information needed would be documented in the chart. If the study is instead focused on patient satisfaction with nursing care during hospitalization or perhaps coordination of multidisciplinary services, other sources would be of greater value. Available sources of data include health care workers, the patient, the chart, and a variety of other records.

Some issues lend themselves to retrospective data collection; others, to concurrent data collection. An issue concerning patient safety should be addressed concurrently so that it can be corrected immediately. Concurrent information should also be collected if data are based on someone's memory, since the information would be most accurate if obtained close to the time of the event. At other times, the only way to obtain unbiased data may be to collect them retrospectively.

The timeliness of the topic may influence certain aspects of study development. If the issue is associated with a critical incident that is time-related, it may be better to develop a study that can be completed quickly. Following a refresher class on problem-oriented records, for example, members of one particular staff wanted to determine whether they were keeping records according to the established guidelines for the hospital. The study was developed so that all data were collected during a one-week period, allowing enthusiasm and participation to remain high. Because of the prompt feedback, the staff was eager to use the results and chose to repeat the study in three months to reevaluate. It was felt that, if this study had taken several months to carry out, the staff would have been less interested in using the results. When it takes a long period of time to plan, implement, and analyze a study, not only decreasing enthusiasm and participation, but also staff turnover and system changes can influence results. The length of time required by studies varies with the topic and the situation, however.

The number in the sample must be chosen based upon a variety of variables. These include available resources such as client population, data collectors, time, money, and assistance in data analysis. Research texts may provide more specifics on selection of sample size dependent on the degree of rigor introduced into the study.

The number of data collectors and the individuals chosen to collect data are determined by the philosophy as well as by the system itself. The quality assurance system may influence the number of data collectors, because some quality assurance committees have limited membership and resources. Sometimes the data resulting from quality assurance studies are less important than the process of addressing the issue. One quality assurance committee conducted a study in which every registered nurse on the unit was required to evaluate three care plans according to a set of criteria. Undoubtedly, the results of the study were somewhat biased, but after the study, the standards were better understood by each registered nurse. A great deal of discussion was stimulated, and the committee felt that care plans showed a greater improvement than they would have shown if more accurate data had been obtained and an in-service class held. This philosophy is not appropriate in all instances, however; accuracy in data collection is important in the vast majority of cases.

The cost-effectiveness of any agency activity has come under increased scrutiny in the past several years. Any of the factors used to determine the method for study can influence cost, not only in terms of money but also in terms of time and other resources. These "costs" may determine the amount of rigor that can be introduced into the study design and must be weighed against the potential benefit of the study.

### Step 7: Pilot Test/Refine Criteria or Instrument

When a study is to be performed, particularly in a clinical setting, it is very important to do a pilot test. In such a test, a representative group member uses the criteria and data collection tool on a small scale in an effort to identify potential problems with the study. Often, there is no other way to get this information. Pilot testing can save a tremendous amount of time and effort, because it decreases the chances that the study will yield unusable data. Furthermore, it makes it possible to test the practical feasibility of the instruments. As a task, it can also stimulate enthusiasm in the study.

Following a pilot test, the group can determine whether the criteria or the instrument needs revision. The pilot test may also reveal information important for data collection, such as the time of day when the client group is more available, an alternate source of data, or the most successful approach in asking a particular question. These strategies can then be incorporated into the actual study.

### Step 8: Collect Data

The process of collecting data is often in itself educational and can do a great deal to improve the practice of those who participate. Involving members of the quality assurance group is very valuable not only in improving their research skills, but also in improving the quality of care that they provide and in increasing their formal and informal influence with peers. Some have gone so far as to say that the process of data collection does more to improve care than do most corrective actions based on the results; they recommend having as many data collectors as possible and appropriate. Others disagree and state that results are more accurate, which is in all cases more desirable, when there are fewer data collectors. In either case, instructions regarding the methodology should be clear enough to yield reliable results from one data collector to the next. In accordance with the unit-based quality assurance philosophy, data should be collected by the staff whose care is being evaluated.

### Step 9: Analyze Data

The purpose of data analysis is to interpret the data collected. Only then can recommendations be made to improve the quality of care. This interpretation must be made by the same representative group that participated in the previous phases of the quality assurance process.

In analyzing any data, there are several key points. The data should be depersonalized as much as possible. It was not collected to identify good nurses, but rather to investigate a specific issue regarding the quality of care. Likewise, it was not collected to evaluate an individual nurse's performance, but rather to examine overall group performance.

Positive as well as negative results should be addressed in the effort to maintain or improve nursing care. A standard of 100 percent achievement is often unrealistic in practice, although it may be appropriate for certain critical criteria. When deficits are identified, they should be labeled according to what their cause may be. For example, deficits may be a systems problem, i.e., time or staff; a knowledge problem, i.e., level of skill of the practitioner; an attitude problem; or even a measurement problem. The categorization of deficits is very helpful in planning and implementing corrective action.

### Step 10: Plan and Implement Corrective Action

According to a report by the ANA Council on Nursing Practice, corrective action can include continuing education, in-service education, peer pressure, administrative changes, environmental changes, research, punitive or reward action, and self-initiated changes.[6] It is necessary to be creative in selecting a corrective action that flows logically from the data. It is also critical that this planning and implementation be done by the unit-based group. Change theories cite the need to include in the planning those who are at the level of the change, because their participation greatly facilitates implementation of the actions and subsequent problem resolution.

In corrective action planning it is important to avoid punitive actions based on quality assurance findings, competition between groups, and reinforcement of unrealistic standards or criteria that, for some reason, have not been changed. These approaches can undermine the quality assurance process. Although they may improve results on follow-up studies, the results are not longstanding; they are based on distorted motives rather than a bona fide commitment to professional nursing practice.

### Step 11: Reevaluate the Issue

The topic of reevaluation is relatively new to the quality assurance process. Previously, it was often assumed that corrective action alone ensured problem resolution. This may or may not be true. For example, an obstetrical unit decided to determine whether all new mothers received consistent information on the proper way to bathe a newborn. This process-oriented study revealed that they did not. As corrective action, the unit developed a written guide describing the procedure, which was given to all new mothers. It was supplemented with individualized instruction by the nurse. Because all new mothers received this guide, it could be assumed that they all received consistent information. No follow-up study was necessary.

Another nursing unit studied selected process criteria regarding the care of patients with in-dwelling catheters. It was found that those providing catheter care did not always adhere to standards and criteria in this area. The group decided that the problem stemmed from staff members' lack of knowledge and, therefore, planned several in-service classes on the care of the patient with an in-dwelling catheter. Because it was impossible to state objectively that subsequent catheter care complied with the standards, a follow-up study was necessary.

The need to demonstrate problem resolution is being more closely addressed by accrediting bodies. It is also of increasing importance to professionals, partly because they want to ensure that their commitment to the quality assurance process achieves results. If corrective action does little or nothing to resolve the problem, the action may not have addressed the actual problem. Perhaps the data were interpreted as indicating a knowledge deficit, but the problem may have been a systems problem or an attitude problem for which very different corrective actions would be appropriate. Clearly, reevaluation of an issue takes time and effort. It may be less exciting than the original study, but without it, all previous work through the quality assurance process may lose its significance.

### Step 12: Report Results

Through the use of a standard report form, studies and results should be documented and communicated. Unless quality assurance activities are shared, at least within the agency, much of their potential benefit is lost. Reports of a study can be most encouraging to peer groups, not only in the study outcomes, but also in the process used. Reports can provide a mechanism for positive feedback or can facilitate the development or refinement of hospitalwide standards and criteria. Reports should also be shared with supervisors. In this way, all levels in the nursing department can identify and work toward resolution of the same priority issues.

Finally, results of the quality assurance activities should be shared with those in other disciplines and those in the overall quality assurance structure of the agency. The sharing of results can stimulate the efforts of others regarding quality assurance and can promote interdisciplinary colleagueship.

## CONCLUSION

Although some of the same steps are inherent in other quality assurance models, the unit-based practice model for nursing quality assurance is somewhat more detailed. With the increasing emphasis on assuring quality of care, more and more nurses are becoming involved in the process. This "decentralization of accountability" is a very important professional step, but it also means that more nurses must be educated in the use of the process. This may be facilitated by a more detailed model.

This model was developed for use in a unit-based quality assurance system. The unit-based philosophy permeates its steps, with such components as the involvement of staff nurses in all phases, evaluation of practice on the group's own unit, and maintenance of an openness in the process so that other nurses may be aware of group activities.

In a review of the steps of any quality assurance model, it is easy to see the similarities of these steps to the problem-solving approach, the nursing process, and the research process. All could probably be placed side-by-side on a continuum of "degree of rigor."[7] Clearly, the same thought processes are being used. When the quality assurance process is used, the degree of rigor appropriate to the situation must be determined. It is then that the process can be seen as a path to growth and the results achieved can be labeled a success.

## NOTES

1. American Nurses' Association Congress for Nursing Practice, *A Plan for Implementation of the Standards of Nursing Practice* (Kansas City, MO: American Nurses' Association, 1975), p. 15.
2. Marlene G. Mayers, Ronald B. Norby, and Annita B. Watson, *Quality Assurance for Patient Care: Nursing Perspectives* (New York: Appleton-Century-Crofts, 1977), p. 1.
3. ANA Congress for Nursing Practice, *Implementation of the Standards of Nursing Practice*, p. 14.
4. Ibid, p. 16.

5. Audrone Vanagunas et al., "Principles of Quality Assurance," *Quality Review Bulletin* 5, no. 2 (1979): 6.
6. ANA Congress for Nursing Practice, *Implementation of the Standards of Nursing Practice*, p. 17.
7. Doris Bloch, "Interrelated Issues in Evaluation and Evaluation Research: A Researcher's Perspective," *Nursing Research*, 29 (March/April 1980): 69.

---

## REFERENCES

### Books

American Nurses' Association Congress for Nursing Practice. *A Plan for Implementation of the Standards of Nursing Practice*. Kansas City, MO: American Nurses' Association, 1975.

Mason, Elizabeth. *How to Write Meaningful Nursing Standards*. New York: John Wiley & Sons, 1978.

Mayers, Marlene G.; Norby, Ronald B.; and Watson, Annita B. *Quality Assurance for Patient Care: Nursing Perspectives*. New York: Appleton-Century-Crofts, 1977.

### Journals

Bloch, Doris. "Interrelated Issues on Evaluation and Evaluation Research: A Researcher's Perspective." *Nursing Research* 29 (1980): 69–73.

Downs, Florence S. "Relationship of Findings of Clinical Research and Development of Criteria: A Researcher's Perspective." *Nursing Research* 29 (1980): 94–97.

Gordon, Marjory. "Determining Study Topics." *Nursing Research* 29 (1980): 83–87.

Harmon, Carol A. "Involving Staff in Nursing Quality Assurance." *Quality Review Bulletin* 6, no. 11 (1980): 26–30.

Horn, Barbara J. "Establishing Valid and Reliable Criteria: A Researcher's Perspective." *Nursing Research* 29 (1980): 88–90.

Howe, Marilyn J. "Developing Instruments for Measurement of Criteria: A Clinical Nursing Practice Perspective." *Nursing Research* 29 (1980): 100–103.

Krueger, Janelle C. "Establishing Priorities for Evaluation and Evaluation Research: A Nursing Perspective." *Nursing Research* 29 (1980): 115–118.

Schroeder, Patricia S.; Maibusch, Regina M.; Anderson, Cheryl A.; and Formella, Nancy Mansheim. "A Unit Based Approach to Quality Assurance." *Quality Review Bulletin* 8 (1982): 10–12.

Vanagunas, Audrone; Egelston, E. Martin; Hopkins, Julie; and Walczak, Regina M. "Principles of Quality Assurance." *Quality Review Bulletin* 5, no. 2 (1979): 3–6.

Woody, Mary F. "Evaluation versus Research: An Evaluator's Perspective." *Nursing Research* 29 (1980): 74–77.

# Chapter 6

# Retrospective Chart Audits

*Margaret A. Smerlinski, M.S., R.N.*

The retrospective chart audit is probably the most common method used to conduct quality assurance studies. Some persons, in fact, equate quality assurance with retrospective chart audits.[1]

## DEFINITION OF METHOD

The retrospective chart audit is an evaluation of patient care that is done after the patient has been discharged. It focuses on the documented evidence of nursing care provided and may include an examination of the structure, process, and/or outcomes of care. This method of assessment is based on the assumption that what is documented is what has been performed or effected. The converse is also assumed, i.e., that a process has not occurred nor an outcome achieved if it has not been documented.[2] It is further assumed that "good" documentation reflects "good" care. Since documentation represents only one measure of care, however, other methods of assessing care practices must also be used.

## LITERATURE REVIEW

Two formats for conducting retrospective chart audits are well documented in the quality assurance literature. The first is described by the Joint Commission on the Accreditation of Hospitals (JCAH), which defines audit as "a review means of looking into the charts of discharged patients to determine the type of care that they have received."[3] The JCAH audit follows a six-point plan that was developed in conjunction with the JCAH's inspection program for nursing services. The points outlined in the plan are summarized by Froebe and Bain as follows:

> (1) establishment of criteria for patient care, (2) comparison of criteria and actual practices, (3) analysis of actual practice findings, (4) correc-

> tive action, (5) follow-up studies to determine whether the corrective action was effective, and (6) report of the results of audit activity to those to whom one is accountable with accompanying notations describing the actions of the governing body in response to all the foregoing.[4]

Since patients are generally classified in terms of medical diagnoses and procedures, the JCAH suggested that criteria be developed around these designated groupings.[5] Examples of designated groupings are numerous, including (1) medical diagnosis, (2) operative procedure, and (3) test procedures. More recently, some designated groupings are being developed around nursing diagnoses, such as alterations in patient comfort or self-concept.[6]

In practice, criteria are developed from the standards of care for the designated patient population. The standards of care may be defined by professional organizations, or they may be defined by institutional policies or procedures. In either case, the chart is reviewed to determine if the documentation of practice demonstrates compliance with predetermined standards. If an analysis of the actual practice findings reveals certain deficiencies in practice, corrective actions need to be identified and implemented. Follow-up studies may be done to determine if the corrective actions were effective. The purpose of the audit procedure is to improve documentation, since it is assumed that documentation reflects quality in practice.

The second retrospective chart audit that is well defined in the quality assurance literature is the Phaneuf Nursing Audit.[7] This comprehensive retrospective process audit contains fifty items that measure the quality of nursing care received by a patient. Items were developed for one dependent and six independent functions of nursing, as described by Lesnick and Anderson.[8] These functions are defined by Phaneuf as follows:

> (1) Application and execution of physicians' legal orders, (2) observation of symptoms, (3) supervision of the patient, (4) supervision of those participating in care, (5) reporting and recording, (6) application of nursing procedures and techniques, and (7) promotion of health by direction and teaching.[9]

Each function has a varying number of items assigned to it with specific numerical values. Each function is evaluated by totaling the scores for the items that comprise it. The audit yelds a total score, as well as individual scores for each of the seven functions defined. In addition, ranges of the scores have been translated into terms that describe quality: excellent, good, incomplete, poor, and unsafe.[10] A manual for use of this audit is available.[11]

The literature includes a number of suggested outcome and/or process criteria sets that can be adapted and used to design retrospective chart audits. These criteria sets are descriptive of a wide variety of nursing problems and populations.

Two particularly useful references for description of such criteria sets are *Guidelines for Review of Nursing Care at the Local Level,*[12] prepared by the American Nurses' Association (ANA), and *Quality Assurance for Patient Care: Nursing Perspectives,* by Mayers and colleagues.[13] For example, in "Discharge Criteria, Vaginal Hysterectomy,"[14] Mayers and associates developed six criteria regarding the patient's verbalization of knowledge about activities to avoid or direct effects of the hysterectomy itself. Among the criteria were (1) verbalizes need to avoid activities that cause pelvic congestion and (2) verbalizes fact that she can no longer expect menstrual periods, but that hormones are still produced. All criteria would be audited from the chart after the patient was discharged. The purpose of such an audit would be to examine the documentation in the chart and measure it against the developed criteria to determine compliance. If consistent deficits were found, the audit committee might develop a teaching tool to be used as a guide for discharge teaching of future hysterectomy patients. A subsequent audit might be done after the teaching tool had been in use for a time to reevaluate the documentation of discharge teaching done with this population group.

## STEPS IN RETROSPECTIVE CHART EVALUATION

Mayers and colleagues delineated the basic guidelines of evaluation as criteria formulation, compliance determination, chart review to assess compliance, data analysis, deficit identification, remedial action planning and implementation, and periodic reevaluation.[15] The retrospective chart audit, which may be selected to study a nursing problem within the unit-based quality assurance system, incorporates all these basic guidelines of evaluation.

### Criteria Formulation

Once the problem has been identified and stated, criteria must be formulated. The criteria are the yardsticks against which judgments can be made.[16] Good criteria are precise, objective, and measurable. Documented evidence of the criteria must also be easily retrievable from the chart.

Before criteria are developed, however, the quality assurance committee must decide what kind of criteria will best answer the questions posed. Criteria are generally one of three types: structure, process, or outcome. Although first described by Donabedian as approaches to the evaluation of medical care,[17] these criteria are equally applicable to the evaluation of nursing care. Any of these types of criteria, singly or in combination, may be used to audit charts retrospectively. The question, objectives, and/or purposes of the study determine which type of criteria or approaches are needed.

For example, if the purpose of the study is to determine the adequacy of the staff to patient ratio on a given unit during a specified period, the criteria needed are primarily structural in nature. Structure criteria describe the physical, fiscal, and organizational characteristics of an agency.[18] If the study focuses on care given to a patient, process criteria are needed. Process criteria measure what was done for the patient during the delivery of care; for example, patients with decubitus ulcers will be turned every two hours. Finally, if the study focuses on the end result of care, outcome criteria are needed. For example, for a population of post–acute congestive heart failure patients, several teaching outcome criteria might be developed, such as "Patient is able to state the significance of daily weight changes." This teaching outcome, along with others, could be retrospectively audited to determine if the outcomes were achieved.

## Compliance Determination

In order to determine compliance, a standard must be set for each criterion measured. The standard is usually expressed as a percentage or ratio of items to be achieved for each criterion.[19]

Recently, there has been a considerable amount of debate around the setting of compliance standards in relation to nursing criteria. Mayers and associates suggested that, since there is little documented evidence of compliance norms in relation to nursing criteria, there is little justification for setting compliance standards below 100 percent.[20] This standard of 100 percent is used by the JCAH and is recommended as a screening standard by the ANA.[21,22] On the other hand, Hover and Zimmer argued that reliance on norms is not always appropriate; a group of individuals may vary greatly in a characteristic to be evaluated, but a particular individual may tolerate little change in this characteristic. Furthermore, where nursing care standards have been poor, the use of such standards as norms might inhibit movement toward achieving quality in care. Thus, Hover and Zimmer recommended waiting until after the completion of the first evaluation to set the compliance standards.[23] Gallant and McLane, following this recommendation, set a compliance standard of 70 percent in their study about the process of validating outcome criteria.[24]

Ultimately, the specific purpose of an audit should determine when the standard is set and at what level. For example, if a population group is to be screened for certain characteristics, it is probably advisable to set the compliance standard at 100 percent before the audit is conducted. In this way, all charts would be examined for the defined characteristics.

## Chart Review

After the appropriate population has been selected and a sample drawn, data are collected by comparing the charts against the established criteria. A typical retrospective audit tool is shown in Exhibit 6–1.

**Exhibit 6–1** Sample Retrospective Audit Tool

| Criterion | Exception(s) | Standard | Met | Met by Exception | Not Met | Comments | Instructions to Auditor |
|---|---|---|---|---|---|---|---|
| 1. | | | | | | | Where data is to be found in the record |
| 2. | | | | | | | |
| 3. | | | | | | | |
| 4. | | | | | | | |

*Source:* Reprinted with permission from St. Michael Hospital, Milwaukee, Wisconsin. Copyright 1980.

## Data Analysis

In the process of data analysis, criteria that were met, met by exception, or not met are totaled for all audited charts. The scores are converted into percentages and compared with the predetermined compliance standard. Those criteria that do not meet the standard are identified as deficits.

The next step in data analysis is to determine the reason for each deficit so that needed remedial action steps can be taken. Factors that may have contributed to a lack of documentation must also be identified.

## Remedial Action Planning and Implementation

Plans to correct the deficiencies must be made and implemented. Remedial actions might be the development of special staff in-service training programs, creation of new chart forms, revision of existing chart forms, or periodic reevaluation.

# CLINICAL EXAMPLES

Retrospective chart audits can be useful within the unit-based quality assurance program under many different circumstances.

## Example #1: Preoperative Teaching of Orthopedic Surgical Patients

Members of the unit-based quality assurance committee on a medical/oncology unit with twenty-five beds observed that a significant number of orthopedic surgical patients were being placed on their unit because of a lack of available beds on the adjacent orthopedic specialty unit. The patient population consisted primarily of patients who were scheduled to have a total hip replacement, hip pinning, or laminectomy. These patients were usually transferred to the orthopedic unit postoperatively. The committee members expressed concern about whether the medical/oncology unit staff had sufficient knowledge to care for these patients preoperatively, especially in regard to preoperative teaching.

In order to determine the staff's knowledge about preoperative teaching for this patient population group, a questionnaire was developed and given to the staff. Because the results of the questionnaire indicated a need for staff in-service training, the staff was then trained in both general and specific preoperative teaching for this population group.

In order to evaluate the effectiveness of the in-service training, the quality assurance committee conducted a retrospective chart audit on all patients who had a total hip replacement, hip pinning, or laminectomy and had been cared for preoperatively on the unit. The sample of audited charts was divided into two groups and compared. Group I consisted of charts that were completed prior to the in-service training, and group II consisted of charts completed after the in-service training. Criteria based on the content of the training were developed (Table 6–1).

While the results of the audit demonstrated improved documentation on those charts completed following the in-service training, the committee was not completely satisfied. The documentation was still spotty, frequently lacking specifics or even mention of "routine preoperative teaching." Because data analysis revealed that the problem may have been a lack of documentation rather than a lack of actual patient teaching, the quality assurance committee developed a structured preoperative teaching form particularly for use with this population group. The committee planned to conduct a reaudit after the teaching form had been in use.

The foregoing is an excellent example of an appropriate use of the retrospective chart audit. The committee defined the problem well. By addressing the staff's knowledge about the care required by the population in the study before conducting the audit, the committee was able not only to control for this knowledge base, but also to determine the effects of the in-service training on the subsequent documentation. Generally, chart audits are done without determining the staff's

**Table 6–1** Preoperative Teaching Criteria for Orthopedic Surgical Patients

| *Criteria* | *Exceptions* |
|---|---|
| 1. Patient received preoperative teaching booklet. | 1. None |
| 2. Patient verbalizes knowledge that she/he is NPO after midnight on night prior to surgery. | 2. None |
| 3. Patient demonstrates the ability to deep breathe and cough. | 3. None |
| 4. Patient demonstrates the ability to perform leg exercises appropriate to surgical procedure. | 4. None |
| 5. Patient demonstrates the ability to log roll using correct body alignment. | 5. None |
| 6. Patient viewed total hip replacement videotape. | 6. Those patients undergoing a laminectomy. |
| 7. Patient demonstrates the ability to get in and out of bed using proper body alignment. | 7. Those patients undergoing hip surgery. |

*Source:* Reprinted with permission from St. Michael Hospital, Milwaukee, Wisconsin. Copyright 1980.

knowledge base. When the results of the audit are found to be poor, it is assumed that staff education will correct the problem. Knowledge is only one determinant of documentation, however. By resolving the knowledge issue first, the committee could identify other ways to improve documentation for this population group.

### Example #2: Documentation of Neurological Assessments by Nurses in the Emergency Department

Members of a unit-based emergency department quality assurance committee were concerned about nurses' documentation of neurological assessments on patients who entered the department with possible neurological deficits. A flow sheet to facilitate the assessment and documentation of changes in neurological status was available, and the committee wanted to determine whether the flow sheet was being used on these patients and whether all parameters, as defined on the flow sheet, were being assessed and documented (Exhibit 6–2). A retrospective chart audit was done on thirty-four charts of patients who entered the emergency department and subsequently were admitted to the hospital with diagnoses suggesting neurological deficits.

The results of the audit indicated that the neurological record was not routinely used. Even when it was used, not all parameters were assessed and documented, nor were the documented parameters consistently described. Further analysis of the results identified several shortcomings in the assessment tool. It was decided that the assessment tool needed revision if documentation was to be consistent. The tool was given to the clinical nurse specialist in neurological nursing for revision.

Retrospective chart audits often lead to the development of flow sheets or tools to remind staff to document certain predetermined criterion-related elements of care.[25] Even when aids to documentation are available, however, they are not always used. The audit reveals only whether something is documented, not the reason for failure to document it. Like knowledge in the previous example, availability of aids to documentation is only one determinant of documentation.

### Example #3: Retrospective Process and Outcome Audit: Children with Harrington Rod Insertion for Treatment of Scoliosis

A retrospective chart audit was completed by a pediatric unit-based quality assurance committee to determine whether the unit was meeting the standards of care outlined in a nursing care plan that had been developed several years earlier for the care of children who needed to have a Harrington rod inserted for the treatment of scoliosis. Committee members were especially interested in how well postoperative physical assessments were being documented. The sample consisted of the last fifteen charts of children, ages one to eighteen, who had

**Exhibit 6–2** Emergency Department Craniotomy Checks Data Collection Sheet

1. Has a craniotomy sheet been initiated? (check one)

   _____ Yes _____ No

2. If not, are all pertinent parameters documented elsewhere?

   | Yes | No | |
   |---|---|---|
   | _____ | _____ | Vital signs |
   | _____ | _____ | LOC |
   | _____ | _____ | Speech |
   | _____ | _____ | Stimuli to awaken |
   | _____ | _____ | Pain response |
   | _____ | _____ | Pupils |
   | _____ | _____ | Movement |

3. Are the parameters being assessed and documented according to stated criteria? (check where appropriate)

   A. LOC

   _____ Oriented/disoriented/restless/combative
   _____ Other ______________________________

   B. Speech

   _____ Clear/rambling/garbled/none
   _____ Other ______________________________

   C. Awakens to

   _____ Name/shaking/light pain/strong pain
   _____ Other ______________________________

   D. Reaction to pain

   _____ Appropriate/inappropriate/decerebrate/none
   _____ Other ______________________________

   E. Pupils

   _____ Size 1-9
   _____ Reaction
   _____ Other ______________________________

   F. Movement

   _____ Normal strength (4)/slight weakness (3)/50% reduction in strength (2)/marked weakness without spontaneous movement (1)/total paralysis (0)
   _____ Other ________________________ _____

**Exhibit 6–2** continued

4. Are there any deviations from the normal neurologic state? Which ones? (list) Were those deviations re-assessed? How often?

| Deviations | Re-assessed<br>Yes/No | How often |
|---|---|---|

*Source:* Reprinted with permission from St. Michael Hospital, Milwaukee, Wisconsin. Copyright 1981.

undergone a Harrington rod insertion over the last year. The tool used to evaluate the documentation for this patient population was developed by identifying process criteria from the standardized nursing care plan and utilizing outcome criteria already established for this population group (Exhibit 6–3). Criteria were divided into three major areas: preoperative teaching, postoperative physical assessment, and discharge teaching.

The results of the audit indicated deficiencies in each of the three major areas audited. The quality assurance committee recommended the following remedial actions:

1. Develop a preprinted preoperative teaching sheet.
2. Facilitate recording of physical assessment data postoperatively through use of the hospital's nursing assessment record form.
3. Post the standardized nursing care plan on the unit to familiarize the staff with this resource.
4. Develop a preprinted discharge instruction sheet.
5. Conduct concurrent spot-check audits on all patients undergoing Harrington rod insertions.
6. Conduct a reaudit of this population within the next calendar year.

A reaudit was conducted the following year. The same tool was used, this time with a sample of nine charts. The results demonstrated improved documentation in the area of preoperative teaching, which was attributed to the use of the preprinted preoperative teaching sheet. Despite the use of the nursing assessment record, however, the documentation in the area of postoperative physical assessment continued to be sporadic. Documentation of discharge teaching also continued to be a problem; it was believed that failure to develop the preprinted discharge instruction sheet as planned was responsible.

This example points out common problems in conducting retrospective chart audits. First of all, the retrospective chart audit is essentially a descriptive study of

**Exhibit 6–3** Data Collection Tool for Retrospective Audit of Harrington Rod Insertions for Treatment of Scoliosis

Population: Children having Harrington Rodding (ages 1-18)

Patient's Hospital Number _________ Sex _________ Age _________

| CRITERIA | MET | NOT MET | MET BY EXCEPTION |
|---|---|---|---|
| PREOPERATIVE<br>1. Preoperative Teaching | | | |
| A. Explain activity limits expected postop | | | |
| B. Practice getting out of bed | | | |
| C. Practice with urinal and fracture pan | | | |
| D. Explain eating on side with straws; practice | | | |
| E. Determine spinal immobilizer to be used and explain | | | |
| F. Evidence that patients included in preop teaching | | | |
| 2. Arrangements for education continuation discussed with parents | | | |
| 3. Primary nurse identified | | | |
| FIRST THREE DAYS POSTOPERATIVE<br>1. Lung Assessment | | | |
| A. Lung fields auscultated (Recorded $\bar{q}$ 4 hrs. x 72 hrs., then $\bar{q}$ shift) | | | |
| B. Skin color assessed (Recorded $\bar{q}$ 4 hrs. x 72 hrs., then $\bar{q}$ shift) | | | |
| C. Respiratory quality and frequency (Recorded $\bar{q}$ 4 hrs. x 72 hrs., then $\bar{q}$ shift) | | | |
| 2. Bowel Assessment | | | |
| A. Bowel sounds auscultated $\bar{q}$ 4 hrs. until bowel sounds present | | | |

**Exhibit 6–3** continued

| CRITERIA | MET | NOT MET | MET BY EXCEPTION |
|---|---|---|---|
| 3. Skin Integrity | | | |
| A. Patient turned at least $\bar{q}$ 2 hrs. until able to be up | | | |
| B. Pressure points massaged and inspected. Recorded daily | | | |
| 4. CMS Checks Recorded | | | |
| A. $\bar{q}$ 2 hrs. first 72 hrs. | | | |
| B. $\bar{q}$ 4 hrs. until discharge | | | |
| 5. Emotional status especially in relation to body image is recorded daily | | | |
| 6. Self-care Progression Recorded | | | |
| A. First three days ⟶ completely dependent | | | |
| B. Second three days (4-7 days postop) ⟶ needs minimal assistance | | | |
| C. Day before discharge ⟶ self-care recorded<br>Exception: Child's developmental level interferes, then parents should be doing care before discharge | | | |
| BEFORE DISCHARGE<br>1. Verbalizes comprehension of the following: | | | |
| A. Activity limitations | | | |
| B. Medications (able to identify meds, state action, side effects, dosages, and times | | | |
| C. Family members demonstrate role in assisting with skin care | | | |
| D. Family members demonstrate correct brace/cast application and adjustment | | | |

**Exhibit 6–3** continued

| CRITERIA | MET | NOT MET | MET BY EXCEPTION |
|---|---|---|---|
| 2. Verbalizes must notify physician of the following: | | | |
| A. Fever ≥ 101° | | | |
| B. Wound drainage or tenderness | | | |
| C. Changes in CMS | | | |
| D. Falls | | | |
| E. Pressure areas from brace/cast | | | |
| 3. Has acquired special equipment needed for home | | | |

*Source:* Reprinted with permission from St. Michael Hospital, Milwaukee, Wisconsin. Copyright 1981.

documentation. For this reason, the retrospective chart audit is useful in discovering trends in patient care.[26] The audit does not reveal the reason for those trends, however.

Second, since retrospective chart audits are usually done with large numbers of patients, it may be difficult for unit-based quality assurance committees that have only small numbers of patients to conduct them. In this example, a total of twenty-four charts were audited over a two-year period. If patients undergoing a Harrington rod insertion are seen so infrequently, it may be unreasonable to expect documentation to improve greatly. Even with the preprinted flow sheets to remind staff of what should be documented, the results of the reaudit, in general, suggest that alternate methods of data collection are needed to determine why problems in documentation with this population group persist.

All retrospective chart audits, as previously stated, are based on the assumption that what is not documented is not done or that good documentation equals good care. Many factors influence what is or is not documented, however. In addition to the knowledge base of the staff and the availability of written aids to documentation, staff to patient ratios and the acuity of patients' illness may also influence documentation. While useful in identifying trends in documentation, the retrospective chart audit does not give a complete picture of documentation, nor can it serve as the only methodology for evaluating the quality of patient care delivered. Multiple methodologies are needed to evaluate both the documentation of care and the quality of care delivered.

## NOTES

1. Norma M. Lang, *Quality Assurance in Nursing: A Selected Bibliography* (Department of Health, Education and Welfare, Publication No. HRA 80-30, 1980), p. vii.

2. Marlene G. Mayers, Ronald B. Norby, and Annita B. Watson, *Quality Assurance for Patient Care: Nursing Perspectives* (New York: Appleton-Century-Crofts, 1977), p. 77.

3. Doris J. Froebe and R. Joyce Bain, *Quality Assurance Programs and Controls in Nursing* (St. Louis, MO: C.V. Mosby, 1976), p. 75.

4. Ibid, p. 76.

5. Ibid.

6. Delores E. Young and Marlene R. Ventura, "Application of Nursing Diagnosis in Quality Assessment Research," *Quality Assurance Update* 4, no. 2 (December 1980): 2.

7. Maria C. Phaneuf, *The Nursing Audit: Profile for Excellence* (New York: Appleton-Century-Crofts, 1972), pp. 20–34.

8. Milton J. Lesnik and Bernice E. Anderson, *Nursing Practice and the Law*, 2nd ed. (Philadelphia: J.B. Lippincott, 1955), pp. 247–293.

9. Phaneuf, *The Nursing Audit: Profile for Excellence*, p. 16.

10. Ibid.

11. Ibid, pp. 1–131.

12. American Nurses' Association, *Guidelines for Review of Nursing Care at the Local Level* (Kansas City, MO: American Nurses' Association, 1976), pp. 1–126.

13. Mayers, Norby, and Watson, *Quality Assurance for Patient Care*.

14. Ibid, p. 81.

15. Ibid, p. 75.

16. Ibid, p. 17.

17. Avedis Donabedian, *A Guide to Medical Care Administration*, Vol. 2, *Medical Care Appraisal—Quality and Utilization* (New York: American Public Health Association, 1969), pp. 2–4.

18. Norma M. Lang, "Quality Care—Individual and Collective Responsibility," *The American Nurse* 6, no. 9 (September 1974): 4.

19. Julie Hover and Marie J. Zimmer, "Nursing Quality Assurance: The Wisconsin System," *Nursing Outlook* 26 (April 1978): 248.

20. Mayers, Norby, and Watson, *Quality Assurance for Patient Care*, p. 28.

21. Joint Commission on Accreditation of Hospitals, *Nursing Audit Workshop*, 2nd ed. (Chicago: Joint Commission on Accreditation of Hospitals, 1974), p. N Audit/12.

22. American Nurses' Association, *Guidelines for Review of Nursing Care at the Local Level*, p. 33.

23. Julie Hover and Marie J. Zimmer, "Nursing Quality Assurance: The Wisconsin System," *Nursing Outlook* 26 (April 1978): 247–248.

24. Barbara W. Gallant and Audrey M. McLane, "Outcome Criteria: A Process for Validation at the Unit Level," *Journal of Nursing Administration* 9 (January 1979): 14–20.

25. Mayers, Norby, and Watson, *Quality Assurance for Patient Care*, p. 77.

26. Ibid.

## REFERENCES

### Books

American Nurses' Association. *Guidelines for Review of Nursing Care at the Local Level.* Kansas City, MO: American Nurses' Association, 1976.

Donabedian, Avedis. *A Guide to Medical Care Administration,* Vol. 2, *Medical Care Appraisal—Quality and Utilization.* New York: American Public Health Association, 1969.

Froebe, Doris J., and Bain, R. Joyce. *Quality Assurance Programs and Controls in Nursing.* St. Louis, MO: C. V. Mosby, 1976.

Ganong, Joan, and Ganong, Warren. *Help . . . With Nursing Audit: A Management Guide.* Chapel Hill: W. L. Ganong, 1975.

Lang, Norma M. *Quality Assurance in Nursing: A Selected Bibliography.* Department of Health, Education and Welfare Publication No. HRA 80-30, 1980.

Lesnik, Milton J. and Anderson, Bernice E. *Nursing Practice and the Law.* 2nd ed. Philadelphia: J.B. Lippincott, 1955.

Mayers, Marlene G.; Norby, Ronald B.; and Watson, Annita B. *Quality Assurance for Patient Care: Nursing Perspectives.* New York: Appleton-Century-Crofts, 1977.

Phaneuf, Maria C. *The Nursing Audit: Profile for Excellence.* New York: Appleton-Century-Crofts, 1972.

Weiss, Carol H. *Evaluation Research: Methods of Assessing Program Effectiveness.* Englewood Cliffs, NJ: Prentice-Hall, 1972.

### Journals

Eddy, Lyndall, and Westbrook, Linda. "Multidisciplinary Retrospective Patient Care Audit." *American Journal of Nursing* 75 (1975): 961–963.

Gallant, Barbara W., and McLane, Audrey M. "Outcome Criteria: A Process for Validation at the Unit Level." *Journal of Nursing Administration* 9 (1979): 14–20.

Hover, Julie, and Zimmer, Marie J. "Nursing Quality Assurance: The Wisconsin System." *Nursing Outlook* 26 (1978): 242–248.

Lang, Norma M. "Quality Care—Individual and Collective Responsibility." *The American Nurse* 6, no. 9 (1974): 4.

Phaneuf, Maria C. "Quality Assurance: A Nursing View." *Hospitals, JAHA* 47 (1973): 62–68.

Rinaldi, Leena Aalto, and Rubin, Charlene F. "Adding Retrospective Audit." *American Journal of Nursing* 75, no. 2 (1975): 256–259.

Wandelt, Mabel A., and Phaneuf, Maria C. "Three Instruments for Measuring the Quality of Nursing Care." *Hospital Topics* 50, no. 8 (1972): 20–29.

Watson, Annita, and Mayers, Marlene. "Evaluating the Quality of Patient Care Through Retrospective Chart Review." *Journal of Nursing Administration* 6, no. 3 (1976): 17–21.

Woody, Mary F. "An Evaluator's Perspective." *Nursing Research* 29 (1980): 74–77.

Young, Delores E., and Ventura, Marlene R. "Application of Nursing Diagnosis in Quality Assessment Research." *Quality Assurance Update* 4, no. 2 (1980): 1–4.

## Chapter 7

# Concurrent Document Review

*Michele M. Malin, M.S.N., R.N.*

A critical examination of patient outcomes and patient care management, as reflected in the documentation, while care is in progress is a concurrent document review. Sources of data include the patient's medical records and the nursing care plan.

On some units, documentation in patient records may be reviewed on an ongoing basis to ensure that policies are adhered to and standards of care are met. This review process might be based on criteria as simple and straightforward as noting a patient's height and weight on admission, or as complex as evaluating whether a nursing diagnosis is stated specifically enough to ensure appropriate nursing management.

For the evaluation of patients' charts and nursing care plans, tools that reflect standards of care and/or outcomes for patients are developed. Members of each unit's quality assurance committee may decide on topics they wish to review through concurrent auditing on a monthly basis. The criteria for review may be the same as those for retrospective chart audits, with the basic process being exactly the same.

## EXAMPLES OF CONCURRENT DOCUMENT REVIEW

A concurrent document review was done on a medical unit at St. Michael Hospital to determine if nursing care plans were being completed properly. During a one-hour period, members of the unit's quality assurance committee collected data from the nursing care plans of each patient on the unit. All criteria on the data collection tool were behaviorally stated; exceptions were explicitly stated (Exhibit 7–1).

After data had been collected and compiled, the committee reviewed the results and made recommendations. Several areas of deficiency were noted: expected outcomes were not consistently identified for each diagnosis, nursing orders were

**Exhibit 7–1** Sample Criteria for Evaluation of Use of the Nursing Care Plan

| CRITERIA | MET | NOT MET | EXCEPTION |
|---|---|---|---|
| 1. Discharge goal is identified in writing. | | | |
| 2. Primary nurse's signature located in appropriate box.<br>Exception: No primary nurse | | | |
| 3. Nursing diagnoses identified on nursing care plan.<br>Exception: "No problem at this time" is written on nursing care plan | | | |
| 4. Expected outcome is identified for each problem. | | | |

*Source:* Reprinted with permission from St. Michael Hospital, Milwaukee, Wisconsin. Copyright 1980.

not signed by the registered nurse who wrote the orders, and deadlines were rarely indicated for diagnoses. It was recommended that (1) the results of the review be shared with nursing staff at a unit meeting and (2) a clinical nurse specialist in the specialty area provide some in-service training on proper utilization of the nursing care plan. The committee also recommended that a reaudit be done in six months to determine the effectiveness of the action taken.

In the process of this review, the committee collected supplemental data indicating any difference between the date the patient was admitted to the hospital and the date the first problem was identified on the nursing care plan. This information was shared with the staff nurses to help them examine their practice.

In another study, nursing practice was assessed in relation to the monitoring of intake and output, and specific categories of patients who require these measurements were identified. Registered nurse data collectors from an oncology unit at St. Michael Hospital each reviewed nine cases on three consecutive Wednesdays.

The reviewers were assigned to collect data from the records of patients for whom they did not provide daily care. Each patient's care plan, medication sheet, chart, and room were reviewed and data recorded (Exhibit 7–2). Also, the patients were questioned to determine whether they were aware that their intake and output were being measured.

After reviewing the results of this study, the unit's quality assurance committee made recommendations to the head nurse and the nursing staff that led to the development of a unit policy in which specific categories of patients who require measurement of intake and output were identified. In addition, an in-service program on the rationale for measuring intake and output in specific groups of patients was presented to unit nursing assistants.

The use of flow sheets for documentation may also be reviewed concurrently. On one critical care unit, the use of the patient teaching record (Exhibit 7–3),

**Exhibit 7–2** Sample Criteria for an Intake and Output Evaluation Study Tool

| CRITERIA | MET | NOT MET | EXCEPTION |
|---|---|---|---|
| 1. Patients are on I & O when on daily diuresis. | | | |
| 2. Patients are on I & O when admitted for urologic surgery. | | | |
| 3. Patients are on I & O when on continuous I.V. fluids. | | | |
| 4. I & O is documented for past 24 hours on flow sheet. | | | |
| 5. An I & O sheet is present on the patient's door when patient is on I & O. | | | |
| 6. Equipment to measure I & O is in room. | | | |

*Source:* Reprinted with permission from St. Michael Hospital, Milwaukee, Wisconsin. Copyright 1980.

**Exhibit 7–3** Patient Teaching Record

St MICHAEL HOSPITAL
milwaukee wisconsin 53209

**PATIENT TEACHING RECORD**

When documenting teaching, consider: explanation of admission, reaction to illness and hospitalization, explanation of diagnosis, discussion of patient's concerns, diet, activity, medications and specific health measures. ✓ Yes or No. If "No" comment in "Patient Response Column."

| DATE: | CONTENT | Verbalizes Understanding YES | NO | PATIENT RESPONSE | INITIAL |
|---|---|---|---|---|---|

SIGNATURES: ____________________

310 625

F23703 - 11-82 - MR

**PATIENT TEACHING RECORD**

which was used by hospital staff to document all teaching done with patients and their families during the hospital stay, was reviewed to determine if the form was being used appropriately. In this study, members of the unit's quality assurance committee collected data from the patient teaching record of all seven patients in the unit on a particular day. The criteria reviewed (Exhibit 7–4) revealed inconsistent use of the teaching record and failure to document those occasions when patients were not teaching candidates because of their condition. The results of this review were discussed at a unit meeting, and a standard was developed regarding patient teaching. It included a statement of the need to orient all patients and their families to the critical care unit and to document this orientation on the patient teaching record.

Sniff described a multidisciplinary effort in concurrently reviewing emergency department care given to patients at a hospital in Illinois.[1] After an initial retrospective study, a concurrent evaluation form that included criteria related to standard nursing and medical procedures in the emergency department was developed for use in weekly concurrent monitoring. The result was improved adherence to predetermined standards of care.

The usefulness of repeated, concurrent review over a number of years is illustrated in a series of studies done at St. Michael Hospital to determine accuracy in recording electrocardiogram (ECG) strips and in measuring and interpreting ECG results. The first review, conducted in 1978, involved all patients being monitored on four units during a three-day period. The results revealed not only a lack of consistency in using abbreviations, signing strips, timing strips, and placing strips in the chart, but also deficiencies in interpretation of results. Corrective action led to the development of hospitalwide policies on the performance, measurement, and interpretation of ECG strips. In-service programs were presented on all units with monitored beds, and a standardized care plan was developed. The most recent review, in 1982, showed a great improvement in adherence to established policy and in the staff's ability to interpret the rhythm strips correctly.

Concurrent document review of the problem-oriented nursing record poses some special difficulties. In auditing these records, the quality assurance committee may want to evaluate the use of the written format as well as the quality of the nursing diagnoses and of the nursing orders that have been developed and implemented for particular groups of patients. As the area of nursing diagnoses evolves, judgments about the adequacy of documentation and care may become especially complex. In order to measure the appropriateness of a particular nursing diagnosis, for example, the reviewers must have more skill than is ordinarily necessary in auditing charts. They are called upon to judge how well care is planned, carried out, and documented in the patient's records.[2]

The use of problem-oriented nursing recording on a pediatric unit was evaluated one year after the system had been implemented. Before beginning the review,

**Exhibit 7–4** Sample Criteria for Evaluation of Use of the Patient Teaching Record

| CRITERIA | MET | NOT MET | EXCEPTION |
|---|---|---|---|
| 1. Explanation of admission to the unit. Procedure is:<br>A. Documented under the "content" column | | | |
| B. Documented under the "patient response" column | | | |
| Exceptions:<br>a. Patient is comatose | | | |
| b. Patient is confused | | | |
| c. Patient is uncooperative | | | |
| In these cases, teaching with family must still be documented. | | | |
| 2. Discussion of patient's concerns related to diet, activity, medication, and specific health measures are documented:<br>A. Under "content" column | | | |
| B. Under "patient response" column | | | |
| 3. Explanation of diagnosis is given to family member or significant other is:<br>A. Documented under "content" column | | | |
| B. Documented under "patient response" column | | | |

*Source:* Reprinted with permission from St. Michael Hospital, Milwaukee, Wisconsin. Copyright 1982.

unit quality assurance committee members participated in a brief training session to review criteria to be used in evaluating the system (Exhibit 7–5) and to ensure the uniformity of data collection. It was decided that both retrospective and concurrent reviews would be done to determine whether use of the documentation system had changed over time. The same criteria were used for both reviews, although criteria related to discharge were excluded from the concurrent review.

The concurrent care review was made of patients hospitalized on the unit during a one-week period. All patients whose care was reviewed had been hospitalized for at least forty-eight hours at the time of the study. Two registered nurses who worked night shifts permanently collected the data from the patient records. This approach allowed easy access to patient records and permitted a degree of objectivity, since the night shift nurses who performed the audit did not normally carry primary patient caseloads.

The results showed several deficient areas, indicating an apparent difficulty in using problem-oriented nursing recording as a tool to document the ongoing process of patient care. This finding was presented to the nursing staff at a unit meeting, and plans were made for the parent-child clinical nurse specialist to hold monthly care plan review sessions on the appropriate use of problem-oriented nursing recording. The use of the system will be monitored on a continuous basis.

## ADVANTAGES AND DISADVANTAGES

The primary advantage of concurrent review is in the immediate feedback provided to the staff about current patient processes and outcomes.[3] The immediate feedback helps motivate nurses to meet expected standards of care. Staff members can relate particular care criteria directly to specific patients. Just as important is the fact that any problems identified may be remedied while the patient is still undergoing care.

Because concurrent review is done while charts are in use, it is difficult to obtain adequate random samples;[4] because sample sizes are small, it is difficult to quantify results and obtain statistics with meaning. Probably the biggest drawback of concurrent review, however, is the potential for reviewer bias. Even when methods are chosen to protect against bias as much as possible, reviewers may neglect to note the errors of their peers. Furthermore, if the criteria to be reviewed are not carefully selected, concurrent review may measure only conformity to standards, not the validity of the care provided. It is easy to overemphasize a few selected, easily measured criteria and not search for ways to review less concrete data objectively.

In a study comparing concurrent and retrospective auditing on the same patients, Trussel and Strand found that concurrent audits "produce more and different information, take more time, and cost more to conduct."[5] Although

**Exhibit 7–5** Sample Criteria Used to Evaluate Use of Problem-Oriented Nursing Recording

Chart Unit Number ______________
Patient Room Number ______________
Name of Auditor ______________
Date of Review ______________

| Criteria | Meets Criterion | Meets Exception | Does Not Meet | Instructions and Comments |
|---|---|---|---|---|
| DATA COLLECTION | | | | |
| 1. A completed data base is present on chart or Kardex (All sections complete and signed.) Exception: None | | | | If does not meet, indicate what data are missing. |
| 2. A head-to-toe assessment was completed within 8 hours of admission. Exception: None | | | | |
| NURSING DIAGNOSIS | | | | |
| 3. The Nursing Diagnoses List was initiated within 24 hours. Exception: R.N. indicated at time of admission that there were none. | | | | |
| 4. The diagnoses on the Nursing Diagnoses List are stated as nursing diagnoses. Exception: Unknown etiology | | | | The nursing diagnosis includes the patient's response to the actual or potential health problems and the etiology. (No medical diagnoses.) |
| 5. Each diagnosis is preceded by number and date of onset. Exception: None | | | | |
| 6. Each diagnosis is signed by an R.N. Exception: None | | | | |
| 7. Identified diagnoses on the List are resolved when outcome is met. Exception: Outcomes achieved to date; "ongoing" deadline. | | | | |

*Source:* Reprinted with permission from St. Michael Hospital, Milwaukee, Wisconsin. Copyright 1981.

concurrent auditing was found to be twice as costly as retrospective auditing and to take more than twice as much time to complete, the data retrieved from concurrent auditing was more valuable to the staff. Twice as many items of information per audit were retrieved in concurrent auditing, and more than three times as many remarks were written by the auditors in the spaces provided on the audit forms. Areas such as patients' "feelings" and "perceptions and emotional needs at the time of interview" were included in comments of concurrent auditors, while none of this type of information was obtained by retrospective audit. The authors suggested that such comments may provide a firsthand source of information for patient care conferences.

In summary, concurrent document review may be used to evaluate adherence to policies and standards. The data retrieved in concurrent review provide a wealth of information about the process of providing patient care and a basis for the development of new standards.

## NOTES

1. David Sniff, "The Evolution of a Quality Assurance Program," *Quality Review Bulletin* 6 (January 1980): 26–29.
2. Marlene G. Mayers et al., *Quality Assurance for Patient Care: Nursing Perspectives* (New York: Appleton-Century-Crofts, 1977), p. 97.
3. Ibid, p. 87.
4. Ibid, p. 89.
5. Patricia Trussel and Nancy Strand, "A Comparison of Concurrent and Retrospective Audits on the Same Points," *Journal of Nursing Administration* 8 (May 1978): 38.

## REFERENCES

### Books

Froebe, Doris G., and Bain, R. Joyce. *Quality Assurance Programs and Controls in Nursing*. St. Louis, MO: C.V. Mosby, 1976.

Mayers, Marlene G.; Norby, Ronald B.; and Watson, Annita B. *Quality Assurance for Patient Care: Nursing Perspectives*. New York: Appleton-Century-Crofts, 1977, pp. 87–125.

Michnich, Marie; Harris, L. Jeff; Willis, Richard A.; Williams, Jamesina E.; and Torrens, Paul R. *Ambulatory Care Evaluation: A Primer for Quality Review*. Los Angeles: University of California, 1976.

Phaneuf, Maria. *The Nursing Audit and Self-Regulation in Nursing Practice*. 2nd ed. New York: Appleton-Century-Crofts, 1976.

### Journals

Beck, Bobbi, and Hardwick, Karen. "A Concurrent Surgical Mini-audit Procedure." *Quality Review Bulletin* 7 (1981): 21–24.

Lindy, Cheryl N. ''A Three-Part Approach to Quality Assurance in Nursing.'' *Quality Review Bulletin* 6 (1980): 12–16.

Mich, Ann B. ''Evaluating the Process of Nursing Care in Long Term Care Facilities.'' *Quality Review Bulletin* Special Edition (1982): 53–59.

Phaneuf, Maria C., and Wandelt, Mabel A. ''Three Methods of Process-Oriented Nursing Evaluation.'' *Quality Review Bulletin* 7 (1981): 20–26.

Sniff, David. ''The Evolution of a Quality Assurance Program.'' *Quality Review Bulletin* 6 (1980): 26–29.

Trussel, Patricia, and Strand, Nancy. ''A Comparison of Concurrent and Retrospective Audits on the Same Patients.'' *Journal of Nursing Administration* 8 (1978): 33–38.

## Chapter 8

# Interviewing: A Valuable Quality Assurance Strategy

*Cathleen K. Wilson, M.S.N., R.N.*
*Regina M. Maibusch, S.S.S.F., M.S., R.N.*

Nurses may use interviews in the assessment of quality nursing care. Loftland defined interview in the following manner:

> The term interview is constructed out of two words, "inter" and "view." To "view" means to look at, to have a perception of. "Inter" means between two objects or points, as in intercity transit. Therefore, the term "interview" refers to the act of perceiving, as conducted between two separate points . . . between two people.[1]

Loftland also emphasized the act of perceiving in the interview process.[2] Other theorists agree that perceptions gained through the interview process make the art of interviewing an important strategy in data collection.[3] The interviewer is in the unique position of observing all elements of the interview situation and often obtains additional data that are useful in the analysis of responses. Nurses considering the use of interview techniques in quality assurance studies must first consider the strengths and limitations of this strategy, however.

## STRENGTHS AND WEAKNESSES OF INTERVIEWING

### Strengths

Interviewing has been described as a valuable strategy because it allows the interviewer not only to probe deeply and obtain a great deal of data, but also to check the perceptions of respondents.[4] Interviewing provides a verbal interaction sequence in which the interviewer can clarify questions about the interview items before the responses are recorded. This process improves the accuracy of data collection.[5] For these reasons, interviewing is an appropriate strategy when nurses are studying complex subjects, such as attitudes, opinions, patient satisfaction, and beliefs about health care.

The fact that interviewing can be used with almost every segment of the population is particularly useful in nursing situations.[6] Patients who cannot read or write or those who are handicapped in some other fashion can be interviewed, because they are required only to respond to the interviewer. Furthermore, more interviews may be completed;[7] nurses, patients, and families dealing with illness may not have enough energy to do much more than talk. In addition, talking to someone about the illness may have some therapeutic effects.

Finally, interviewing may be a researcher's only way to retrieve information about a patient's history,[8] and a knowledge of the history might be critical to an understanding of the reason for a patient's particular belief, such as a health care belief. In psychiatric nursing, history is clearly an important variable.

## Limitations

Although interviewing can be a valuable strategy in evaluating nursing care, it takes more time and is more costly than many other evaluation strategies. The training required for interviewers, the time needed for the interview and for the interview process, and the number of respondents necessary to ensure reliability contribute to the time and cost of the evaluation endeavor.

The possibility of collecting biased data is another frequently described limitation of the interview method. Social interactions between human beings are complex, and either the interviewer or the respondent may have characteristics and behaviors that result in highly biased data (Table 8–1). There have been attempts to check for bias in data by repeating interviews with a random number of respondents,[9] but obviously, the reliability of the interview method is not as great as that of an objective questionnaire.

Interview techniques are also limited by the memory of respondents, which may be faulty. Memory is influenced by the amount of time since the particular event occurred, the frequency with which the event occurs in the respondent's life, and the event's relative importance to the respondent.[10]

Finally, when the data collected are highly objective and quantifiable, clear relationships among variables in the nursing situation can be identified by the evaluator. Causal relationships are very difficult to establish in evaluation situations, however, because multiple complex factors are studied and the information is subject to considerable bias.[11] If the evaluator's purpose is to establish the effects of a particular treatment, other strategies of data collection are preferable.

## Implications of Strengths and Weaknesses

It is clear that interviewing is a sophisticated social interaction skill. Those who select persons to function as interviewers must take this into consideration.

**Table 8–1** Characteristics of Interviewers and Respondents That May Bias the Information Collected

| *Interviewer* | *Respondents* |
|---|---|
| Tendency to lead respondents in a particular direction<br>Lack of interpersonal skills to deal with complex social interaction situations<br>• shy, paranoid, uncooperative respondents<br>• sensitive subject materials<br>Dislike of certain characteristics of respondent<br>Feeling of urgency to complete interview<br>• time pressures<br>• dislike of respondent | Eagerness to please the interviewer<br>• prestige needs<br>• fear of authority figures<br>• enjoyment of social contact<br>Poor communicator<br>• use of multiple defense mechanisms<br>• underreporting<br>• inability to articulate feelings<br>Dislike of interviewer<br>Lack of insight (self-diagnosis may require that subject make personal evaluation and inferential judgments about self)<br>Embarrassment or irritation at interview content |

Interviewers must possess good interpersonal skills, such as active listening skills, clarifying skills, and feedback skills. Any evaluation study involving this strategy of data collection should include a plan for training the interviewers.

The time and cost factors of interviewing must also be considered. At St. Michael Hospital, the unit-based model provides opportunities for nurses to plan and conduct evaluation studies, but the realities of the clinical setting sometimes make it necessary to use less timely strategies of data collection.

The complexity of nursing situations sometimes makes them difficult to study. For example, the patient dependency in the nurse-patient relationship may prevent patients from making negative comments about nursing care.[12] In such situations, interviews might include probes to facilitate patients' frank discussions about their nursing care concerns, or interviewers who are not involved in the patients' daily care might conduct the study.

Social-psychological variables seem to influence nursing care consistently. Cognitive, emotional, behavioral, and social variables all affect nurses' feelings about resuscitating terminally ill patients, the communication patterns of health teams caring for special patient populations, and patients' expectations of nursing care. The interview is an ideal method by which the evaluator can collect the information that will ultimately guide nursing practice.

## TYPES OF INTERVIEWS

Interviews can be unstructured, semistructured, or structured.[13] In spite of its name, the unstructured interview is not without a purpose. The interviewer tries to obtain specific information; because the information desired may be personal or sensitive, however, direct questioning might not elicit truthful responses. Therefore, the interview is allowed to proceed as a conversation, with the interviewer using subtle questioning to obtain the desired information. This requires great skill and previous training.

In the semistructured interview, the interviewer has a set of well-defined questions that serve as a springboard for more in-depth probing. If the interview were conducted with only the original questions, the client response might be superficial and incomplete. Questions for a semistructured interview allow the interviewer to raise the topic and to obtain additional responses as the client becomes comfortable with the subject.

The structured interview, in contrast, is designed to obtain clearly defined and specific information. This type of interview is suitable when shades of meaning or feelings are not needed or depth is not required in the response.

## CLINICAL EXAMPLES

Miller and Russell used interviews with the residents of a nursing home to identify the elements in their environment that promote or prevent their satisfaction.[14] Other researchers had examined the effect of safety, medical treatment, and nutrition on a resident's satisfaction.

The questionnaire used was the Life Satisfaction Index developed by Neugarten, Havighurst, and Tobin and modified by Adams.[15,16] The eighteen items involved the residents' feelings about their current situation, such as "I am just as happy as when I was young." or "The things I do are as interesting to me as they ever were."[17] Both positive and negative statements about the resident's present situation in life were provided as a check on consistency. Each item was read to the resident, and the interviewer recorded the response. Three responses were possible for each item: "agree," "disagree," and "not sure." Although these items examined feelings, the emotional content was already expressed and the resident had only to choose. Like an objective questionnaire, the Life Satisfaction Index typifies a structured interview. It obtains rather precise information about feelings that might be difficult to assess objectively if an unstructured approach had been used.

In their study, Miller and Russell also used a second instrument, called an open-ended questionnaire, that was based on what their review of the literature identified as the elements older people most often felt contributed to their satisfaction, e.g., leisure time, the residence, security, meal time, significant others, religion, and health status. Again, there were three possible responses, i.e., "yes," "no," and "don't know," for each of the twenty-four major questions. This portion of the questionnaire was not open-ended, but rather forced a choice. Most of the twenty-four questions were followed by probe questions, however, to assist the data collector in conducting the interview and to allow for depth and self-expression by the resident responder.

This, then, was a combined typology of the structured and semistructured interview. The twenty-four major questions comprised a structured interview; the probe questions, a semistructured interview. For example, the major question related to leisure read, "Do you enjoy your leisure?" The respondent was forced to choose an answer. The probe questions to that major question: (1) "Where do you spend most of your leisure time?" (2) "What do you enjoy doing most?" (3) "Are the materials (for leisure time stated) readily available?" and (4) "If reading, what type of reading do you do?" are open-ended.[18]

Hover and Zimmer have described the system in use at the University of Wisconsin Hospitals in the middle to late 1970s.[19] Five overall criteria formed the basic framework for each criteria set: "(1) knowledge of illness and its treatment, (2) skills, (3) knowledge of medications, (4) adaptive behavior, and (5) health or physiologic status."[20] Measures specific to varying patient populations were developed for each of these major criteria.

Several methods were used to obtain data about these criteria, including a chart review, observation of the patient, and interview. For example, an interview guide was used to obtain data specific to the third criterion, knowledge of medications (Exhibit 8–1). The questions asked are specific for each medication prescribed. This is another example of the use of the structured interview to determine the quality of nursing care that a patient received, in this instance, teaching. A factor not measured is the patient's ability and motivation to learn.

The literature reports numerous nursing interventions that assist postpartum families in integrating a new baby into the family. Rhode and Groenjes-Finke described a study involving several structured questionnaires, one of which was used as an interview guide for a telephone contact.[21] Using an experimental design, Rhode and Groenjes-Finke compared nurse-initiated postdischarge telephone contact to six-week postpartum checkup counseling for their effects on the new mothers' ability to deal with crisis and stress. Ninety-nine mothers were randomly assigned to the experimental and/or control group. A valid data tool was used to assess stress in all the mothers on the second postpartum day. Two days after discharge, the mothers in the experimental group were contacted by telephone. The telephone conversation was allowed to develop naturally, but information was obtained in eight areas. Specific questions relating to these eight areas had been developed earlier to ensure that identical questions were asked by the experimenters (Exhibit 8–2), and an effort had been made to reduce bias by establishing

**Exhibit 8–1** Medication Knowledge Test

Population: Adult patients going home on medications.
Caretakers of children going home on medication.

Point in Time: Discharge from hospital.

Patient's Initials__________ Date of Discharge__________

Medical Service__________ Date of Discharge Meds Ordered__________

Nursing Unit__________ Medication List From Chart__________

Age__________ Sex__________

Medical Diagnosis__________

1. What is(are) the name(s) of your medication(s)?

2. Can you describe for me what your medicine looks like? (color, shape, size)

3. How much of the medicine do you take at one time? (1 tablet, 1 tsp.)

4. Do you know what the prescribed dose of your medicine is? (mg., Gm., ml.) __________ If yes, what is it?

5. How do you take your medicine?

6. How many times a day do you take your medication(s)?

7. Do you know why you should take the medication on a specific time schedule?

8. What does the medication do?

9. Why is it important for you to take this particular medicine?

**Exhibit 8–1** continued

10. Do you know of any undesirable effects that this medication produces? __________________ If yes, can you name some?

11. What will you do if you notice that you are having side effects from your medication?

12. How long do you have to keep taking the medication?

13. Where will you keep the medication.

14. What will happen if you stop taking the medication without your doctor knowing?

15. What would you do if you missed 1 dose of medication?

16. What would you do if you missed 2 doses of medication?

*Source:* Reprinted with permission of Nursing Department, University of Wisconsin Hospitals, 1977.

agreement among the experimenters on their responses to the mothers. Although the questions were specific, the interview was semistructured because the interview guide was not rigidly adhered to without diversion in order or extraneous content.

In 1981, a surgical nursing unit at St. Michael Hospital undertook an evaluation study to determine whether preoperative teaching was done, whether it was effective, and whether it was documented. The study sample consisted of fifty-two patients who underwent general surgery and remained hospitalized for forty-eight hours or more. Eleven professional nurses were used as interviewers. A structured interview guide of eighteen questions was developed (Exhibit 8–3). The first sixteen questions were used for the interview; the last two required chart review. Responses to the questions required a simple "yes" or "no." Because of the directness of the questions and the unambiguous answers required, little training was needed for the interviewers.

As a result of this study, a new slide/tape program on preoperative teaching was developed by St. Michael Hospital personnel. Attractive posters were displayed

**Exhibit 8–2** Protocol for Telephone Calls

1. What questions or problems do you have now concerning the care of your baby?
2. How much rest have you been able to get since you have been home?
3. Have you had a problem with too many visitors?
4. Do you have enough help at home?
5. What effect is the new baby in the house having on your family?
6. What questions or problems do you have concerning care of yourself as your body recovers from pregnancy and delivery?
7. Have you noticed any problems with the "baby blues"?
8. Have you thought of any questions about your method of birth control since you left the hospital?

*Note:* To ensure comparability between mothers' responses and between experimenters, identical questions were asked at each telephone call (above). Ten calls by each experimenter were taped and analyzed by an experienced independent faculty member to establish comparability of the experimenters' responses to mothers.

*Source:* Reprinted with permission from Mary Ann Rhode and Jean M. Groenjes-Finke, "Evaluation of Nurse-Initiated Telephone Calls to Postpartum Women," *Issues in Health Care of Women* 2, no. 2 (April 1980): 33. Permission of Hemisphere Publishing Corporation, 1983.

on the unit to advertise the nightly program. The format for a written invitation for each patient was developed. In-service programs incorporating research findings on the value of preoperative teaching were presented. Standards were developed for the nightly classes, which were taught by a registered nurse assigned by the head nurse on a rotating basis.

In three months, the study was repeated on a smaller population. Twenty-four patients were interviewed by four registered nurses in this reaudit. All criteria were met at a higher percentage than in the original evaluation. For example, 75 percent of the interviewed patients now attended preoperative classes versus 13 percent in the first study. The intent is to conduct periodic reaudits to determine whether criteria continue to be met.

Medical and nursing personnel at St. Michael Hospital conducted a study to evaluate the adequacy of instructions given to patients with lacerations that had been sutured in the emergency department. The study objective was to determine the knowledge patients had of wound care, as well as the effectiveness of the instruction sheet given to each patient. In conjunction with the medical director of

**Exhibit 8–3** Preoperative Teaching Evaluation Study

Interviewer: ________________ Date of Interview: _________

Type of Surgery: ______________________________________

Patient's Age ________________ Date of Surgery: ___________

Interview Guide

1. Did you attend preop class? Yes___ No___ If no, why?

2. Was the class helpful? Yes___ No___ If no, why?

3. Did your nurse show you how to deep breathe and cough? Yes___ No___

4. Did you have to show her that you could do it? Yes___ No___

5. Did the nurse show you how to splint your incision before surgery? Yes___ No___ Does not apply___

6. Did you have to show her that you could do it? Yes___ No___ Does not apply___

7. Did the nurse show you how to get in and out of bed appropriately? Yes___ No___ Does not apply___

8. Did you have to show her that you could do it? Yes___ No___ Does not apply___

9. Did the nurse show you how to do leg exercises? Yes___ No___

10. Did you have to show her that you could do it? Yes___ No___

11. Were you told before surgery that you would have an I.V.? Yes___ No___

12. Were you told before surgery that you would wear surgical stockings? Yes___ No___ Not ordered___

13. Were you told before surgery that you would not be able to eat or drink anything after midnight? Yes___ No___

**Exhibit 8–3** continued

14. Were you told before surgery that you would wake up in the Recovery Room? Yes___ No___

15. Were you told before surgery that you would be getting up to walk the evening of surgery? Yes___ No___ Does not apply___

16. Were you told before surgery about how to get pain relief? Yes___ No___

17. Preop teaching is documented? Yes___ No___

18. If yes, where? In the Nurses' Notes___ Patient Teaching Record___ Preop Patient Teaching Record___

*Source:* Reprinted with permission from St. Michael Hospital, Milwaukee, Wisconsin. Copyright 1981.

the emergency department, the nursing quality assurance committee developed an instrument of six questions (Exhibit 8–4). Responses were obtained by means of a telephone interview conducted by a registered nurse twenty-four to forty-eight hours after discharge from the emergency department. Data collection continued until sixty-three patients were included in the study (fifty had been determined as the minimum). It took approximately five weeks to collect the information on the study sample.

Because this study was the emergency department's first venture into a multidisciplinary audit, it was significant not only for its positive findings concerning patient education, but also for its positive effect on physician-nurse collaboration. The medical directorship of the emergency department was a new position, and the quality assurance effort provided the two health care disciplines involved an opportunity to build a respect for each other.

More recently, the interview method was used to gather data in a study of post-myocardial infarction patients transferred from the cardiac care unit. The purpose of the study was to determine what patients knew about their myocardial infarction at the time of the transfer. Again, a structured interview guide was used (Exhibit 8–5). The questions had been previously tested to ensure that they were clear and easily understood by the patient.

Four members of the quality assurance committee of the cardiac care unit interviewed eleven patients the evening before or the morning of their transfer from the unit. The findings showed that patients answered from 0 percent to 100 percent of the questions correctly. Many variables could have caused the dif-

**Exhibit 8–4** Quality Assurance Study of Discharge Instructions

Patient Number ____________________

Date and time of discharge from Emergency Department ________

Date and time of interview ________________________

Interview Guide

1. Did you receive a printed instruction sheet telling you how to take care of your sutured wound? _____ Yes _____ No

2. Did you receive any instruction regarding care of your wound besides the printed sheet? _____ Yes _____ No

   If so, by whom? _____R.N. _____M.D.

3. When are your sutures to be taken out?

4. Who is going to take them out?

5. Describe how you are taking care of your wound now.

6. How could you tell if your wound was infected?

*Source:* Reprinted with permission from St. Michael Hospital, Milwaukee, Wisconsin. Copyright 1982.

**Exhibit 8–5** Questionnaire on Knowledge of Patients with Myocardial Infarction

| Patient Questions | Factors from the Chart | Patient Responses Correct/Incorrect |
|---|---|---|
| 1. What did the tests show was wrong with you? | Type of M.I. | |
| 2. What type of physical activities are you allowed to do now? | Rehab level or M.D. activity order | |
| 3. Which medications are you taking now and what are they for? (List the name of the pill, if you know it, otherwise describe the way it looks or what it does.) | List the meds from the med sheet | |
| 4. What is a heart attack? | Definition from printed information given to patient | |
| 5. What past or present illnesses or life-styles do you feel have caused your present illness? | Risk factors | |
| 6. How long do you think you will be in the hospital? | Name of physician ______ Time told by physician______ | |
| 7. What will your treatment be for this illness between now and the time you go home? | Rehabilitation program?; classes?; rest? | |

**Exhibit 8–5** continued

| Patient Questions | Factors from the Chart | Patient Responses Correct/Incorrect |
|---|---|---|
| 8. After you go home from the hospital, will you need to change your daily activities? (example - job, hobbies, etc.) | On special diet?; any restrictions that you know of? | |
| 9. Could this ever happen to you again? | | |
| 10. What questions do you have that were not answered during your stay in this unit? | | |

Did the patient get any printed information? How many days ago?

Teaching documented?

*Source:* Reprinted with permission from St. Michael Hospital, Milwaukee, Wisconsin. Copyright 1982.

ferences in patient responses, such as age, sex, first myocardial infarction, what was taught versus what was learned, attending physician, and primary nurse. These were not correlated. However, patients who received the printed material about heart health entitled *Take Heart*[22] scored an average of 69 percent, while patients who did not receive this material scored an average of 29 percent.

The quality assurance committee's recommendations included (1) revision of the patient teaching record for patients with myocardial infarction so that the record consists of more realistic outcomes, (2) development of a slide/tape presentation for patients that focuses on early concerns and questions, and (3) revision of the interview guide to ensure clarity.

## NOTES

1. John Loftland, *Analyzing Social Settings* (Belmont, CA: Wadsworth, 1971), p. 75.
2. Ibid.
3. Stephen Isaac and William B. Michael, *Handbook in Research and Evaluation* (San Diego: Edits, 1971), p. 96.
4. Claire Selltiz, Lawrence Wrightsman, and Stuart Cook, *Research Methods in Social Relations*, 3rd ed. (New York: Holt, Rinehart and Winston, 1976), pp. 291–330.
5. Ibid.
6. Ibid.
7. Smith, *Strategies of Social Research*, pp. 170–171.
8. Michael Patton, *Qualitative Evaluation Methods* (Beverly Hills, CA: Sage Publications, 1980), pp. 195–264.
9. Selltiz, Wrightsman, and Cook, *Research Methods in Social Relations*, pp. 291–330.
10. Smith, *Strategies of Social Research*, p. 170.
11. Thomas Bouchard, Jr., "Field Research Methods: Interviewing, Questionnaires, Participant Observation, Systematic Observation, Unobtrusive Nurses," in Marvin D. Dunnette (ed.), *The Handbook of Industrial and Organizational Psychology* (Boston, MA: Houghton Mifflin, 1976), pp. 363–373.
12. Diane S. Moore and Karen Cook Hubbard, "Comparison of Methods for Evaluating Patient Response to Nursing Care," *Nursing Research* 24, no. 3 (May-June 1975): 202.
13. Isaac and Michael, *Handbook in Research and Evaluation*, p. 96.
14. Sister Patricia Miller and Dorothy A. Russell, "Elements Promoting Satisfaction," *Journal of Gerontological Nursing* 6, no. 3 (March 1980): 121–129.
15. Bernice L. Neugarten, Robert J. Havighurst, and Sheldon S. Tobin, "The Measurement of Life Satisfaction," *Journal of Gerontology* 16, no. 2 (April 1961): 134–143.
16. Donald L. Adams, "Analysis of a Life Satisfaction Index," *Journal of Gerontology* 24, no. 4 (October 1969): 470–474.
17. Miller and Russell, "Elements Promoting Satisfaction," p. 126.
18. Ibid, p. 127.
19. Julie Hover and Marie J. Zimmer, "Nursing Quality Assurance: The Wisconsin System," *Nursing Outlook* 26 no. 4 (April 1978): 242–248.
20. Ibid.
21. Mary Ann Rhode and Jean M. Groenjes-Finke, "Evaluation of Nurse-Initiated Telephone Calls to Postpartum Women," *Issues in the Health Care of Women* 2, no. 2 (April 1980): 23–41.
22. *Take Heart*, produced by Cardiac Care Committee, St. Michael Hospital, 1979.

## REFERENCES

### Books

Bouchard, Thomas, Jr. "Field Research Methods: Interviewing, Questionnaires, Participant Observation, Systematic Observation, Unobtrusive Nurses." In Marvin D. Dunnette (ed.), *The Handbook of Industrial and Organizational Psychology*. Boston, MA: Houghton Mifflin, 1976, pp. 363–373.

Isaac, Stephen, and Michael, William B. *Handbook in Research and Evaluation*. San Diego: Edits, 1971.

Loftland, John. *Analyzing Social Setting*. Belmont, CA: Wadsworth, 1971.

Patton, Michael. *Qualitative Evaluation Methods*. Beverly Hills, CA: Sage Publications, 1980, pp. 195–264.

Selltiz, Claire; Wrightsman, Lawrence; and Cook, Stuart. *Research Methods in Social Relations*, 3rd ed. New York: Holt, Rinehart and Winston, 1976, pp. 291–330.

Smith, Herman W. *Strategies of Social Research*. Englewood Cliffs, NJ: Prentice-Hall, 1975.

**Journals**

Adams, David L. "Analysis of a Life Satisfaction Index." *Journal of Gerontology* 24 (October 1969): 470–474.

Hover, Julie, and Zimmer, Marie J. "Nursing Quality Assurance: The Wisconsin System." *Nursing Outlook* 26 (1978): 242–248.

Miller, Sister Patricia, and Russell, Dorothy A. "Elements Promoting Satisfaction." *Journal of Gerontological Nursing* 6 (1980): 121–129.

Moore, Diane S., and Hubbard, Karen Cook. "Comparison of Methods for Evaluating Patient Response to Nursing Care." *Nursing Research* 24 (1975): 202.

Neugarten, Bernice L.; Havighurst, Robert J.; and Tobin, Sheldon S. "The Measurement of Life Satisfaction." *Journal of Gerontology* 16 (April 1961): 134–143.

Rhode, Mary Ann, and Groenjes-Finke, Jean M. "Evaluation of Nurse-Initiated Telephone Calls to Postpartum Women." *Issues in the Health Care of Women* 2 (1980): 23–41.

# Chapter 9

# Using a Questionnaire

*Peggy L. Wagner, M.S.N., R.N., CCRN*

One method of collecting data on quality assurance issues is the questionnaire, which solicits written information directly from individuals. When appropriately constructed and administered, questionnaires generate data useful in making decisions about care. The results of questionnaires may have a direct impact on the person completing the questionnaire, or the results may not personally affect respondents.

## RESPONDENT IMPACT QUESTIONNAIRES

Questionnaires can be used to solicit several types of information to meet multipurpose goals. With respondent impact questionnaires, individuals or groups completing questionnaires receive feedback and are directly involved in resultant actions. Respondents have a personal interest in the timeliness of their response and the accuracy of their answers. Data collection tools can be designed to document current knowledge and attitudes or intentions related to future actions. By compiling this type of information, immediate action can be taken to correct information, prevent unsafe behavior or undue emotional hardship, or stimulate changes in attitude or behavior (Table 9–1). Questionnaire data can stimulate action regarding both patient and staff needs in the clinical setting.

Depending on the specific purpose of the questionnaire, the answers solicited may affect individuals, groups, or both. If respondents are to receive personal feedback, anonymity must be sacrificed. If lack of confidentiality would affect the accuracy of answers, feedback can be given to the group. Both anonymous and nonanonymous questionnaires are useful in the appropriate situation.

### Knowledge

Teaching protocols or programs are designed for many patient populations. One important reason for testing knowledge is to provide a baseline for supplementing

**Table 9–1** Respondent Impact Questionnaires

| *Information Solicited* | *Application of Results* |
|---|---|
| Knowledge | Correction of misinformation |
| Attitudes/feelings | Provision of additional knowledge |
| Intentions related to future | Counseling regarding positive self-care; beneficial coping mechanisms |
| | Problem solving |
| | Behavior modification |

or correcting knowledge so that the patient can develop safe and productive self-care practices before leaving the health care system. At St. Michael Hospital, for example, patients who have participated in the inpatient cardiac rehabilitation program are asked to complete a quiz before discharge (Exhibit 9–1). The primary nurse is responsible for reviewing the quiz with the patient, since the quiz is meant to stimulate discussion and reveal potential problems before the patient goes home.

Staff knowledge and needs can also be determined by a questionnaire. The education program for cardiopulmonary resuscitation (CPR) at St. Michael Hospital is a self-learning program used in conjunction with the American Heart Association Basic Life Support Certification. Knowledge is reviewed and tested by means of a quiz (Exhibit 9–2) that is self-corrected for immediate feedback, then sent to the head nurse who validates completion and notes any areas in which additional education is needed.

## Attitudes

Data that are collected during the time frame of the experience when involvement is high generally reveal a great deal about attitudes, but they may be colored by emotions. If the sources of attitude can be isolated, however, constructive and specific intervention can be instituted.

When the quality of care was threatened by nonspecific anxiety and malcontent in the coronary care unit, nurses on the unit staff directed the quality assurance committee to study the sources of stress so that action could be taken to resolve the problems. A questionnaire was sent to all nurses to identify stressors in five areas: (1) interpersonal communication, (2) knowledge base, (3) environment, (4) patient care, and (5) personal events affecting work. These identified stressors were compiled and reissued to registered nurses, who scored them on a least to

## **Exhibit 9–1** Sample Quiz for Cardiac Patients

**We hope the information in this booklet has been helpful to you and your family. We'd like you to review some of these facts and ask that you complete the following quiz and give it to your nurse before you leave the hospital.**

# HOW MUCH DO YOU KNOW ABOUT YOUR HEART ATTACK?

**(In the following questions, circle all of the correct answers.)**

1. The length of time for your heart attack to heal after a heart attack is:
   a. One week
   b. Two to four weeks
   c. Two to three months
   d. Six months

2. Cholesterol can be described as:
   a. A fatty substance found in foods
   b. A fatty material found only in egg yolk, liver and shrimp
   c. A form of tryglycerides
   d. A fatty substance produced by the body

3. Which of the following is lowest in saturated fat?
   a. Broiled pork chop
   b. Broiled white fish
   c. Grilled sirloin steak
   d. Fried chicken

4. Which of the following statements about smoking are true?
   a. There is no risk in smoking if you don't inhale.
   b. Smoking is not a health hazard for women.
   c. Everyone will gain weight if they quit smoking.
   d. Smokers who stop smoking reduce their risk of heart attack.

5. After the scar has formed over the damaged portion of your heart and you have resumed activities, you should avoid:
   a. Yard work in very hot or very cold weather
   b. Sexual relations
   c. Situations that make you very angry, tense or afraid
   d. Cigarettes

6. Which of the following concerning high blood pressure (hypertension) are true?
   a. People only get high blood pressure if they have a heart attack or are over forty.
   b. High blood pressure is not always related to stress.
   c. People only have hypertension occasionally. It goes away by itself.
   d. The way to take blood pressure pills depends on the way you feel.

7. For which of the following should you notify your doctor or go to the nearest emergency room?
   a. Fainting or dizziness
   b. Palpitations (rapid heart rate) 30 minutes after intercourse
   c. Increased shortness of breath
   d. A change in the pattern of angina

8. Dietary changes your family needs to make are:
   a. Eat to maintain ideal weight.
   b. No change is necessary, the diet is only for someone with heart disease.
   c. Reduce total intake of fat.
   d. Substitute skimmed milk for whole milk and cream.

9. Factors that could cause a normal increase in your pulse are:
   a. An argument with your best friend
   b. Jogging
   c. Sleeping
   d. Sexual activity

10. Which of the following statements concerning activity are true?
   a. Sitting to do an activity requires less activity than standing.
   b. While your heart is healing from a heart attack, it must work harder to perform your usual daily activities.
   c. Regular walking and jogging are excellent exercises for your heart when performed in moderation as directed by your physician.
   d. Competitive sports are good for your heart.

---

Circle true **(T)** or false **(F)** for each question.

**T or F** 1. Treatment for heart attack is aimed at giving your heart time to mend itself.

**T or F** 2. Filters or low tar and nicotine cigarettes make smoking safe.

**T or F** 3. Coconut oil is a polyunsaturated fat.

**T or F** 4. Everyone who has a heart attack will have angina afterwards.

**T or F** 5. The competitive, time-oriented personality can be changed.

ANSWERS FOR QUIZ
Multiple Choice:
1. c 5. a,c,d 8. a,c,d
2. a,d 6. b 9. a,b,d
3. b 7. a,b,c,d 10. a,b,c
4. d
True or False:
1. T 3. F 5. T
2. F 4. F

*Source:* Reprinted with permission from Barbara Johnston, John Cantwell, and Gerald Fletcher, "Eight Steps to Inpatient Cardiac Rehabilitation: The Team Effort—Methodology and Preliminary Results." *Heart and Lung* 5 (1976): 97–111. Adapted by Cardiac Rehabilitation Staff at St. Michael Hospital, Milwaukee, Wisconsin, for use in *Take Heart,* 1979, page 11.

**Exhibit 9–2** CPR Review Quiz

1. If you found an unconscious patient, describe in order the steps you would take immediately to diagnose and treat cardiopulmonary arrest.

Answer the following questions by circling all correct responses

2. Appropriate ways of getting help once you have found a victim of cardiopulmonary arrest in the hospital are:

   a. Turn on the patient call light
   b. Dial 8111
   c. Run to summon the closest person
   d. Shout for help

3. If you found a patient with a heartbeat but no respirations, you would:

   a. Call a Code 4
   b. Continue to assess for cardiac arrest
   c. Give 1 breath every 5 seconds
   d. Do cardiac massage

4. In diagnosing a cardiac arrest, it is important to palpate a carotid pulse:

   a. Briefly, this is an emergency
   b. For 1 full minute
   c. For 5-10 seconds
   d. While listening for respirations

5. When defibrillating, you must remember the following points:

   a. No one must be in contact with the bed or the patient
   b. The monitoring leads must be in place
   c. Patients are always defibrillated at 400 watt/second in a Code 4
   d. Both buttons must be depressed simultaneously to discharge the unit

6. The commonly used dosage of Lidocaine drip is:

   a. 1 gm in 1000 ml D/5/W
   b. 1 gm in 500 ml D/5/W
   c. 50 mgm in 1000 ml D/5/W
   d. 50 mgm in 500 ml D/5/W

7. Drugs that can be given through the ET tube during a Code 4 are:

   a. Epinephrine, Bicarb, Dextrose
   b. Lidocaine, Epinephrine, Atropine
   c. Bicarb, Bretylol, Atropine
   d. Lidocaine, Bicarb, Epinephrine

**Exhibit 9–2** continued

8. Which of the following are responsibilities of the staff nurse in a Code 4:

   a. Defibrillation
   b. Medication administration
   c. "Traffic control"
   d. Completion of the CPR record and evaluation

9. After the crash cart arrives, in which order would nursing personnel assume the following responsibilities:

   a. Start an IV
   b. Place the arrest board under the patient and continue with CPR
   c. Place the monitoring leads
   d. Record
   e. Monitor vital signs

10. Which of the following monitoring leads should be used regularly during a Code 4:

    a. Lead I
    b. Lead II
    c. Lead III
    d. $MCL_1$

Answer the following questions true or false.

1. T F The crash cart must be checked every shift.

2. T F The only time a precordial thump should be delivered is in a monitored arrest.

3. T F CPR may be interrupted for 1 minute during intubation.

4. T F The nursing staff may give any appropriate drug IV push under the direct supervision of a physician at a a Code 4

5. T F Defibrillator pads can be used for multiple defibrillations.

6. T F Vasopressors, such as Intropin, should be run wide open to increase the blood pressure.

most stressful scale. Items and clusters of items were then discussed by staff, and specific interventions defined and implemented. A repeat study showed significantly less stress related to most items and a general reduction in unit anxiety, facilitating renewed energy in patient care.

### Intentions Related to Future

Questionnaires regarding behavior planned for the future can make it possible to intervene immediately if behavior modification is necessary. These data can also be used in conjunction with a later questionnaire to determine long-term impact of programs, such as stop smoking clinics or weight loss programs.

## NONRESPONDENT IMPACT QUESTIONNAIRES

Questionnaires can also be designed to elicit information with ramifications for a more global population than those who respond to the questionnaire or for a future population. Information may be collected from large numbers of persons in order to test the impact of a changing variable or to change future actions within groups. Individual, immediate intervention is not an outcome of this type of questionnaire. Information that might be gathered in this type of questionnaire includes personal facts; facts about events or conditions; beliefs related to these facts; attitudes, opinions, and feelings; level of knowledge; intentions related to future actions; or behaviors (Table 9–2).

**Table 9–2** Nonrespondent Impact Questionnaires

| *Information Solicited* | *Application of Results* |
| --- | --- |
| Personal facts | Test of the impact of a changing variable |
| Facts about events or conditions | Program evaluation/implementation |
| Beliefs related to facts | Change in future actions within groups or departments |
| Attitudes, opinions, and feelings | Identification and comparison of population characteristics |
| Knowledge | |
| Intentions related to future | |
| Behaviors | |

### Personal Facts

Demographic data involve factual information about individuals, e.g., date of birth, sex, race, place of birth, and residence. Such data may be collected to define group characteristics or to identify variables that affect other information on the questionnaire. In quality assurance activities, demographic data may be used to identify characteristics such as age, education, or nationality, of groups to whom programs or written materials are to be directed; to identify changes within populations as the result of an intervention; or to establish a basis for program development or modification (for example, to determine the average age or education of a target group).

### Facts about Events or Conditions

Incident reports that provide data on medication errors and patient accidents are one means of collecting facts about events or conditions and are closely bound to quality assurance and risk management. Johnson and Pachano described a questionnaire in which nurses and patients from an acute care setting were polled separately to determine their perceptions of facts related to discharge planning.[1] As part of a project to determine the effectiveness of quality assurance in a mental health setting, Sinclair and Frankel published a questionnaire that asked for specific information about individual case studies for comparison between programs with quality assurance activities and programs without them.[2]

### Beliefs Related to Facts

Questionnaires that solicit facts about events or conditions can easily be expanded to include related subjective information. Perceptions about the causes or consequences of facts may be helpful in analyzing information and making recommendations for any needed corrective actions.

### Attitudes, Opinions, and Feelings

There has been a great deal of emphasis on using questionnaires to determine attitudes, opinions, and feelings in health care settings. Most often, data have been used for evaluating the system and making changes in it.

Patient satisfaction surveys of various designs are commonly used. One unique questionnaire was administered to families of hospice patients who had died to determine the families' opinions of the program.[3] Another focused on the humanistic, nonmedical aspects of care.[4] Taylor and associates developed an extensive survey designed to gather measurable patient perceptions from all departments with patient contact.[5] Another questionnaire concentrated on general ratings of all services related to specific nursing units.[6]

Program evaluation can readily be done by questionnaire. An opinion survey, sometimes in conjunction with knowledge testing, provides information valuable for program modification. For example, patients in the inpatient cardiac rehabilitation program at St. Michael Hospital complete an open-ended questionnaire that is directed routinely to the program coordinator (Exhibit 9–3). Hansen and Lavandero used a questionnaire to evaluate a teaching program for patients undergoing cardiovascular surgery.[7] A questionnaire that was developed for the evaluation of an oncology self-help group collected demographic data, factual data about program participation, and data on perception of quality and benefits of the program.[8]

Employee opinions are also valuable in evaluating quality issues within a system. Caldwell described an employee attitude survey in which employees and managers were surveyed by questionnaire to identify institutional problems; this has a wide application in a variety of hospitals.[9] A survey that could be easily applied to nursing was developed within the radiology departments of a multihospital group to obtain staff perceptions of potential problems and to prioritize those problems.[10] Harmon used an opinion survey before and after an in-service program to test attitudes of nurses toward standards of care.[11] Chavasse published a questionnaire designed to reveal nurses' attitudes toward a change in their patient delivery system.[12]

Questionnaires can also be helpful in achieving consensus of opinion among several people. The Delphi technique is one method involving questionnaires that could have wide application to quality issues. In this approach a series of questionnaires is used to stimulate ideas and prioritize them according to the direction of the group.[13,14] Critical care nurses at St. Michael Hospital used the Delphi technique to design flow sheets mutually acceptable to nurses and physicians in both intensive and coronary care units.

## Knowledge

Questionnaires that assess patients' level of understanding can indicate program effectiveness or test the impact of program changes on learning. Hover and Zimmer described a questionnaire that sampled the knowledge of mothers and children after cleft palate repair and that could be retained on the chart for retrospective review.[15] Another study administered postdischarge to patients with lumbar disc derangement measured their knowledge as an evaluation of the program.[16] Many of these same knowledge tests, administered differently, could also be used as a guide for concurrent patient education.

The effectiveness of staff education programs can also be assessed by questionnaire. At St. Michael Hospital, nurses in the intensive care unit who had reviewed

**Exhibit 9–3** Program Evaluation

# PROGRAM EVALUATION

**Your opinions and feelings are most important to the cardiac rehabilitation staff in evaluating and revising the program for future patients. Please share them with us below.**

## TO THE PATIENT:

**1.** Did you attend the classes for cardiac patients?

Comments: ______________________________

______________________________

**2.** Did you participate in the exercise program during your stay in the hospital?

Comments: ______________________________

______________________________

**3.** How will you continue your rehabilitation at home (e.g., smoking, diet, activity, stress, medications)?

______________________________

______________________________

## TO THE FAMILY (Relationship ______________):

**1.** Did you attend the discussion for families while your relative was in the CCU?

Comments: ______________________________

______________________________

**2.** Did you attend the cardiac classes with your relative?

Comments: ______________________________

______________________________

**3.** What will your role be in the rehabilitation of your relative after discharge?

______________________________

______________________________

______________________________

## OTHER REMARKS:

______________________________

______________________________

______________________________

______________________________

______________________________

*Source:* Reprinted with permission from Cardiac Rehabilitation Staff, *Take Heart*, St. Michael Hospital, Milwaukee, Wisconsin, 1979, page 12.

the American Association of Critical Care Nurses Standards for Critical Care subjectively identified a general gap in their knowledge regarding electrical safety, despite yearly in-service programs. A questionnaire was designed to test their knowledge and to provide structure for future programs.

### Intentions Related to Future

Choices that individuals have made for their future can be expressed on a questionnaire. This information could be obtained from a group of persons in collective action studies designed to estimate the impact of teaching or programming or to determine needs. No intervention can be accomplished, however, without losing anonymity and, possibly, some honesty and openness of responses.

### Health Care Practices

In reporting their own health care practices, patients can give valuable information for evaluation purposes. For example, a questionnaire on return to sexual activity after myocardial infarction was administered to St. Michael Hospital patients postdischarge with the promise of anonymity. The study results confirmed literature reviews regarding patients' failure to return to their previous level of sexual functioning and led to the expansion of St. Michael Hospital's cardiac rehabilitation program to fill the gap in teaching and counseling.

## CHOOSING A QUESTIONNAIRE AS A DATA COLLECTION TOOL

When a questionnaire is being considered as a data collection tool in an evaluation study, it is important to examine all the pros and cons. Generally, questionnaires are fairly economical. Costs involved include

- salary of the person developing the tool
- typing
- duplicating
- distribution costs (e.g., envelopes and postage)
- salary of the person compiling and analyzing the data (perhaps also computer costs)

Because of the low cost and brief time needed to administer a questionnaire, the distribution or sample size is potentially very large. If the questionnaire is well designed, it should be easy to process the information obtained, either by hand or by computer. In addition, the data retrieved by questionnaire are free of interviewer bias if administered correctly. Anonymous return may also increase the accuracy of some types of information.[17-19]

Although questionnaires have many advantages, their disadvantages can outweigh their advantages unless care is taken in structure and administration. Respondents may answer all items similarly based on feelings related to one part of the experience; this halo effect may color results. For example, the patient who has had one bad experience when a nurse does not answer a call light quickly enough may give a lower rating to other items, such as food service or general satisfaction. Likewise, respondents may rate all items high if they believe that their answers will affect a kind but ineffective caregiver's salary or job security. Questionnaires administered "after the fact" require an element of recall that could significantly affect results. Timing the administration of a questionnaire to solicit fresh information or feelings is crucial, unless, of course, retention is being tested.[20,21]

Finally, depending on the method of questionnaire collection, the rate of return may be poor. Methods suggesting duty or implying commitment, such as including stamped, self-addressed return envelopes or offering other rewards and incentives, may have a positive effect on the rate of return. One researcher even included coins for the respondent to buy a cup of coffee to drink while answering the questionnaire! Personal collection of questionnaires or the promise of immediate feedback may increase the rate of return, but it may produce guarded responses. The return of the questionnaire hinges largely on the interest of the respondent in the subject under study, the ease of completion, and the clarity of the intent. In short, return is dependent on the construction of the questionnaire.

## QUESTIONNAIRE CONSTRUCTION

### Closed-ended versus Open-ended Questions

Careful consideration of format style on a questionnaire is essential in view of the complexity and application of data analysis. Questionnaires can be designed with either closed-ended (fixed alternative) or open-ended items.[22] Each format has specific applications and limitations.

Closed-ended questionnaires can be written in several styles:

1. yes/no (true/false)
2. multiple choice
3. rank order, in which items are placed in order of importance or rated
4. checklists or matrix
5. graphic rating scales[23]

These types of questionnaires are quick and easy to complete, and collation of the data can be simple (Exhibit 9–4). Scaled questionnaires may unwittingly eliminate

**Exhibit 9–4** Examples of Closed-ended Questionnaire Styles

*True/False*

Circle the correct response.

True/false Questionnaires are an appropriate instrument for evaluating patients' opinions about their care.

*Multiple Choice*

Circle the letter of the correct answers:

Which of the following valuable information is solicited through use of respondent impact questionnaires:

a. Knowledge
b. Attitudes
c. Intentions related to future

*Rank Order*

Order the following steps in questionnaire construction by inserting the appropriate number (1-5) in the blank:

______ Pilot test
______ Decision on format
______ Revision
______ First draft
______ Final draft

*Checklists or Matrix*

Compare closed-ended and open-ended styles by completing the spaces:

| | *Closed-ended Questionnaire* | *Open-ended Questionnaire* |
|---|---|---|
| Cost | | |
| Data interpretation | | |
| Completeness | | |
| Accuracy | | |

*Graphic Rating Scales*

Rate your opinion of the patient satisfaction survey in use at your hospital:

| 1 | 2 | 3 | 4 | 5 |
|---|---|---|---|---|
| Poor | | | | Excellent |

information or alternatives, however, thus suppressing true expression and forcing a choice between poor alternatives. Superficial information may result. Respondents may also guess, responding to items where they have no knowledge of the truly appropriate answer.[24]

Data can be collected through the use of open-ended questions or by the diary method (Exhibit 9–5). This type of tool permits the evaluator to see the world as it

**Exhibit 9–5** Open-ended Questionnaire Styles

| |
|---|
| *Open-ended Questions* |
| Describe the use of questionnaires in program evaluation. |
| *Diary Method* |
| As you complete a questionnaire study, document all costs that you incur. |

is seen by the respondent and does not predetermine or eliminate possible points of view. The goal of manageable open-ended questionnaires is to provide a framework within which people can respond accurately and thoroughly from their own points of view.[25]

Problems may arise with open-ended questions. For example, written information may be misinterpreted; accuracy depends on the writing skills of the respondent. In addition, descriptive information is often difficult to collate. Statistics may be inappropriately applied, especially if categorization of data is not rigorous. The extent to which categories are accurately generated by use of raw data facilitates analysis. These types of questionnaires are also usually very time-consuming for the respondent to complete, which may reduce motivation to respond and return rate. Finally, it is impossible to probe or extend responses with any questionnaire, as can be done in an interview (see Chapter 8).

## Process of Construction

An organized process of construction is important in realizing a concise, applicable questionnaire that will reveal analyzable data. There are five steps in questionnaire construction.

### *1. Decision on Format*

The initial step involves determining the objectives of the study, selecting the population to be questioned, and deciding on specific areas to be covered. Other factors to be determined include the appropriate number of questions and length of the questionnaire, and whether a closed-ended or open-ended approach is best suited for the needs and purposes of this particular study.

### *2. First Draft*

The actual construction of the questions requires special attention. Ambiguous questions result in inadequate or misleading data. Questions should be carefully worded to avoid leading the respondent to a predetermined bias of the investigator. It is also best to eliminate slang, objectionable wording, or phrases that evoke an emotional response. In writing multiple choice questions, all alternatives must be. expressed at the risk of producing misleading data. The order of responses should follow a logical pattern; for example, from least to greatest.

Depending on the length of the proposed questionnaire, the time available, and the opportunities of those who are constructing the items to attend meetings, the first draft can be constructed by the group together either at a single meeting or a series of meetings. Individuals can also bring their work to the meeting(s) to be compiled within the structure of the format determined earlier.

*3. Revision*

The initial questionnaire should be analyzed for wording of the questions, position of the questions in relationship to one another, parallel construction in language, and complete coverage of all areas to be tested. It should be reviewed in terms of decisions previously made regarding format.

*4. Pilot Test*

When a more rigid study design is desired, e.g., for broader applicability of results, a pilot test is an essential step in questionnaire construction. Although it may not always be practical within the financial constraints or timeframe of unit-based evaluation studies, errors in construction will reveal themselves within the actual data collection and analysis period if no pilot test has been conducted. A trial can be used to test reliability and validity of questions, as well as to fine-tune methodology.

Reliability is the ability of an instrument to obtain consistent results, while validity is the ability of the instrument to test what it was designed to test.[26] Although evaluation studies in quality assurance historically have not been subjected to these tests, reliability and validity are becoming more and more important as significant practice changes are being based on the results of evaluation studies. Generalizability of study results, i.e., the applicability of findings outside the study area, is a function of group external validity and affects the application of study results between patient groups or hospital units. As quality assurance becomes a key for progress in nursing practice, instrumentation should be assessed more rigorously. A general guide to reliability and validity tests is presented in Tables 9–3 and 9–4.

*5. Final Draft/Instructions*

When all potential concerns and weak points in methodology and style have surfaced, the questions and instructions to the respondent can be drafted in final form. This is the last step before actual data collection begins.[31,32]

**Table 9–3** Testing Reliability[27,28]

| *Method* | *What It Tests* | *How It Works* |
|---|---|---|
| Test-Retest | Trait stability | The instrument is readministered at a later date and scores compared. |
| Split-half | Internal consistency | Items on a test are split into two groups, scored separately, and compared. |
| Kuder-Richardson Procedure | Internal consistency | Formula is applied to test results. |
| Equivalence | Inter-rater reliability | Variables recorded are compared simultaneously and independently by multiple observers. |
| | Consistency of multiple instruments | Instruments to be tested are administered randomly in immediate succession. |

**Table 9–4** Testing Validity[29,30]

| *Type of Validity* | *What It Tests* | *How to Test It* |
|---|---|---|
| Content validity | Adequate number and appropriate balance of questions to test content | Review of instrument by experts |
| Predictive validity | Accuracy of predictions of future behavior | Comparison of test prediction to actual results |
| Concurrent validity | Accuracy of description of present behavior | Comparison of results with demonstrated behavior |
| Construct validity | Ability of an instrument to test the critical concept | Correlation of results with those of another instrument thought to test the same thing; use of a group of "judges" to observe and document the behavior, using predetermined criteria; administration of instrument to groups who would be expected to differ regarding the attribute |
| Face validity | Overall focus of instrument | Subjective observation and review of the instrument |

## DISTRIBUTING THE QUESTIONNAIRE

Before distributing a questionnaire, the researcher must determine respondent eligibility. Since the intent of respondent impact questionnaires is immediate feedback, lack of discrimination in distribution can only result in embarrassment. Three practical methods of distribution are: (1) delivery by the evaluator with pick up and discussion at a later date, (2) delivery to a group for individual or group feedback after questionnaire completion, and (3) delivery by mail with discussion to be at a future time set either by the respondent or the evaluator. Any of these methods facilitates individual feedback and intervention. Finally, it is necessary to obtain permission to circulate questionnaires within the health care structure.

Nonrespondent impact studies may involve different methods of distribution. The population sample may be identified through medical records, if the questionnaire is for patients. Distribution of a questionnaire to employees may be determined by job status. Group characteristics must be determined in identifying the population. Permission is also necessary for these studies. Permission may be easy to obtain, perhaps through the quality assurance mechanism, but those who are potentially interested should be notified as a courtesy.

Questionnaires for collective action may be distributed through hospital mail or the postal service. Cost, of course, is quite different. Questionnaires could be distributed by hand, providing interface for explanation, solicitation of commitment, and return.

## ANALYZING THE DATA

Once the questionnaires have been distributed and returned, data must be reviewed. Results of respondent impact studies must be dealt with as soon as possible. Individual responses on all types of questionnaires must be compiled for collective analysis when an adequate sample has been obtained. The analysis of the data differs, depending on study design, but predetermined criteria or standards and statistical methods facilitate the use of questionnaire information. If the questionnaire has been effectively designed, corrective actions can be taken and the study easily and economically readministered later for comparison and assessment of the effectiveness of the intervention or program changes.

---

### NOTES

1. Jeanne Johnson and Audrey Pachano, "Planning Patients' Discharge," *Supervisor Nurse* 12, no. 2 (February 1981): 44–50.

2. Carole Sinclair and Mark Frankel, "The Effect of Quality Assurance Activities on the Quality of Mental Health Services," *Quality Review Bulletin* 8, no. 7 (July 1982): 7–15.

3. Nancy L. Bohnet, "Quality Assurance as an Ongoing Component of Hospice Care," *Quality Review Bulletin* 8, no. 5 (May 1982): 7–11.

4. Gerald P. Turner, "Representing the Patient: A Canadian Hospital's Approach," *Quality Review Bulletin* 6, no. 3 (March 1980): 2–5.

5. Paul Taylor et al., "Development and Use of a Method of Assessing Patient Perception of Care," *Hospital and Health Services Administration* 26 (Winter 1981): 89–104.

6. Barbara J. Morrison et al., "Consumer Opinion Surveys," *Quality Review Bulletin* 8, no. 2 (February 1982): 19–24.

7. Marian Hansen and Ramón Lavandero, "A Multidisciplinary Education Program for Patients Undergoing Cardiovascular Surgery," *Quality Review Bulletin* 7, no. 5 (May 1981): 19–24.

8. Richard Maisiak et al., "Evaluation of TOUCH: An Oncology Self-help Group," *Oncology Nursing Forum* 8, no. 3 (1981): 20–25.

9. George B. Caldwell, "Use of Employee Surveys in Quality Assurance Programs," *Quality Review Bulletin* (July 1981): 19–22.

10. David Raymond, "Departmental Review: Identification and Analysis of Problems in Diagnostic Radiology," *Quality Review Bulletin* 6, no. 9 (September 1980): 5–10.

11. Carol A. Harmon, "Involving Staff in Nursing Quality Assurance," *Quality Review Bulletin* 6, no. 11 (November 1980): 26–30.

12. Judith Chavasse, "From Task Assignment to Patient Allocation: A Change Evaluation," *Journal of Advanced Nursing* 6 (1981): 137–145.

13. Kae Hentges and Michael C. Hosokawa, "Delphi: Group Participation in Needs Assessment and Curriculum Development," *Journal of School Health* 15, no. 8 (October 1980): 447–450.

14. Linda A. Lewandowsky, "Research Priorities for Critical Care Nursing: A Study by the American Association of Critical Care Nurses," *Heart and Lung* 12, no. 1 (January 1983): 35–44.

15. Julie Hover and Marie Zimmer, "Nursing Quality Assurance: The Wisconsin System," *Nursing Outlook* 26 (April 1978): 242–248.

16. Ann A. Kuntavanish and Patricia Curran Ostrow, "The Outcomes of Back Conservation Education," *Quality Review Bulletin* 6, no. 4 (April 1980): 22–26.

17. Marlene G. Mayers, Ronald B. Norby, and Annita B. Watson, *Quality Assurance for Patient Care: Nursing Perspectives* (New York: Appleton-Century-Crofts, 1977), pp. 82–84.

18. Faye G. Abdellah and Eugene Levine, *Better Patient Care Through Nursing Research* (New York: MacMillan, 1980), p. 342.

19. Denise Polit and Bernadette Hungler, *Nursing Research: Principles and Methods* (Philadelphia: J.B. Lippincott, 1978); pp. 351–352.

20. Mayers, Norby, and Watson, *Quality Assurance for Patient Care: Nursing Perspectives*, pp. 82–84.

21. Abdellah and Levine, *Better Patient Care Through Nursing Research*, p. 341.

22. Polit and Hungler, *Nursing Research: Principles and Methods*, p. 327.

23. Ibid, pp. 342, 346.

24. Ibid, pp. 327–330.

25. Michael Quinn Patton, *Qualitative Evaluation Methods* (Beverly Hills, CA: Sage Productions, 1980), pp. 28–30.

26. Eleanor Walters Treece and James William Treece, Jr., *Elements of Research in Nursing* (St. Louis, MO: C. V. Mosby, 1982), p. 119.

27. Ibid, pp. 122–126.

28. Polit and Hungler, *Nursing Research: Principles and Methods,* pp. 424–433.

29. Treece and Treece, *Elements of Research in Nursing,* pp. 126–132.

30. Polit and Hungler, *Nursing Research: Principles and Methods,* pp. 434–441.

31. Claire Selltiz, Lawrence S. Wrightsman, and Stuart W. Cook, *Research Methods in Social Relations,* 3rd ed. (New York: Holt, Rinehart and Winston, 1976), pp. 542–563.

32. Polit and Hungler, *Nursing Research: Principles and Methods,* pp. 346–347.

---

## REFERENCES

### Books

Abdellah, Faye G., and Levine, Eugene. *Better Patient Care Through Nursing Research,* 2nd ed. New York: MacMillan, 1980, pp. 341–342.

Mayers, Marlene G.; Norby, Ronald B.; and Watson, Annita B. *Quality Assurance for Patient Care: Nursing Perspectives.* New York: Appleton-Century-Crofts, 1977, pp. 82–84.

Patton, Michael Quinn. *Qualitative Evaluation Methods.* Beverly Hills, CA: Sage Productions, 1980, pp. 28–30.

Polit, Denise, and Hungler, Bernadette. *Nursing Research: Principles and Methods.* Philadelphia: J. B. Lippincott, Company, 1978, pp. 342–441.

Selltiz, Claire; Wrightsman, Lawrence; and Cook, Stuart W. *Research Methods in Social Relations,* 3rd ed. New York: Holt, Rinehart and Winston, 1976, pp. 542–563.

Treece, Eleanor Walters, and Treece, James William, Jr. *Elements of Research in Nursing.* St. Louis, MO: C. V. Mosby, 1982, pp. 122–132.

### Journals

Bohnet, Nancy L. "Quality Assurance as an Ongoing Component of Hospice Care." *Quality Review Bulletin* 6, no. 5 (1982): 7–11.

Caldwell, George B. "Use of Employee Surveys in Quality Assurance Programs." *Quality Review Bulletin* 7, no. 7 (1981): 19–22.

Chavasse, Judith. "From Task Assignment to Patient Allocation: A Change Evaluation." *Journal of Advanced Nursing* 6 (1981): 137–145.

Darr, Marilyn S.; Self, Timothy H.; Ryan, Michael R.; Vanderbush, Ross E.; and Boswell, Richard C. "Content and Retention Evaluation of an Audiovisual Patient Education Program on Bronchodilators." *American Journal of Hospital Pharmacy* 38 (1981): 672–675.

Hansen, Marian, and Lavandero, Ramón. "A Multidisciplinary Education Program for Patients Undergoing Cardiovascular Surgery." *Quality Review Bulletin* 7, no. 5 (1981): 19–24.

Harmon, Carol A. "Involving Staff in Nursing Quality Assurance." *Quality Review Bulletin* 6, no. 11 (1980): 26–30.

Hentges, Kae, and Hosokawa, Michael C. "Delphi: Group Participation in Needs Assessment and Curriculum Development." *Journal of School Health* 50, no. 8 (1980): 447–450.

Hover, Julie, and Zimmer, Marie. "Nursing Quality Assurance: The Wisconsin System." *Nursing Outlook* 26 (1978): 242–248.

Johnson, Jeanne, and Pachano, Audrey. "Planning Patients' Discharge." *Supervisor Nurse* 12, no. 2 (1981): 44–50.

Johnston, Barbara; Cantwell, John; and Fletcher, Gerald. "Eight Steps to Inpatient Cardiac Rehabilitation: The Team Effort—Methodology and Preliminary Results." *Heart and Lung* 5 (1976): 97–111.

Kuntavanish, Ann A., and Ostrow, Patricia Curran. "The Outcome of Back Conservation Education." *Quality Review Bulletin* 6, no. 4 (1980): 22–26.

Lewandowsky, Linda A. "Research Priorities for Critical Care Nursing: A Study by the American Association of Critical Care Nurses." *Heart and Lung* 12 (1983): 35–44.

Maisiak, Richard; Cain, Marilyn; Yarbro, Connie Heuke; and Josof, Louis. "Evaluation of TOUCH: An Oncology Self-help Group." *Oncology Nursing Forum* 8 (1981): 20–25.

Moores, Brian, and Thompson, Andy. "Getting Feedback." *Health and Social Science Journal* 29, May 1981, pp. 634–636.

Morrison, Barbara J.; Rehr, Helen; Rosenberg, Gary; and Davis, Samuel. "Consumer Opinion Surveys." *Quality Review Bulletin* 8, no. 2 (1982): 19–24.

Raymond, David. "Departmental Review: Identification and Analysis of Problems in Diagnostic Radiology." *Quality Review Bulletin* 6, no. 9 (1980): 5–10.

Sinclair, Carole, and Frankel, Mark. "The Effect of Quality Assurance Activities on the Quality of Mental Health Services." *Quality Review Bulletin* 8, no. 7 (1982): 7–15.

Taylor, Paul; Nelson-Wernick, Eleanor; Currey, Hal S.; Woodbury, Marion E.; and Conley, Lois E. "Development and Use of a Method of Assessing Patient Perception of Health Care." *Hospital and Health Services Administration* (1981): 89–104.

Tersine, Richard J., and Riggs, Walter E. "The Delphi Technique: A Long-Range Planning Tool." *Business Horizons* (1976): 51–56.

Turner, Gerald P. "Representing the Patient: A Canadian Hospital's Approach." *Quality Review Bulletin* 6, no. 3 (1980): 2–5.

# Chapter 10

# Observation as an Evaluation Tool

*Mary A. Bruskewitz, M.S., R.N.*

Nurses may use the observation method to collect data for quality assurance studies. Weick defined the observation method as "the selection, provocation, recording, and encoding of that set of behavior and setting concerning organisms 'in situ' which is consistent with empirical aims."[1] Observation is the actual recording of an event in part or in whole as it occurs in its natural setting.

Polit and Hungler clarified Weick's definition by explaining the terms *selection, provocation, recording,* and *encoding.*[2] Selection is the identification of specific behaviors that are to be observed, the establishment of criteria or standards. Provocation identifies the role of the nurse-observer in the event as it occurs. Recording is the documentation, according to the established criteria or selection of behaviors, of the event as it occurs. Encoding is simplifying the data into a form in which they can be analyzed to reach conclusions.

## STRENGTHS OF THE OBSERVATION METHOD

Observation can provide the researcher with data that cannot be collected through other means. For example, physical characteristics, traits, or appearances can be observed. Any procedure or task that nurses do for or with the patient and its outcome can be observed. Observation of verbal and nonverbal behavior provides data on the interactions among nurses, patients, families, and other health professionals. The interactions between the patient and the environment can be observed to determine what variables in the environment influence patients' behaviors.

Observation produces a large quantity of data relatively easily. Problems with recall are minimized, since observations are recorded at the time the event occurs. The method is adaptable to the acute care facility, the long-term care facility, the rehabilitation center, and the public health setting—almost any setting. The event being observed can be recorded by cameras and tape recorders for later review.

The observer may participate in the event. Nurses can easily use the technique, as they already have the skill and training for assessment and observation.

## LIMITATIONS OF THE OBSERVATION METHOD

The observation method has limitations that must be considered in determining its appropriateness for a particular study. In identifying the limitations, three areas must be considered: the event, the observer, and the instrument or tool.

As Weick defined observation, it is the recording of the event in its natural setting. Therefore, the observer must wait for the event to occur. The event may occur so infrequently, however, that it is difficult to obtain an adequate sample. Waiting for the event to occur naturally may also be costly, but staging the event may alter it, thus biasing the results. Furthermore, the length of the observation period is important. If the time period is too short for all the observations to be made, the observer may make decisions without adequate information. There are also circumstances in which confidentiality and privacy requirements make observations for evaluation studies inappropriate.

The mere presence of the observer may influence the event and, thus, the data. Polit and Hungler identified this as reactivity, or the Hawthorne effect.[3] If the observer participates in the event, objectivity may be lost, and the event may no longer be natural.

Observations have a built-in bias that must be identified prior to implementation of the observation method. The observer's emotions, values, attitudes, and expectations may affect the way in which the event is recorded and, thus, the data. Weick identified six observer biases that can alter the observations:[4]

1. Central tendency bias is the distortion of the event to a middle ground.
2. Enhancement of contrast effect bias is the distortion of observations into clear-cut entities.
3. Assimilation bias is the recording of the data toward orderliness and regularity or identifying the observations with previous experiences. Expectations and attitudes of the observer are common assimilation biases.
4. The halo effect occurs when the observer is influenced by characteristics of the observer's personality.
5. Severity bias is rating the observee too negatively.
6. Leniency bias occurs when the observer rates too positively.

If the data are recorded on a prepared form, the instrument may lead to many problems. If it is long and very detailed, the observer spends more time in note taking and less time in the actual observations. In addition, the observer may interpret the event instead of just recording it. If more than one observer is to observe the event, some inter-rater and intrarater reliability must be established prior to data collection. Inter-rater reliability is established through a training program. Although this adds time to the study, it is a vital step in the process to ensure accuracy of the data. The longer or the more detailed the tool, the more important the training period is for a successful study. Intrarater reliability is developed through practice in using the tool.

## ROLE OF THE OBSERVER

The relationship and the interaction between the observer and the observee are crucial to minimizing the limitations and maximizing the strengths of the observation method. Polit and Hungler identified two variables in this relationship: concealment and intervention.[5] Concealment is defined as the amount of information the observee is given prior to the observation period, i.e., the observee's awareness of being observed. Intervention refers to the role of the observer in the event. The role may vary from passive observation to full participation. Jackson also identified this relationship between the observer and the observee.[6] The variable in this instance is the observer's participation in the event.

Polit and Hungler, as well as Jackson, described four similar types of interactions dependent on the degree of concealment and the degree of observer intervention or participation. The first two relationships occur when the observee has no knowledge of being observed. "Concealment-no intervention" or "complete observer" occurs when the observer is a passive bystander and does not participate in the event; in contrast, "concealment-intervention" or "complete participation" occurs when the observer participates in the event in varying degrees. In the other two types of relationships, the observee is aware of being observed at the time of the observation period. In a "no concealment-intervention" or "participant-as-observer" relationship, the observer participates in the event in varying degrees as a natural part of the event and records the event. "No concealment-no intervention" describes a relationship in which the observer is a passive bystander and only records the event. Jackson defined this relationship somewhat differently, calling it "observer-as-participant"; the observer is a person outside the event, but may participate in the event. For example, the nurse providing care to a patient and observing the patient plays the role of "participant-as-observer"; if a second nurse observes the first nurse providing the care and participates in the care, the second nurse plays the role of "observer-as-participant."

Before determining what the observer's role is to be and whether the observee is to be aware of the observation period, investigators must discuss the advantages and disadvantages of each situation. Certain ethical questions arise in regard to concealment. Is it morally right to observe a person without informing that person of the study, its purpose, and that person's role in it? The American Hospital

Association's *A Patient's Bill of Rights* guarantees the right of all patients to be informed of their role in any research study.[7] Privacy and confidentiality must be maintained, both for patients and for nurses as observees. Concealment decreases the reactivity factor, however, thus enhancing the reliability of the data. An awareness of this dilemma when they develop the instrument and plan the implementation helps observers to maintain the rights of the observee and the patient while still obtaining the data.

## EXAMPLES OF USE OF THE OBSERVATION METHOD

Nurses have used the observation method to identify and clarify patient care problems, to identify areas where continuing education and in-service programs are needed, to supply data for management decision making, and to write nursing standards of care.

### Slater Scale and Qual PACs

Two published instruments in which observation is used to assess the quality of nursing are the Slater Scale and the Quality Patient Care Scale (Qual PACs).[8,9] They were the first two instruments designed to assess the quality of care given by nurses. Their purposes were multifold: self-evaluation, identification of educational needs and nurse competencies for promotion, evaluation of progress made in an educational program, examination of the relationship between the nurse and the patient, and assistance in administrative decision making.

Although the Slater Scale has eighty-four items and the Qual PACs has sixty-eight items, both divide nursing activities in patient care into the same six subsections:

1. psychosocial, individual
2. psychosocial, group
3. physical
4. general
5. communication
6. professional implications

While the Slater Scale focuses on the individual nurse's performance, the Qual PACs focuses on the care received.

One advantage of these two instruments is that they are adaptable to any setting, from the acute care setting to the nursing home to rehabilitation centers. The authors claim to have established reliability and validity through repeated testing. Each item on the instrument has additional cues given to aid the observer in the recording process (Exhibit 10–1). Studies using these tools have shown that a

**Exhibit 10–1** Slater Scale and Quality Patient Care Scale Cue Sheet

"Is a Receptive Listener"

Cues:

1. "Facial expressions indicate interest and understanding."
2. "Gives patient time to talk."
3. "Waits for the patient to complete sentence before speaking or moving away from the patient."
4. "Encourages conversation by using brief comments or loading questions to let the patient know she [sic] is listening and interested."
5. "Terminates conversation in a manner such that patient understands reasons for termination, leaving patient with feeling of satisfaction about discussion."

*Source:* Reprinted with permission from Mabel A. Wandelt and Doris Slater Stewart, *Slater Nursing Competencies Rating Scale* (New York: Appleton-Century-Crofts, 1975), p. 11.

sample size as small as 15 percent of the population gives reliable data. Studies have also shown that the instruments identify learning that has occurred in as short a period of time as two weeks.

The limitations of the instruments revolve around the standard of measurement and the frame of reference developed by each observer. The standard of measurement is the quality of performance expected from the first-level staff nurse. Wandelt and Stewart, in developing their standard, stated that those who are knowledgeable in the field know what is meant by a first-level staff nurse's performance, so they gave no further explanation or guidelines.[10] Because the standard of measurement is not well-defined and because the individual observer develops a frame of reference based on personal experiences with other nurses, the instruments are limited in their generalizability and adaptability on a large scale. The data collected may be biased.

## Clinical Evaluation of Nursing Care

Observation is also used to assess the quality of nursing care in an instrument developed by Munley.[11] With this instrument, interview, observation, and chart audit methods are used to collect the data. In the interview section, the patient is asked whether his or her physical, cognitive, emotional, and spiritual needs are being met by the nursing staff. Observation is used in the second section to complete seventy items divided among six patient care categories: physical, safety, medication, socioeconomical, environmental, and spiritual. The nurse-observer collects data by observing the patient's present health status regarding each of the categories. The third section involves a chart audit to obtain current information on forty-three items in the six patient care categories that correspond to those in the second section. Teaching and patient discharge planning are also assessed in the third section.

Munley's instrument was designed to be used on a general medical-surgical unit. It has since been adapted to the critical care setting, the obstetrics-gynecology unit, and the operating room. It has been used to observe 5 to 8 percent of the patient population. The observation time was approximately twenty minutes, once the observer became familiar with the tool.

In addition to its adaptability to other units, this instrument has other advantages. A minimal amount of training is needed to administer it, because the tool for observation is in a checklist design. There is less chance for observer interpretation, because each item is rated as "yes, no, or nonapplicable." Reactivity is decreased, because the observer does not participate in the event. The question of concealment is not relevant, because the patient participates in the evaluation process through the interview.

The instrument is designed to assess the patient's status or the outcome of nursing care at a given time. The instrument is not useful in assessing a process or the quality of the nursing care as it is being given. It only identifies what nursing actions are on the care plan and the patient's perception of that care.

## Professional Practitioner Rating Tool

Dunn developed a tool to measure nurses' application of specific principles to specific nursing procedures.[12] The instrument, the Professional Practitioner Rating Tool, was developed at a Veterans Administration hospital. Content validity was established by a panel of nursing experts. Inter-rater reliability was established as the instrument was tested in the study.

Two nursing supervisors observed thirty-five nurses who had been selected to participate in this study. Each nurse took a written test, the Nursing Principles Test, developed by the Veterans Administration hospitals prior to the study. Five procedures were selected for observation: (1) tracheal suctioning, (2) tube feeding administration, (3) oral medication administration, (4) intramuscular medication administration, and (5) intravenous medication administration. These procedures were selected because each was based on several nursing principles. The procedures were stated in behavioral, measurable terms in a checkoff design on the tool. Each nurse was observed performing each procedure four times. Observations were done on all three shifts within a one-week period.

Results of the study showed that proficiency with one procedure did not indicate proficiency with another. The task steps were not readily transferable from one procedure to another. Furthermore, nurses who scored high on the written test did not necessarily show proficiency with the procedures.

The application of nursing principles to procedures is definitely an advantage of this study. The complexity of the observations and the few procedures used are limitations, however. The observees were aware of the observation period, since they had volunteered to participate in the study. The effect that this awareness may have had on the study is not discussed.

It would be relatively easy to apply this instrument to a quality assurance study. Any nursing procedure that integrates the physical sciences with nursing principles could be observed in a patient care setting. For example, nurses performing peripheral intravenous site care integrate the principle of aseptic technique with their skills in assessing the site and the skin integrity. To conduct a study of this procedure, one nurse-observer on each shift on the unit would observe all the intravenous site care performed within a one-week period to determine if the care met certain criteria (Exhibit 10–2). The nurse-observer would not participate in the care. The patient would be informed of the study and the observation period prior to the study. The nurse-observee would be aware of the study and observation period as a unit quality assurance project. According to the classification discussed earlier, this would then be a "no concealment-no intervention" relationship between the nurse-observer and the nurse-observee.

**Exhibit 10–2** Criteria for the Peripheral Intravenous Site Care Study

1. Procedure is explained to the patient. yes/no

   Exception: Patient is comatose.

2. The old dressing is removed. yes/no

3. Insertion site is cleaned with alcohol swab. yes/no

4. Iodophor ointment is applied to the insertion site. yes/no

   Exception: Patient is allergic to Iodophor ointment.

5. Sterile dressing is re-applied. yes/no

6. Documentation on the chart indicates I.V. site care done and the assessment of the skin integrity. yes/no

*Source:* Reprinted with permission from St. Michael Hospital, Milwaukee, Wisconsin. Copyright 1980.

## Recovery Room Behavior and Postoperative Convalescence

Observation was also used with the interview and chart audit methods in a study reported by Elms.[13] Surgical patients undergoing general anesthesia were observed in the recovery room to determine if their immediate postoperative behavior could be used to predict the course of their convalescence. Recovery room behavior was identified as spontaneous behavior, which had no outside stimulation, or response behavior, which was a result of external stimulation. Both types of behaviors were rated according to the amount of discomfort observed.

The patients agreed preoperatively to participate in the study. Their behavior was observed during the entire time they were in the recovery room. The patients were also interviewed every other day during their convalescence, beginning the first postoperative day. The interview covered four areas: (1) physical complaints and discomforts, (2) physical independence, (3) social interaction and diversional activity, and (4) emotional responses. Data were also collected from the charts and from the head nurses. The chart audit focused on the general medical indices that reflect adaptation postoperatively, such as number of fever days, number of pain medications, postoperative complications, and the length of postoperative hospitalization. Following each patient interview, the head nurse was asked to complete a questionnaire that corresponded to the patient's interview guide and was used to correlate the nurse's perception of the patient's adjustment with the patient's perception of adjustment.

It was found that patients who had a large percentage of negative responses to stimuli in the recovery room tended to have a more difficult convalescence. Postoperative convalescence, as measured by the patient interviews, correlated strongly with the nurse's assessment and the general medical indices of adjustment. This study showed the relationship between the patient's recovery room behavior and the patient's behavioral response to the surgical patient's convalescence period.

This same tool could be used to study the relationship of preoperative teaching to recovery room behavior and postoperative convalescence. Preoperative teaching would be the independent variable in such a study. All patients undergoing general anesthesia would be observed in the recovery room, and observations would be recorded according to the Elms' instrument. The patient's perception of the convalescence, the nurse's perception of the patient's convalescence, and the medical indices would be assessed by means of the same instrument. Then data could be collected to determine whether preoperative teaching made a difference in the patient's recovery room behavior and convalescence. A quality assurance study such as this is a good opportunity for two units to collaborate on a project.

### Bath Demonstration Study

Observation was also used in an evaluation study on the obstetrical unit. The purpose of the study was to review the content of the newborn bath demonstration class and identify areas of inconsistent teaching. Based on the literature describing what parents need to know about newborn bath care, twenty-five criteria were developed (Exhibit 10–3). Two nurses from the obstetrical unit observed fourteen class demonstrations over a two-month period. The nurses were passive observers in the class, i.e., "no intervention." The patients were not aware of the study, since they were not being observed, but the nurses conducting the classes were aware of the project as a quality assurance study, i.e., "no concealment."

As a result of this study, the following changes were made in the bath demonstration class: (1) the class content was expanded to include all the criteria developed in the tool, (2) the content was changed to include information on alternatives when needed, (3) audiovisuals used in the class were refined to reflect the criteria, (4) an in-service program on the content was held for the instructors, and (5) patient education handouts were developed to supplement the teaching in the classes.

In the examples given, observation has been used as the method of choice to evaluate patient teaching, to determine nurses' proficiency in procedures, to develop standards of care, and to assess the interactions between the patient and the environment.

### Management of Patients with In-dwelling Catheters

The final example is a study in which the nursing management of patients with an in-dwelling catheter was evaluated in terms of outcome criteria (Exhibit 10–4). The study was conducted on a gerontology unit over a two-month period. One nurse-observer collected the data on eight separate days during the two months. Every patient on the unit who had an in-dwelling catheter that day was observed. Following the study, the results were shared at a unit meeting, and recommendations were made regarding ways in which the staff could continue to meet the criteria. The results were also shared hospitalwide through the Quality Assurance Coordinating Committee (see Chapter 2).

## CONCLUSION

The observation method can provide important data regarding nursing care as it is given to the patient and the outcomes of that care. The technique is an integral

**Exhibit 10–3** Evaluation of Bath Demonstration

AUDITOR: TEACHER:

DATE:

CRITERIA

Yes No

A. Eye Care

1. Demonstrated with cotton balls and washcloths
2. Washes from inner to outer
3. No soap
4. Explains no drainage is normal after discharge

B. Cord Care

1. Use alcohol
2. Three times every day or with each diaper change
3. Move stump to clean
4. Don't cover with diaper
5. Don't position infant on abdomen until cord falls off
6. Don't submerge infant in tub until after cord has been off for two days

C. Genital Care

Female

1. Wash from front to back
2. Separate labia; wash in creases
3. Mucus drainage is normal

Male

1. Wash under scrotum and around
2. Wash penis after circumcision gently and firmly
3. Demonstrate foreskin retraction
4. Explain reason for retraction

D. Rectal Temperature

1. How to read thermometer
2. Shake down
3. Lubricate
4. Insert 1/2 inch
5. Restrain legs
6. Demonstrate two positions for taking temperature

E. How Often to Bathe

1. Minimum of two to three times per week
2. Flexible time of day (scheduling)

*Source:* Reprinted with permission from St. Michael Hospital, Milwaukee, Wisconsin. Copyright 1981.

**Exhibit 10–4** Criteria for the Nursing Management of Patients with In-dwelling Urinary Catheters

| | | |
|---|---|---|
| 1. | Is this Foley catheter stabilized? | yes/no |
| 2. | How is it stabilized? | yes/no |
| | Tape? Strap? Non-applicable | |
| 3. | Is there slack between the exit point and the point where it is stabilized? | yes/no |
| 4. | Is the bag below bladder level? | yes/no |
| 5. | Is the tubing in good drainage position? | yes/no |
| 6. | Is the collection bag off the floor? | yes/no |
| 7. | Is the drainage spout correctly in its holder? | yes/no |
| 8. | Is the clamp on the drainage bag closed all the way? | yes/no |
| 9. | Is the tubing clear enough to evaluate the condition of the urine? | yes/no |
| 10. | Is the patient on any type of urine acidifier? | yes/no |

*Source:* Reprinted with permission from St. Michael Hospital, Milwaukee, Wisconsin. Copyright 1981.

part of the nursing process, as nurses are trained and skilled in using observation in providing care for their patients. Observation is a method that nurses can easily adapt to use in quality assurance.

## NOTES

1. Karl Weick, "Systematic Observational Methods," in *The Handbook of Social Psychology*, vol. 2, ed. Gardner Lindzey and Elliot Aronson (Reading, MA: Addison-Wesley, 1968), p. 360.
2. Denise Polit and Bernadette Hungler, "Observational Methods," in *Nursing Research Principles and Methods* (Philadelphia: J.B. Lippincott, 1983).
3. Ibid.
4. Weick, "Systematic Observational Methods," pp. 428-431.
5. Polit and Hungler, "Observational Methods."

6. Bettie S. Jackson, "Participant Observation in Nursing Research," *Supervisor Nurse* 4, no. 5 (May 1973): 30–40.

7. American Hospital Association, *A Patient's Bill of Rights* (Chicago: American Hospital Association, 1973).

8. Mabel A. Wandelt and Doris Slater Stewart, *Slater Nursing Competencies Rating Scale* (New York: Appleton-Century-Crofts, 1975).

9. Mabel A. Wandelt and Joel W. Ager, *Quality Patient Care Scale* (New York: Appleton-Century-Crofts, 1974).

10. Wandelt and Stewart, *Slater Nursing Competencies Rating Scale.*

11. Mary Jane Munley, "An Evaluation of Nursing Care by Direct Observation," *Supervisor Nurse* 4, no. 4 (April 1973): 28–34.

12. Margaret A. Dunn, "Development of an Instrument to Measure Nursing Performance," *Nursing Research* 19, no. 6 (November-December 1970): 502–510.

13. Roslyn R. Elms, "Recovery Room Behavior and Postoperative Convalescence," *Nursing Research* 21, no. 5 (September-October, 1972): 390–397.

---

**REFERENCES**

**Books**

American Hospital Association. *A Patient's Bill of Rights*. Chicago: American Hospital Association, 1973.

Isaac, Stephen. *Handbook in Research and Evaluation*. San Diego: Knopp, 1971.

Polit, Denise, and Hungler, Bernadette. "Observational Methods." In *Nursing Research Principles and Methods,* Philadelphia: J.B. Lippincott, 1983.

Wandelt, Mabel A., and Ager, Joel W. *Quality Patient Care Scale*. New York: Appleton-Century-Crofts, 1974.

Wandelt, Mabel A., and Stewart, Doris Slater. *Slater Nursing Competencies Rating Scale*. New York: Appleton-Century-Crofts, 1975.

Weick, Karl. "Systematic Observational Methods." In *The Handbook of Social Psychology,* edited by Gardner Lindzey and Elliot Aronson. Reading, MA: Addison-Wesley, 1968.

**Journals**

Block, Doris. "Evaluation of Nursing Care in Terms of Process and Outcome: Issues in Research and Quality Assurance." *Nursing Research* 24, no. 4 (July-August 1975): 256–263.

Clough, Dorothy H., and Derdiarian, Anayis. "A Behavioral Checklist to Measure Dependence and Independence." *Nursing Research* 29, no. 1 (January-February 1980): 55–58.

Distel, Lori. "More Than Chart Review." *Quality Review Bulletin* 7, no. 1 (1981): 26–29.

Downs, Florence S., and Fitzpatrick, Joyce J. "Preliminary Investigation of the Reliability and Validity of a Tool for the Assessment of Body Positions and Motor Activity." *Nursing Research* 25, no. 6 (1976): 404–408.

Dunn, Margaret A. "Development of an Instrument to Measure Nursing Performance." *Nursing Research* 19, no. 6 (1970): 502–510.

Elms, Roslyn R. "Recovery Room Behavior and Postoperative Convalescence." *Nursing Research* 21, no. 5 (1972): 390–397.

Gaymor, Alan K., and Berry, Rosalie K. "Observations of a Staff Nurse: An Organizational Analysis." *Journal of Nursing Administration* 3, no. 3 (1973): 43–49.

Jackson, Bettie S. "Participant Observation in Nursing Research." *Supervisor Nurse* 4, no. 5 (1973): 30–40.

Lindeman, Carol A. "Measuring Quality of Nursing Care: Part One." *Journal of Nursing Administration* 6, no. 5 (1976): 7–9.

Lindeman, Carol A. "Measuring Quality of Nursing Care: Part Two." *Journal of Nursing Administration* 6, no. 7 (1976): 16–19.

Munley, Mary Jane. "An Evaluation of Nursing Care by Direct Observation." *Supervisor Nurse* 4, no. 4 (1973): 28–34.

Munley, Mary Jane. "Direct Observation Tool." *AORN Journal* 22, no. 2 (1975): 191–194.

Pearsall, Marion. "Participant Observation as Role and Method in Behavioral Research." *Nursing Research* 14, no. 1 (1965): 37–42.

Phaneuf, Maria C., and Wandelt, Mabel A. "Three Methods of Process-Oriented Nursing Evaluation." *Quality Review Bulletin* 17, no. 8 (1981): 20–26.

Schick, D'Anne. "Steps for Evaluating Patient Care." *AORN Journal* 20, no. 2 (1974): 237–240.

Ventura, Marlene R., and Crosby, Frances. "Preparing the Nurse Observer to Use the Quality Patient Care Scale: A Modular Approach." *The Journal of Continuing Education* 9, no. 6 (1978): 37–40.

Wandelt, Mabel A., and Phaneuf, Maria C. "Three Instruments for Measuring the Quality of Nursing Care." *Hospital Topics* 50 (1972): 20–29.

# Chapter 11

# Combining Techniques in Data Collection

*Margaret A. Skocir, M.S.N., R.N.*

Selecting the appropriate method for any evaluation study may be difficult. There are many sources of data available, and many factors can and do influence the methods of data collection utilized. Abdellah suggested that the following elements be considered in selecting a method of data collection:

> the research problem; the design of the study—experimental versus non-experimental, prospective or retrospective; the variables being studied and how they are defined, and how they are measured; the amount of time in which the study can be completed; the sampling units to be included—their type, number and location; and the amount of resources available to do the study.[1]

After all these factors have been considered, more than one method may be found to be appropriate. In some cases, a combination of methods may be required.

Combining methods may be defined as utilizing several approaches to gather data about specific variables. This technique may also be used to validate findings. For example, an interview may be used to follow up a written questionnaire or to validate data obtained from a record audit. Three major categories of studies lend themselves to the utilization of combined methods. These include studies designed to evaluate a system or program, studies intended to validate roles, and studies based on multiple sources of data.

## TECHNIQUES THAT MAY BE COMBINED

The most common techniques to be combined are questionnaire and interview, questionnaire and record audit, and observation and interview. In order to combine methods appropriately, the researcher must have an understanding of each method, its uses, its advantages, and its disadvantages (Table 11–1).

**Table 11–1** Overview of Common Research Techniques

| | *Questionnaire* | *Interview* | *Observation* | *Record Audit* |
|---|---|---|---|---|
| Uses | To obtain factual data, such as demographic data or behavioral characteristics | To gather data through verbal skills<br>To identify variables and relationsips<br>To supplement other data collection methods | To conduct prospective studies<br>To obtain data by instrumentation, such as blood pressure cuffs, thermometers<br>To record responses to variables<br>To document effects of interventions upon individual or groups<br>Sociological research | To evaluate the care of individual patients<br>To evaluate effects of a delivery system<br>To evaluate effects of programming and planning for a group of patients<br>To obtain demographic information |
| Requirements for use | Concise statement of the problem<br>Precise wording of questions | Trained interviewer<br>Topic suitable for interview<br>Questions clearly stated | Data collection very specific to the study<br>Observer highly trained | None |
| Advantages | Simple to use and easy to process<br>Low cost<br>Little time investment | Probing into data allowed<br>Data easily processed<br>Data of greater depth obtained | High level of precision using quantitative measurements | Data easily obtainable<br>Reduced time lag between decision to collect data and the availability of data in concurrent audit |

| | | | | |
|---|---|---|---|---|
| | | | | Data usable before problem becomes great<br>Data obtained retrospectively, if necessary |
| Disadvantages | Errors in interpretation<br>Skillful design required<br>Objectivity required | Time-consuming and expensive<br>Validity affected by interviewer subjectivity and bias | Data influenced by Hawthorne effect<br>Need to train observers | Differences between definition of variables for which data are available and definition of variables in the study<br>More information about caregiver than about patient in the record |
| Reliability | Testing to determine inter- and intrarater reliability | | High level of control needed to ensure reliability of observations | |
| Validity | Pretest required | Extensive interviewer training required | | |

## Questionnaire

The single most widely used instrument for data collection is the questionnaire. Questions are designed to elicit data on a great many variables, such as demographic information, behavioral characteristics, or specific events. A questionnaire requires a clear and concise statement of the issue being investigated.

Objectivity is essential in constructing a questionnaire. In order to facilitate the analysis of data, questions should be simply asked. Questions that are wordy, ambiguous, in any way intimidating or threatening to the respondent must be avoided. Questions that evoke predictable response biases and obscure information should also be avoided. Depending on the nature of the data, anonymity may be extremely important; in this case, however, other information may be lost.

Major advantages of the questionnaire include its simplicity in use, the ease with which the data obtained can be processed, its relatively low cost, and the little time investment. A major disadvantage is the great potential for error in interpretation. To avoid these errors, a questionnaire must be skillfully designed. A pilot test is also required to assess the validity of the instrument.

## Interview

In an interview, an observer collects data on the variables being investigated by means of verbal questioning of the study subjects. Interviews are most commonly used to identify variables and their relationships. Many times, an interview is used in combination with other data-collecting methods. Interviews vary from the highly structured, in which the interviewer reads the question and records the subject's response verbatim, to the highly unstructured, in which the instrument provides only the outline for question content. In the latter, the interviewer has more freedom to elicit data from the subjects. Validity of the interview method can only be ensured with adequate training of the interviewer and pretested questions from which ambiguities, inadequate wording, and hidden biases have been eliminated.

The major advantages of the interview technique are that it allows the interviewer to establish rapport with study subjects and to probe deeply into the data; to validate communication between interviewer and subject, and the resulting data can be easily processed. Its several disadvantages include high costs, substantial time investment, interviewer bias, and subject's desire to please the interviewer.

## Observation

A technique that can readily be combined with others is observation. An observer gathers data through the use of quantitative scales, qualitative measures, or active participation in the activity. Reliability can be ensured only through adequate training of observers. In addition, any tool used must be well tested, clear, and concise.

Observation techniques are often utilized in prospective studies and in studies that use equipment (e.g., blood pressure cuffs, thermometers, or cardiac monitors) as sources of data. In nonparticipant observation the data collector remains outside of the event and records responses to particular variables. Participant observation techniques utilize the data collector as an integral part of the activity being investigated. They are often used in studies that require documentation of a particular intervention's effects on an individual or a group. This method is quite popular in research designed to evaluate a service, such as those provided in health care.

The major advantage of nonparticipant observation is the accuracy that can be obtained when an observer uses mechanical instruments to record data. However, the observer must be well trained to ensure accurate data.

The Hawthorne effect, which is the psychological effect of an observer upon those being studied, must be acknowledged when selecting the nonparticipant observation technique. This can be reduced by having the researcher take an active role in the situation to be observed.

### Record Audit

The primary role of the medical record is to provide a continuous account of an individual patient's progress. It is the foundation for evaluating past care and planning future care. By grouping the records of many patients together, the effects of an entire delivery system can be evaluated through retrospective review. Lastly, the medical record provides raw data, such as demographic information.

A record audit has several advantages. For example, data can be obtained easily. Concurrent audits greatly reduce the time lag between the decision to collect data and the availability of the data. Audits also make the data on a specific problem available before problems become more serious. Definitions of variables for which the data are available may differ from the definitions of the variables identified in the study, however. Furthermore, the record may reflect the nurses' activities, but fail to identify patient problems and patient responses. A careful review of the documentation system may help to avoid this problem.

## COMBINING METHODS

The decision to combine methods is largely determined by the nature of the problem being studied. Combining techniques should be considered whenever there are multiple sources of data. If the objective of the study is to examine the impact of a change in the system of care delivery, for example, the many groups of people affected (i.e., patients, nurses, physicians, administrators, and other departments) may all be able to provide valuable data. Questionnaires might be combined with interviews; record audits might be combined with observations. Another system change that would lend itself to study by combined techniques is the documentation system. Obviously, a record audit would be the primary method of data collection, but a questionnaire might also be used to measure the effects of such a system change on the nurses involved.

Combined techniques might be used in studies that validate roles or role changes. In a study of changes in the head nurse role as a new system of care delivery is implemented, a questionnaire combined with an interview and observation both before and after the change in the care delivery system can provide data on aspects of the role that have changed. In addition, the effects of nursing interventions on the patient's level of comfort can be determined from observation of the patient, questionnaire and/or interview of the patient, and documentation on the record. All these sources can validate the effects of the variable being studied.

## LITERATURE REVIEW

Many nursing studies have been done using combined techniques. The three major areas that have been studied in this way are (1) evaluation of methods of care delivery, (2) patient care evaluation, and (3) nursing management.

### Evaluation of Methods of Care Delivery

In 1973, Marram studied the effects of primary nursing on a pilot unit.[2] She combined methods to obtain data from multiple sources: statistical records provided the raw data on costs for the unit that she studied; questionnaires were used to obtain data from both patients and nurses; and informal, unstructured interviews were used to obtain spontaneous comments from staff nurses. All the data validated the positive effects of primary nursing.

Daeffler utilized questionnaires and a record audit to compare patients' perceptions of care under a nursing team with their perceptions of care under a primary nursing system.[3] Questionnaires were distributed to patients, and the responses were correlated with the demographic, medical, and nursing data obtained from the record audit. Results indicated that patients were more satisfied with care under the primary nursing system.

Marram and associates studied the cost-effectiveness of primary and team nursing, using questionnaires for nurses, patients, and nurse-administrators, as well as a record audit.[4] Staff questionnaires focused on nurse satisfaction with work organizations, perceptions of key nursing functions, time spent on specific tasks, and involvement with patients. Patient questionnaires were aimed at determining patients' levels of satisfaction with the nursing care that they received. Record audit was used to determine the extent to which nursing assessment was used in care planning and the degree to which the care plan was individualized. All the sources of data helped to validate that primary nursing was a cost-effective system of care delivery.

As a member of the staff at Beth Israel Hospital in Boston, Hegedus and associates conducted a four-phase quality assurance study to review the delivery system of primary nursing.[5] The overall purpose was to identify patterns of nursing care provided to patients. Using the framework of structure, process, and outcome, data were collected by means of various techniques. Structural data were obtained by observational methods; process data were obtained by concurrent record review of the nurses notes, nursing assessment records, and nursing care plans; and outcome data regarding patients' knowledge of their primary nurse and their care plan were gathered by the interview method. Findings demonstrated many positive patterns of patient responses and nursing practice, as well as areas requiring corrective action.

A similar study was done by Kent and Larson to determine to what degree primary nursing had been implemented throughout a 350-bed acute care university hospital.[6] The study was also intended to identify the degree of staff satisfaction and the degree of patient knowledge of care. The structure of primary nursing, the process of delivering nursing care, and its outcome in patient knowledge, as well as the relationship between nursing process and staff satisfaction and that between nursing process and patient knowledge, were examined. Because of the many sources of data, the observation, record audit, interview, and questionnaire methods were combined. Structural data were obtained through observation; process data, through record audit and interview with staff; and outcome data, through patient interviews. The questionnaire method was used to obtain staff satisfaction data.

Data analysis indicated a correlation between the degree to which primary nursing had been implemented and patient knowledge. There was also a strong relationship between nurse job satisfaction and nursing process scores. It was concluded from the study that "there is a statistically significant relationship between the extent of primary nursing implementation and improved patient care."[7]

## Patient Care Evaluation

Routhier developed a tool that uses combined methods to evaluate quality of care before and after a change in structure in which several ancillary positions were added to the staff on a given unit.[8] This tool could be used to evaluate many aspects of direct patient care, such as the admission procedure, discharge planning, and the management of psychosocial needs, and some elements of indirect care, such as the care plans, patient care conferences, and nursing assignments. Four methods were combined in this study: (1) interview of the patient and his or her family and the nursing staff, (2) questionnaire completed at the interview, (3) observation of patient care and safety, and (4) review of the patient's records. The study was explained to all personnel on the selected unit. It was emphasized that the purpose was the evaluation of the care received by the patient rather than the care given by an individual nurse. By using multiple sources of data and combining methods, the researchers identified strengths and weaknesses in total patient care, along with areas of potential for change. Furthermore, the results of this study established a standard of care for the nursing department.

Blair and associates conducted a study to test and refine an instrument designed to examine the outcomes of ambulatory maternal-child nursing.[9] The instrument that was developed to measure maternal outcomes combined the methods of questionnaire and observation. In an approach slightly different from Routhier's, nurses completed a questionnaire on their observations relative to patients' behavior. The patients then completed a questionnaire regarding knowledge and attitudes. The third measurement was a nurse's response form that elicited data relative to tasks and attitudes and an assessment of patient and infant health status. A complex data analysis was done in search of correlations among all the data. The study resulted in the validation of the instruments as measures of quality assurance outcomes.

Since teaching is an essential part of nursing care, determination of a patient's knowledge base is fundamental. In order to assess the parent/guardian knowledge of fever control in children, the emergency department at St. Michael Hospital conducted a study in which the combined methods of questionnaire and observation were used. Parents were asked first to answer the questions presented in Exhibit 11–1 and then to demonstrate temperature taking on their child while the nurse observed. After the demonstration was completed, the nurse provided information and taught skills found to be deficient. As a result of the study, information provided on the teaching sheet for families with febrile children was improved. In addition, a standard nursing care plan entitled Fever Control in the Emergency Department that included assessment of specific areas identified as deficient in the study was implemented. Lastly, thermometers were made available for purchase by parents through the emergency department.

Another example of a study utilizing combined methods of record review, observation of the environment, and patient questionnaire was done to assess current practices in relation to the monitoring of intake and output. Secondly, the study attempted to identify categories of patients who require assessment of intake and output. On three consecutive Wednesdays, six registered nurse data collectors selected nine patients for whom they were not caring. The Kardex and the medication sheets were reviewed to determine current therapy and diagnoses. The data collection tool presented in Exhibit 11–2 was completed.

**Exhibit 11–1** Emergency Department Quality Assurance Subcommittee Evaluation Study Questionnaire

Directions: Administer this questionnaire to the responsible parent or guardian of a child admitted with fever who meets the following criteria:

1. Child less than 16 years of age
2. Temperature greater than 101° rectally or 100° orally

1. In your home, who is the person responsible for taking the child's temperature?
2. Do you have a thermometer in your home? If so, what kind (oral or rectal)?
3. Do you use any other methods of checking the fever?
4. What is a normal temperature?
5. What do you do if the temperature is abnormal?
6. How do you treat an abnormal temperature?
7. How often do you re-check the temperature?
8. When would you call a physician to get help for fever reduction?

Demonstration

Ask the parent to show you how to take the child's temperature.

1. Is the thermometer shaken down? _____ Yes _____ No
2. Is the thermometer in the right place? _____ Rectal _____Yes _____No
   _____ Oral _____Yes _____No
3. How long is the thermometer kept in? _______ minutes

*Source:* Reprinted with permission from St. Michael Hospital, Milwaukee, Wisconsin. Copyright 1982.

The data collector proceeded to each patient's room to determine if the equipment for measuring intake and output was present along with a green intake and output recording sheet. Lastly, the patient was asked if he or she was aware of the fact that his or her intake and output was being measured and recorded.

The results of the study indicated problems with intake and output measurement with several levels of staff. Problems were identified with collection of accurate intake and output records by nursing assistants. The study indicated that appropriate patients were not being placed on intake and output by the primary nurse.

**Exhibit 11–2** Intake and Output

| | PATIENT ON DIURETIC THERAPY | | | PATIENT ADMITTED FOR G.U. SURGERY | | | PATIENTS ON CONTINUOUS I.V. FLUIDS | | | PATIENTS WITH INDWELLING CATH | | | MISCELLANEOUS | TOTALS |
|---|---|---|---|---|---|---|---|---|---|---|---|---|---|---|
| | Day 1 | Day 2 | Day 3 | Day 1 | Day 2 | Day 3 | Day 1 | Day 2 | Day 3 | Day 1 | Day 2 | Day 3 | | |
| Number of patients | | | | | | | | | | | | | | |
| Not on I & O | | | | | | | | | | | | | | |
| I & O - Nursing order | | | | | | | | | | | | | | |
| I & O - M.D. order | | | | | | | | | | | | | | |
| Collected X 24 hours<br>Yes | | | | | | | | | | | | | | |
| No | | | | | | | | | | | | | | |
| Less than 24 hour order | | | | | | | | | | | | | | |
| No comment | | | | | | | | | | | | | | |
| Sheet on door<br>Yes | | | | | | | | | | | | | | |
| No | | | | | | | | | | | | | | |
| No comment | | | | | | | | | | | | | | |
| Equipment in room<br>Yes | | | | | | | | | | | | | | |
| No | | | | | | | | | | | | | | |
| No comment | | | | | | | | | | | | | | |
| Patient aware<br>Yes | | | | | | | | | | | | | | |
| No | | | | | | | | | | | | | | |
| No comment | | | | | | | | | | | | | | |

*Source:* Reprinted with permission from St. Michael Hospital, Milwaukee, Wisconsin. Copyright 1980.

### Nursing Management

Pearsall combined observation with interviews to study nursing supervisors and their role in relation to the hospital organization.[10] Observation techniques were used to identify the role of these supervisors within the organization, and interviews provided data on their attitude toward their position, philosophy of supervision, and process of integrating self into the role of supervisor. Many had to adjust to a new role alone and on the job, and the rigidity that often exists in supervisory roles within hospitals may lead to role conflict and confusion. The study identified the basic dilemma faced by individuals as they assume supervisory positions. Those who were able to maintain an equilibrium between professional standards and organizational expectations were able to remain in supervisory positions.

Sansam explored the applicability of various management principles to the role of the head nurse.[11] Specific areas investigated included the nurse's ability to manage, her basic nursing education, employment practices, and in-service training. Thirty-five head nurses and fifteen physicians were interviewed and asked to complete a questionnaire. Results indicated that management principles were not learned in basic nursing education, but were most often acquired through role modeling, experience, and on-the-job educational sessions. It was found that there was little support and direction for a staff nurse as she assumed the role of head nurse. Again, this study identified areas of role conflict within nursing's supervisory positions.

In Kovner's study,[12] utilization of nursing resources was investigated. A four-week observation of nursing activities, with identification of similarities among patients admitted to selected units, was combined with a staff questionnaire and interview. The nurses' level of activities varied from unit to unit. The units in which nursing outcomes were highly predictable and patient populations varied little did not require expert levels of nursing care; therefore, from an organizational perspective, expert nurses were not well utilized in this unit. Units in which outcomes were highly unpredictable and patient populations were extremely variable, however, utilized all professional and nonprofessional personnel to the fullest and occasionally required a greater number of professional staff. It was found that goals were achieved more often on these units as nurses' knowledge and skills were utilized to the greatest potential.

## AN EVALUATION STUDY USING COMBINED METHODS OF DATA COLLECTION

Those who work in hospitals today face the constant challenge of maintaining quality nursing care. They have accepted this task. At St. Michael Hospital, primary nursing was instituted as a method of care delivery in the mid-1970s. It began with a pilot unit and, within a two-year period, was implemented throughout the hospital. In-service education was provided, and group sessions with staff were often held to discuss problems and concerns.

After primary nursing had been implemented, several unit-based studies were conducted to evaluate the care being given on these primary nursing units. McCarthy and Schifalacqua used questionnaires that were sent to patients as a method of evaluating and comparing care given on a primary nursing unit with that given on a team nursing unit.[13] A similar study was done by Skocir.[14] She used questionnaires completed by patients to compare the level of satisfaction with care on a primary nursing unit with that on a team nursing unit.

In this same institution, a hospitalwide study that combined methods was undertaken to obtain answers to the following questions (see Appendix 11–A):

1. structure items
   - Does every patient have a primary nurse after twenty-four hours of admission?
   - Is the primary nurse identified on the primary board, as well as on the Kardex?
2. process items
   - Has a care plan been initiated?
   - Was the care plan initiated by the primary nurse?
   - Does the documentation reflect an admission note and an admission head-to-toe assessment?
   - Does the documentation reflect the teaching that has been done?
   - Has the teaching been done by the primary nurse?
   - Is the appropriate documentation done on transfer?
3. outcome items
   - Can the patient identify the assigned primary nurse?
   - Can the patient identify the primary nurse's role in helping to plan his or her care and preparing for discharge?

Upon completion of data collection and analysis of these structure, process, and outcome criteria within a primary nursing system, the degree to which primary nursing had been successfully implemented could be validated.

## Preparation of the Study

Even though the need for the study was identified at an administrative level of the organization, representatives of all levels of professional staff were asked to participate in committee activities. The first task to be accomplished was to identify the various sources of the data required. Structural data could be obtained from the primary nursing assignment board, which is present on all units and would identify both primary and associate nurses, and the Kardex, which would support the information obtained from the primary nursing board. It was decided that the full name or first initial and last name of the primary nurse would be the only acceptable identification on the Kardex. Full name, or first initial and last name, are most appropriate since this part of the Kardex is part of the permanent record for legal purposes. Sources of process data included the face sheet on each patient's chart, the nursing data base, the nursing assessment record, the patient teaching record, and the Kardex. The principal source of outcome data was the patient.

The next task facing the committee was to develop a tool that could be used to gather data from multiple sources. Review of the literature provided some assistance. The study by Marram and associates,[15] and the study done at Beth Israel Hospital[16] proved to be especially helpful. In fact, the committee's eventual tool was an adaptation of that used by the Beth Israel staff.

It was decided that the observation method would be used to validate structural data; the record audit, to obtain demographic data and process data from the documentation on the chart and the care plan; and the interview, to collect outcome data. Four questions were prepared to solicit information from patients regarding their knowledge of their primary nurse. Except for the question asking for the name of the primary nurse, the questions could be answered with a "yes" or "no" response. Patients who had been transferred were asked to identify the primary nurse on their current unit.

Since patients are frequently transferred from unit to unit or from a specialty unit to the general medical-surgical unit, a separate section of the tool was prepared for this population. Sources of structure data for these patients were the same, but sources of process data differed slightly in that the admission note and head-to-toe assessment had to be dated since transfer and the care plan had to contain nursing diagnoses dated since transfer or the statement "Kardex reviewed" along with the date. Outcome data were obtained from the patient.

The tool was then pilot-tested on ten patients and their charts. Several revisions were made and a set of instructions developed to standardize the use of the tool. Because the pilot test revealed that the term *primary nurse* was not familiar to the patients, the interviewers were instructed to explain its meaning as "one who gives your care most of the time." In many cases, the patient was then able to identify the primary nurse correctly.

Pilot testing also revealed problems with the record audit. For example, when reviewing the Kardex, the data collectors had a tendency to use their own judgment and decide that the nursing diagnoses were not always valid. The committee decided that the purpose of this study was to determine the presence of documentation, not its content. Validation of nursing diagnosis could be a study of its own. Therefore, for purposes of this study, the presence of documentation, not its content, was emphasized.

## Implementation of the Study

In order to minimize the Hawthorne effect, staff nurses were not informed of the study. Head nurses were told only that a data collector would be present on their units on the date identified for implementation of this study and that a list of patients admitted for at least twenty-four hours would be needed.

Volunteer data collectors randomly selected their units, although great care was taken to ensure that they did not collect data in their own unit. After they proceeded to the unit and received a list of all patients who had been admitted for at least twenty-four hours, a random sample was selected. The sample size had been preset at 25 percent of the capacity of the unit or a minimum of ten. The data collector first reviewed the primary nursing board to determine if the patient had a primary nurse, then validated this by reviewing the Kardex. The presence of nursing diagnoses, outcomes, deadlines, and nursing interventions was determined by a review of the nursing care plan. The chart was then reviewed for the presence of a complete data base, a complete head-to-toe assessment, documentation of patient teaching, and documentation of the teaching done by the primary nurse. Again, content was not reviewed, simply the presence of documentation.

If a primary nurse was identified either on the board or the Kardex, patients were asked to answer four questions about the nurses caring for them. On certain units, such as intensive care, coronary care, and/or pediatrics, patients were unable to answer the questions, and parents or significant others were asked to participate.

In most cases, data collection was completed within one day. In several of the smaller specialty areas, however, the data collector had to return on subsequent days in order to obtain a sample of the designated size.

Data were analyzed by means of simple frequency distribution. Scores were computed for each item for each unit and again for the entire sample. It was found that, on many units, the structure of primary nursing had been well implemented; many patients had a primary nurse after twenty-four hours of admission. In addition, as determined by overall process data, the nursing process was being practiced quite consistently, and that practice met the standards identified by the nursing department. The results of the outcome data analysis were less impressive. Only a small percentage of the patients could identify their primary nurse. Many patients indicated, however, that care had been discussed and that plans for discharge had been addressed. Those units that scored high on the structure elements also scored high on process and outcome elements.

## Critique of the Study

The study provided a wide variety of data. All results were shared with staff and discussed at the unit level. Structure data showed that several units did not use the primary nursing board while others used it simply to note daily assignments.

Patients on those units in which the full names of primary nurses were not identified on the Kardex tended to have a lower score on the identification of primary nurses.

Review of patient charts for process data was problematic. Credit was given for the presence of any type of documentation on the data base, regardless of content, which may have skewed the results. If only one diagnosis was identified, credit was given. Perhaps the number of complete nursing diagnoses should have been identified.

The outcome data obtained from the patients revealed that the nurses did not identify themselves as "primary nurses" or, at least, this term was unfamiliar to the patients. However, the patients could identify their regular caregiver, and they were able to indicate that their care had been discussed with them.

The extent to which primary nursing had been implemented varied from unit to unit. This sparked much discussion among the staff. In some areas, needed changes were identified and implemented. One that was easily implemented was a change in identification of the primary nurse to full name or first initial and last name on the Kardex. All could understand the rationale for this change in procedure. Several in-service topics were identified as a result of this study. One was to review the philosophy of primary nursing and thus increase the frequency with which primary nurses are identified to the patient.

The instrument had several limitations. The patient interview portion posed the problem of misinterpretation of terms. What was self-explanatory to the data collector was often quite foreign to the patient. Perhaps the questionnaire could be reworded. As has been previously stated, ambiguity in terms can be a problem with the interview method. Reluctance of the patient to provide negative feedback is also a limitation with this type of instrument.

Several recommendations for future studies evolved from this study. The interview portion of the instrument could be expanded into a study to validate outcomes of nursing care. Several aspects of the patient's care, such as individualization of care, satisfaction with care, knowledge of medications, knowledge of disease processes, and discharge teaching, could be examined from the patient's perspective.

The chart review could become a study of its own. Admission and transfer notes, along with the data base information, could be reviewed for content. The frequency of assessments and the appropriateness of this frequency could be examined. Assessment data might be reviewed in light of nursing problems identified on the Kardex. Since problem-oriented recording has now been implemented, documentation should be studied for consistency with the standards developed by the nursing department.

Process data obtained from the Kardex are potentially material for another study. The nursing diagnoses could be compared with those identified by the Fourth and Fifth National Conferences on Nursing Diagnosis. New nursing diagnoses might be identified. A study of discharge outcomes might make it possible to identify parameters for discharge planning. Lastly, a critique of the nursing orders for appropriateness as well as completeness would be an interesting review. A more extensive tool would have to be devised in order to conduct each of these studies, however.

## NOTES

1. Faye G. Abdellah, *Better Patient Care Through Nursing Research* (New York: Macmillan, 1965), p. 321.
2. Gwen Marram, "Innovation on Four Tower West/What Happened?" *American Journal of Nursing* 73, no. 5 (May 1973): 814–816.
3. Reidun Juvkam Daeffler, "Patient Perceptions of Care Under Team and Primary Nursing," *Journal of Nursing Administration* 5 (March/April 1975): 20–26.
4. Gwen Marram et al., *Cost Effectiveness of Primary and Team Nursing* (Wakefield, MA: Contemporary Publishing, 1976), pp. 1–91.
5. Kathryn Stewart Hegedus and Sharon Bourdon, "Evaluation Research: A Quality Assurance Program," *Nursing Administration Quarterly* 5, no. 3 (Spring 1981): 26–30.
6. Linda A. Kent and Elaine Larson, "Evaluating the Effectiveness of Primary Nursing Practice," *Journal of Nursing Administration* 13 (January 1983): 34–41.
7. Ibid, p. 40.
8. R. Wilda Routhier, "Tool for the Evaluation of Patient Care," *Supervisor Nurse* 3, no. 1 (January 1972): 15–27.
9. Eunice M. Blair et al., "Instrument Development: Measuring Quality Outcomes in Ambulatory Maternal Child Nursing," *Nursing Administration Quarterly* 2, no. 4 (Summer 1978): 81–93.
10. Marion Pearsall, "Supervision: A Nursing Dilemma," *Nursing Outlook* 9, no. 2 (February 1961): 91–92.
11. P.G. Sansam, *Management Capabilities of the Head Nurse in General Hospitals* (unpublished master's thesis, Xavier University, 1969).
12. Anthony Roger Kovner, *The Nursing Unit: A Technological Perspective* (unpublished doctoral dissertation, University of Pittsburgh, 1966).
13. Donna McCarthy and Marita Schifalacqua, "Primary Nursing: Its Implementation and Six Month Outcome," *Journal of Nursing Administration* 8, no. 5 (May 1978): 29–32.
14. Margaret A. Skocir, *Patients' Perceptions of Satisfaction with Nursing Care on a Primary Versus Team Nursing Unit* (unpublished master's thesis, Marquette University, 1979).
15. Marram et al., *Cost Effectiveness of Primary and Team Nursing,* pp. 1–91.
16. Kathryn Stewart Hegedus and Sharon Bourdon, "Evaluating the Effectiveness of Primary Nursing Practice," pp. 26–30.

## REFERENCES

### Books

Abdellah, Faye G., and Levine, Eugene. *Better Patient Care Through Nursing Research*. New York: Macmillan, 1965.

Cantor, Marjorie Moore. *Achieving Nursing Care Standards: Internal and External*. Wakefield, MA: Nursing Resources, 1978.

Isaac, Stephen, and Michael, William B. *Handbook in Research and Evaluation*. San Diego: Edits, 1971.

Marram, Gwen; Flynn, Kathleen; Abaravich, Wendy; and Carey, Sheila. *Cost Effectiveness of Primary and Team Nursing*. Wakefield, MA: Contemporary Publishing, 1976.

**Journals**

Bailet, Howard; Lewis, Judy; Hockheiser, Louis; and Bush, Nancy. "Assessing the Quality of Care." *Nursing Outlook* 23 (1975): 153–159.

Blair, Eunice M.; Hauf, Barbara; Loveridge, Catherine; Murphy, Juanita; and Roth, Mildred. "Instrument Development: Measuring Quality Outcomes in Ambulatory Maternal Child Nursing." *Nursing Administration Quarterly* 2 (1978): 81–93.

Clifford, J.C. "On the Scene: Beth Israel Hospital." *Nursing Administration Quarterly* 5, no. 3 (1981): 1–5.

Daeffler, Reidun Juvkam. "Patient Perceptions of Care Under Team and Primary Nursing." *Journal of Nursing Administration* 5 (1975): 20–26.

Hegedus, Kathryn S., and Bourdon, Sharon M. "Evaluation Research: A Quality Assurance Program." *Nursing Administration Quarterly* 5, no. 3 (1981): 26–30.

Kent, Linda A., and Larson, Elaine. "Evaluating the Effectiveness of Primary Nursing Practice." *Journal of Nursing Administration* 13, no. 1 (1983): 34–41.

Lindeman, Carol. "Measuring Quality of Nursing Care: Part 1." *Journal of Nursing Administration* 6, no. 6 (1976): 7–9.

Marram, Gwen. "Innovation on Four Tower West/What Happened?" *American Journal of Nursing* 73 (1973): 814–816.

McCarthy, Donna, and Schifalacqua, Marita. "Primary Nursing: Its Implementation and Six Month Outcome." *Journal of Nursing Administration* 8 (1978): 29–32.

McLeis, Afaf, and Benner, Patricia. "Process or Product Evaluation." *Nursing Outlook* 23 (1975): 303–307.

Nehring, Virginia, and Geach, Barbara. "Patients' Evaluation of Their Care: Why They Don't Complain." *Nursing Outlook* 21 (1973): 317–321.

Pearsall, Marion "Supervision: A Nursing Dilemma." *Nursing Outlook* 9, no. 2 (1961): 91–92.

Routhier, R. Wilda. "Tool for the Evaluation of Patient Care." *Supervisor Nurse* 3 (1972): 15–27.

**Unpublished Works**

Kovner, Anthony Roger. *The Nursing Unit: A Technological Perspective*. Doctoral dissertation, University of Pittsburgh, 1966.

Sansam, P.G. *Management Capabilities of the Head Nurse in General Hospitals*. Master's thesis, Xavier University, 1969.

Skocir, Margaret A. *Patients' Perceptions of Satisfaction with Nursing Care on a Primary Versus Team Nursing Unit*. Master's thesis, Marquette University, 1979.

# Appendix 11–A

# Primary Nursing Evaluation Tool*

Date: ______________________ Unit: ______________________

**I. Primary Nurse Identification**

A. Primary nursing board gives name of patient and primary nurse ............................ Y _____ N _____

B. Primary nursing board gives name of associate nurse ...................................... Y _____ N _____

C. Primary nurse identified on Kardex.................... Y _____ N _____

**II. Description of Initial Nursing Note**

A. Admission note

1. Data base complete ................................ Y _____ N _____
2. Care plan established ............................ Y _____ N _____
3. Head-to-toe physical assessment complete ......... Y _____ N _____

**III. Nursing Care Plan**

A. Kardex

1. Nursing diagnosis identified ..................... Y _____ N _____
2. Expected outcomes identified ..................... Y _____ N _____
3. Deadlines identified ............................. Y _____ N _____
4. Nursing orders present ........................... Y _____ N _____
5. Discharge goals identified ....................... Y _____ N _____
6. Signature on nursing orders ...................... Y _____ N _____

*Reprinted with permission from St. Michael Hospital, Milwaukee, Wisconsin. Copyright 1981.

IV. Nursing Notes and Kardex Upon Transfer

A. Nursing note present .................................. Y _____ N _____

1. Head-to-toe assessment complete within 24 hours of transfer ............................ Y _____ N _____

B. Nursing Care Plan

1. Primary nurse on receiving unit identified ....... Y _____ N _____

2. Care plan reviewed .............................. Y _____ N _____

a. Nursing diagnosis identified ................. Y _____ N _____

b. Expected outcomes ............................ Y _____ N _____

c. Deadlines identified ......................... Y _____ N _____

d. Nursing orders present ....................... Y _____ N _____

e. Discharge goals identified ................... Y _____ N _____

f. Signature on nursing orders .................. Y _____ N _____

V. Patient Teaching Record

A. Documentation of teaching ............................ Y _____ N _____

B. Documentation by primary nurse ....................... Y _____ N _____

VI. Patient Interview

A. What is the name of your primary nurse? (acceptable if either first or last name given) ...... Y _____ N _____

B. If answer to A is yes:

1. Did you receive a card with your primary nurse's name on it? ..................................... Y _____ N _____

2. Has your primary nurse discussed any plans or concerns regarding your care? .................... Y _____ N _____

3. Has your primary nurse discussed any plans or concerns regarding your discharge from the hospital? ...................................... Y _____ N _____

Information obtained from patient _____ significant other _____

In the event that the patient is unable to answer the above questions, his/her significant other may be interviewed.

Demographic Data

Age: __________

Sex: __________

Admitting Diagnosis: _________________________

Status on Unit: Direct Admission: ___________

Transfer: ___________________

# Chapter 12

# A Practical Guide to Multidisciplinary Auditing

*Robin Reading Mosleth, R.N., M.S.*

As more and more emphasis is placed on measuring the quality of patient care, health professionals have become increasingly aware of the need to expand their evaluations to the total patient care system. Obviously, one professional is not totally responsible for a patient's health status at the time of discharge. Two, three, or more health professionals from various disciplines are involved to varying degrees. Therefore, an evaluation of total patient care should clearly demonstrate the accountabilities, achievements, and deficiencies of all health team members.

## DEFINITION

Multidisciplinary audits have various definitions, based on the process by which they are carried out. The term *multidisciplinary audit* is often used interchangeably with other terms, such as *interdisciplinary audit, parallel audit,* and *joint audit*; such an audit is also categorized with utilization review, peer review, and research. It is important to look closely at the terminology, as well as the purpose and the method of what is to be evaluated.

Knudson defined a multidisciplinary audit as "a retrospective evaluation of the outcome of services provided by every member of the health care team to the patient population under study."[1] She further stated that "health care professionals together evaluate patient care" and that this collaboration "encourages professional interaction and changes the scope of audit into a patient-centered review."[2] Ideally, by focusing on quality patient care as a shared responsibility, professionals become less concerned with professional autonomy and feel less threatened personally. Because patient care reflects professional practice, feelings do not remain neutral, and communication among all health care professionals does not always proceed efficiently and smoothly. Furthermore, it is important to retain some degree of professional autonomy.[3] For example, in writing criteria, professionals in each discipline must delineate the performance expectations for their colleagues. The multidisciplinary approach will later help to overcome role barriers.

Some authors speak about interdisciplinary audits, in which a number of professionals from the involved health disciplines together determine criteria specific to each other's discipline. The criteria are focused on the care the team members agree should be performed by one or more of the disciplines involved, in regard to a specific diagnosis. This is very time-consuming and demands highly developed communication among disciplines, however. The interdisciplinary audit can also be expanded from a patient-centered audit into a personal or discipline-related evaluation and review.

Parallel audits are monodisciplinary studies performed simultaneously on the same topic by two or more disciplines. The same patient population is used, but the criteria are developed independently. Although no multidisciplinary committee functions in the parallel audit process, a parallel audit is often a beginning step toward collaboration on a multidisciplinary audit.

The term *joint audit* is used synonymously with either multidisciplinary audit or parallel audit when only two disciplines are involved.

Like a multidisciplinary audit, utilization review is concerned with patient care, but it focuses primarily on reasons for admission, reasons for procedures, length of stay, and mortality; it is directed primarily toward the evaluation of physician practice. A utilization review may be performed by a technician or a nurse. Although it may involve the staff, it is limited and does not include as many variables or directly involve as many professionals from various disciplines as does a teamwork effort.

A multidisciplinary audit is not a peer review and should not be done with this hidden purpose in mind. When completed, however, a multidisciplinary audit may be taken further within each separate discipline to examine and evaluate practice in that discipline in a specific institution. This should be done only if this purpose was specified from the onset.

Sell and Goldstein noted that the focus of audit differs from that of research: "The question of which patient management technique is clinically superior is not appropriately handled through audit. However," they continue, "audits can allow committees to evaluate compliance with the quality of an established regimen."[4] In addition, it can generate ideas for research.

## PURPOSE

The multidisciplinary audit has two primary purposes, i.e., to support the care given when it is effective and to provide objective evidence when change is needed. Because the data are collected from the patient chart, the methods of documentation are investigated in the evaluation process. The audit process is an excellent opportunity to improve communication among professionals in different departments, who may be accustomed to working more independently. According to Carter and Sweeney, the audit also "highlights the indispensable contributions of each health care practitioner in accomplishing a common desired goal"[5] An excellent example of working together toward a desired patient goal is given by Carter and Sweeney:

> A criterion states that a patient admitted for uncontrolled diabetes should have a blood sugar of 90-160 mg% at discharge. . . . Prescription of the type and amount of insulin and the diet and overall direction of therapy are physician responsibilities. Administration of insulin, education of the patient in self-administration, and observation of patient compliance with dietary regimen are nursing functions, whereas instruction in diet is the domain of the dietician. Whether the patient's record documents the desired blood sugar at discharge may even be influenced by the laboratory personnel who collect blood and interpret test results.[6]

Therefore, a patient's attainment of this criterion is dependent on the cooperation of several health care professionals, each contributing to the patient's care from a different area of competency.

## PRELIMINARY STEPS

A multidisciplinary audit must have staff support, since commitment to evaluation is the key to its success. Furthermore, in order to conduct such an audit, many professionals in the different disciplines will have to take time away from direct patient care. A good place to start looking for support is in the hospital administration, via nursing administration, and in department meetings and multidisciplinary patient staffings. The idea can be proposed to individuals and in meetings dealing with patient care evaluation.

It is crucial to the audit that the multidisciplinary team members have a working, communicative relationship; a positive attitude; and a willingness to work together.[7] This requires a high-level functioning team. Those who have only a beginning skill in working with others might be wise to attempt a parallel audit first in order to become more confident in the evaluation process. It may help to start with members of two or more disciplines who have a mutual respect and appreciation for the unique contribution that the other can make to the team and the audit topic. Also, it is not necessary for all disciplines to be involved in every multidisciplinary audit.

A good way to become proficient in the multidisciplinary audit process is to work with those who are knowledgeable and skilled in the process. Knudson suggested holding seminars to teach techniques of group process, to review audit methodologies and criteria development, and to explain the benefits and difficulties of a multidisciplinary audit.[8] Such educational experiences, together with workshops, provide an opportunity to practice the skills. These experiences will also spark enthusiasm and encourage interested individuals to become involved in future audits.

Established, regular multidisciplinary staffings facilitate multidisciplinary evaluations. At these times, all health team members involved in a patient's care are present to review and discuss the care being given, the patient's goals, and the health team's goals for their patients. They also discuss how the team can work together to meet these goals. The persons in the staffings can be an ideal group to conduct an audit, since they are already gathered to plan optimal patient treatment and are working with various disciplines to improve patient care.

Good record keeping and problem-oriented charting further simplify a multidisciplinary audit. Because multidisciplinary audits have been primarily retrospective, they have been dependent on good records. In some systems of problem-oriented charting, those in all disciplines chart on the same narrative sheet under titled and numbered patient problems, which makes it easier to retrieve data. The problem-oriented chart should contain a plan for discharge that was begun on the day of admission and is modified and updated continuously. Not only is discharge planning a must for utilization review, but also it is the beginning of good charting, demonstrating efforts toward good patient care and facilitating meaningful audits. If charting is not orderly and there are multiple forms with repeated information, the committee may suggest a documentation workshop immediately[9] or may proceed with the audit and recommend improved documentation of care, as well as more efficient utilization of forms, after the audit has been completed.

## GETTING STARTED

The first step in a multidisciplinary audit is to form a multidisciplinary committee. One purpose of this committee is to "facilitate communication when disciplines cross lines, so that, for example, the head of lab isn't going to the head of nursing to suggest a topic for a nursing audit."[10] A second is to ensure that necessary follow-up activities are completed. A summary of the audit proposal that is brief and can be understood by the administration and the governing board should be prepared.

Members of the committee should come from the disciplines most involved with the group of patients under study, one (at most, two) representative from each discipline. The ideal working group has six to eight members. It is helpful to have one member from outside the patient care disciplines (often the quality assurance coordinator in an institution) to facilitate the group audit process and be the team coordinator. The team members may wish to elect a coordinator from among themselves, however. Represented by this coordinator, the team is responsible to the audit committee or the quality assurance committee, which reports to administration.

It is helpful to designate a ''liaison person'' to answer any questions that the individual from the medical records department (or whoever is retrieving the data) may have.[11] A committee may also appoint a liaison person from each discipline to answer questions regarding the criteria for that discipline. However, this may make it difficult to gain perspective on problems with the study, because more than one person may be making decisions independent of the others on the team. These problems may best be solved by holding a team meeting before the person gathering the data proceeds further. As Tan stated, ''this assures that individual committee members do not reinterpret or redefine criteria set by the group."[12]

Before writing the criteria, the committee members should take some time to become acquainted, if they do not already know each other. Johnson stated that ''feedback from informal exchanges and professional interaction will determine audit productivity and influence effective communication."[13] Each professional should listen to and understand the standards of patient care governing the different disciplines involved. This is particularly true about nursing.[14,15] According to Johnson, ''nurse representatives should be clear about the areas in which nurses make independent decisions on patient care, and they should be prepared to support nursing standards and inform physicians about the effect of these standards on patient outcomes."[16]

After becoming acquainted, the committee must delineate the topic, divide the tasks, decide how often to meet, and establish a timetable. The topic should be a ''multidisciplinary topic,'' one involving care given by professionals from a number of disciplines.[17] The tasks include writing collaborative criteria, performing a pilot study, retrieving data with a designated liaison person, tabulating and reporting results, and determining methods of follow-up on the findings. Meetings are scheduled according to the way in which these functions are divided (if they are), time budgeted for the evaluation, the effectiveness of the group's communication, and the preferences of the committee members. Meetings must last long enough for the committee to develop criteria and instructions completely so that one or two persons are not personally interpreting or trying to recall decisions made during the meetings.

## WRITING CRITERIA

If the evaluation process is carried out by experienced, high-level multidisciplinary groups, the criteria are written by all members of the audit committee. If the number of disciplines involved is not large, more criteria from each discipline can be evaluated; however, care must be taken to avoid including so many items that data collection becomes unwieldy. These criteria are brought together to be discussed, changed, combined, or eliminated until all criteria represent a multidisciplinary evaluation of patient-centered care.[18]

Not all multidisciplinary groups are experienced enough to work through and combine criteria, nor do they all have the time. With groups that are only learning to evaluate care from a multidisciplinary perspective, it may be helpful to have the discipline representatives write two to eight criteria with collaboration from peers within their respective disciplines. This approach maintains some autonomy among disciplines, which may enhance "the equally necessary joint appraisals of quality of care received by patients."[19] Knudson suggested that patients may be good sources of patient-centered audit criteria. In one case, for example, patients from a colostomy club provided input on the care and teaching of colostomy patients prior to discharge.[20]

The criteria are distributed to committee members for review prior to the meeting. Each representative comes to the committee meeting prepared to discuss the rationale for each criterion, as well as its role in patient outcomes.[21,22] The committee reviews all criteria for clarity and overlap. For example, physicians may believe that nurses were performing certain duties, while nurses believe that the physicians were performing these duties. In collaborating on the writing of the criteria, it may be realized that no one was performing them. Perhaps medicine, nursing, and social work all have the criteria that a patient verbalizes an understanding of the need to continue taking medications at home and to come in for a follow-up appointment after discharge. Obviously, the three criteria can be combined.

Although the criteria are multidisciplinary and may be combined, it is still important to indicate who or which discipline has the greatest impact on each criterion. The persons in each discipline involved are held accountable for the criteria specific to and expected of their discipline. These indicated committee members will take action for follow-up, depending on the compiled data results.

The type of criteria used in multidisciplinary retrospective evaluations have primarily been outcome criteria, i.e., they have focused on patient health status, behavior, or knowledge changes that occurred because of care given and were documented in the chart. Multidisciplinary audits can include a few process items,[21] which could be quite informative. Knudson discussed the use of process criteria to investigate patient outcomes.[22] Each criterion should, when possible, be clearly stated as a single question that can be answered "yes" or "no." In this way, the data will be more accurately retrieved, since no individual will have to make interpretive judgments as to whether the criterion was met.

Tan pointed out that various disciplines may write criteria with differing expectations. In a study she described,

> physicians tended to develop criteria for items of practice which they expected to see documented in patients' charts, [while others] fre-

> quently wrote criteria covering items which they did not expect to be documented or which they felt should be documented in the future (usually to demonstrate a need for a new form, procedure or policy).[23]

This will obviously affect the results of the study. Tan further stated that, when the disciplines participating in the audit are competitive, the committee coordinator should clarify the reasons for "wide variations in the rates of deficiencies" and "should explain to representatives of the disciplines how differing expectations can affect compliance rates."[24]

Allowance must be made in the criteria for the fact that each person progresses at his or her own rate. The highest degree of functioning obtained by one patient at discharge may be only half that obtained by another patient at discharge, yet both worked hard and met individualized goals. Kulpa found that criteria were sometimes set low and did not allow for the highest degree of patient function.[25] For example, her study in a rehabilitation setting showed that patients were discharged when they were independently capable of dressing, eating, transferring from a sitting position, and performing a minimum of one personal hygiene task with verbal or physical assistance. However, the criteria were not set to measure the number or ability of patients who were discharged as completely independent. If criteria describe the optimal discharge status rather than the probable one, they are truly patient-centered and can be used to isolate areas that need improvement.[26]

Not only is it important to determine if the criteria have been met, but also how long it took to meet them; if there were any complications; and, if so, whether they were treated and whether they could have been prevented. Therefore, more than one criterion is often needed to obtain a complete picture of a problem, yet word the criterion question to be answered in a "yes" or "no" fashion.

Kulpa found little evidence of the family response to the patient's illness. The committee involved in this study realized that no specific discipline was "directly responsible for assessing, planning or implementing action for this aspect of family involvement."[27] Most patients are intricately involved in their family system, however, and their progress or lack of it in the hospital and at home is related to their family's response and the patient's relationship with family members. Hence, criteria that specifically designate which discipline is to meet this need may be added.

Once the criteria have been written and reviewed, and responsibility for them has been assigned to specific disciplines, it is helpful to do a pilot study with a small sample to see if the data can be retrieved in an orderly and timely fashion. Questions to be asked of the data collector include

- Are the criteria understandable?
- Can the data be easily located in the chart?
- Do the questions follow a "yes" or "no" format?

A pilot study is a quick and easy way to identify and resolve any difficulties that would cause problems and delays in the actual study.

The finished, numbered criteria are placed on a data collection sheet with the responsible party noted. The sheet should have columns for marking "yes" or "no," as well as for indicating exceptions and reasons. Another column for notes is helpful, as the data collector may need to raise a question or the audit directions may require an additional remark.

## RETRIEVING THE DATA

The multidisciplinary audit committee usually works with an assistant, most often a person from the medical records department. This person meets with the committee to review the criteria and the rationale for them, as well as to learn where to look in the chart for the data needed. The assistant is also told whom to contact if any questions arise. After the assistant has pulled the charts and completed the data collection sheets provided, the multidisciplinary committee reconvenes to review the collected data and to answer any additional questions or to search for data that were difficult to find. The committee may wish to tabulate the results as a team, or it may delegate the job to one or two committee members.

In some instances, clinicians choose to retrieve their own data or simply do not have an assistant available to them. If the committee members are all reviewing charts, more problems may occur, such as "personal clinical bias, overlooking and misinterpreting recorded events, a reluctance to criticize confreres despite anonymity, and variations in stringency of judgment both between reviewers and in the same reviewers at different times."[28] This may shift the focus of a patient-centered evaluation into a peer review in which inter-rater reliability is a problem. Therefore, it is recommended that a quality assurance coordinator or a medical records assistant be used.

Data are sought in the patients' charts, which are pulled in the medical records department. After a patient has been discharged, the medical records department retains all physicians' forms and all forms approved by the medical records or chart committee. Other forms are discarded, unless hospital policy states otherwise. This can be a problem, as is well documented by Tan.[29] She reported that some nonmedical disciplines, unaware that forms must be approved in order to be retained in the patient's permanent record, had devised and were using unapproved forms to document important data. Therefore, the information sought by the committee was nowhere to be found, and there was no documented evidence that the care had been given.

As the results are tabulated, achievements and deficiencies are generally identified. This is a critical point at which the group members must work through and evaluate causes for results, all taking responsibility to help each other without pointing accusatory fingers. Because the discipline responsible for each criterion was noted, professionals in a discipline responsible for a criterion that showed variations can determine if the variations are justifiable or if they need to be analyzed further. Discussion by the whole committee may be most helpful, as perhaps other disciplines are also responsible. Perhaps the criterion was worded incorrectly, resulting in outcomes very different from those expected by team members. All must strive to deal with the data in a way that does not elicit defensive behavior.

At this point in the evaluation process, the audit can become a peer review. In some institutions, variations that cannot be clearly justified may be turned over to a hospital peer review committee. The majority of hospitals either do not have a peer review committee or do not follow this route, however. Especially in the first few multidisciplinary audits, when professional defensiveness may be just beneath the surface, it seems best to adhere to the defined purpose of the audit—patient care evaluation—unless otherwise indicated prior to data retrieval.

Results of the audit are reported to the peers of the committee members in the different departments, to the hospital or institutional quality assurance committee, and to hospital administration in accordance with institutional policy. The multidisciplinary committee recommends actions based on patterns of deficiencies found by the audit data. These recommendations may be supplemented by the department heads.

The quality assurance committee transmits the audit summary, with a brief explanatory narrative of the process and findings, to the president of the hospital. The results are reported in person, in both oral and written form. This provides an opportunity for the committee members to work more closely with administration, to take credit for the work, and to clarify any final questions. The written copy is kept on file for further reference, repeat audit, and hospital audit purposes.

As mentioned earlier, the entire multidisciplinary audit committee is responsible for follow-up on deficiencies, unless responsibility for various follow-up proceedings has been delegated. The follow-up is an integral part of the audit, and time for it should have been allotted in the initial time schedule. Although it is difficult to budget time for follow-up at that point, i.e., when the audit results are unknown, it is reasonable to allot several hours for presentations of results and discussion for improvement, continuing education, or for reaudit.

## CRITIQUING THE PROCESS

Certain results are commonly found in multidisciplinary evaluations. For example, a frequently cited result is the need for improved documentation of practice. The patients and their families may be receiving care and services, but unless such care and services are documented, there is no way a retrospective audit can be used to credit care given or to discover deficiencies.

There is often a need to limit the number of criteria.[30,31] Tan wrote after her experience with a multidisciplinary group auditing six professional groups that optimally each discipline sets only two or three criteria. Although this is limiting, the most significant criteria are included, which makes the audit process a more time-effective evaluation.

Study results indicate where procedure or policy changes are needed and whether professional "performance or care on a patient unit needs to be reviewed or evaluated."[32] They are clear and specific indicators of priority needs for in-service and continuing education programs. Research committees may gain insight into possible areas of study based on both deficiencies and achievements.

One advantage of a multidisciplinary audit is that the patient and the patient's family are truly the center of concern. These audits are more effective than single discipline audits, according to Eddy and Westbrook, because they focus on total patient care.[33] Performance of care given is reviewed in several disciplines, from one set of charts, and without duplication of criteria. Because a multidisciplinary committee works together closely, communication improves among disciplines. Also, as each audit is done, more effective methods are discovered for future audits of this kind.

There are also disadvantages to multidisciplinary evaluations. Some are the disadvantages of any type of retrospective audit; others are more specific to multidisciplinary audit. For example, it may take longer to develop relationships and establish communication among members of different disciplines. There may be personal clinical biases that cause committee members to overlook and misinterpret recorded events. Inherent in this may be a reluctance to criticize peers, despite anonymity, as well as poor inter-rater reliability. The entire committee, as well as the entire department, becomes aware of deficiencies in a discipline. In a multidisciplinary audit, however, this awareness can be advantageous; although one, two, or three persons from different disciplines are responsible for follow-up, they work together. Changes or improvements in care given by those in one discipline affect not only the patient and/or the patient's family, but also the care given by other professionals in that health care system.

Two nationwide studies raise many questions about the cost-effectiveness of audit activity, as well as its impact on patient care and outcomes. Both cite a need for improved methodologies to evaluate health care.[34,35] With these issues in mind, Tan advised caution; she recommended limiting studies to a manageable size, using published or experienced knowledge of identified problems, and modifying the approach to multidisciplinary audits as new techniques are found.[36]

## NOTES

1. Maureen Knudson, "Teamwork: The Crux of Multidisciplinary Audit," *Quality Review Bulletin* 2, no. 12 (December 1976): 22.

2. Ibid.

3. Maria C. Phaneuf and Mabel A. Wandelt, "Obstacles to and Potentials for Nursing Quality Appraisal," *Quality Review Bulletin* 7, no. 4 (April 1981): 3.

4. Heiner Sell and W. Zacharius Goldstein, "Evolution, Not Revolution," *Quality Review Bulletin* 4, no. 11 (November 1978): 31.

5. Joan H. Carter and Jeanne Sweeney, "Patient Focus in Multidisciplinary Review," *Quality Review Bulletin* 2, no. 12 (December 1976): 21.

6. Ibid.

7. American Nurses' Association, *A Plan for Implementation of the Standards of Nursing Practice* (Kansas City, MO: American Nurses' Association, 1975), p. 11.

8. Knudson, "Teamwork: The Crux of Multidisciplinary Audit," p. 23.

9. Lyndall Eddy and Linda Westbrook, "Multidisciplinary Retrospective Patient Care Audit," *American Journal of Nursing* 75, no. 6 (June 1975): 962.

10. "HPR Roundup: Multidisciplinary Audit," *Hospital Peer Review* 3, no. 1 (January 1978): 6.

11. Marva West Tan, "Problem Areas in Multidisciplinary Audit," *Quality Review Bulletin* 4, no. 11 (November 1978): 33.

12. Ibid, p. 34.

13. Arlene Johnson, "Communication as the Key to Effective Joint Practice Audit," *Quality Review Bulletin* 2, no. 12 (December 1976): 7.

14. Ibid, p. 6.

15. Julie Hover and Marie Zimmer, "Nursing Quality Assurance: The Wisconsin System," *Nursing Outlook* 26, April 1978, p. 248.

16. Johnson, "Communication as the Key to Effective Joint Practice Audit," p. 7.

17. Marjory Gordon, "Determining Study Topics," *Nursing Research* 29, no. 2 (March/April 1980): 86.

18. Knudson, "Teamwork: The Crux of Multidisciplinary Audit," p. 22.

19. Phaneuf and Wandelt, "Obstacles to and Potentials for Nursing Quality Appraisal," p. 3.

20. Knudson, "Teamwork: The Crux of Multidisciplinary Audit," p. 22.

21. "HPR Roundup: Multidisciplinary Audit," p. 7.

22. Knudson, "Teamwork: The Crux of Multidisciplinary Audit," p. 24.

23. Tan, "Problem Areas in Multidisciplinary Audit," p. 34.

24. Ibid.

25. Judith Kulpa, "Interdisciplinary Review in Long Term Care," *Quality Review Bulletin* 4, no. 11 (November 1978): 20.

26. Knudson, "Teamwork: The Crux of Multidisciplinary Audit," p. 24.

27. Kulpa, "Interdisciplinary Review in Long Term Care," p. 20.

28. Eddy and Westbrook, "Multidisciplinary Retrospective Patient Care Audit," p. 961.

29. Tan, "Problem Areas in Multidisciplinary Audit," p. 35.

30. Ibid.

31. Eddy and Westbrook, "Multidisciplinary Retrospective Patient Care Audit," p. 962.

32. Ibid, p. 963.

33. Ibid.

34. Institute of Medicine, *Assessing Quality in Health Care: An Evaluation* (Washington: National Academy of Sciences, 1976).

35. National League for Nursing, Department of Baccalaureate and Higher Degree Programs, *Quality Assurance—A Joint Venture* (New York: National League for Nursing, 1975).

36. Tan, "Problem Areas in Multidisciplinary Audit," p. 35.

## REFERENCES

### Books

American Nurses' Association. *A Plan for Implementation of the Standards of Nursing Practice.* Kansas City, MO: American Nurses' Association, 1975.

Benedicter, Helen. *From Nursing Audit to Multidisciplinary Audit.* New York: National League for Nursing, 1977.

Institute of Medicine. *Assessing Quality in Health Care: An Evaluation.* Washington: National Academy of Sciences, 1976.

National League for Nursing, Department of Baccalaureate and Higher Degree Programs. *Quality Assurance—A Joint Venture.* New York: National League for Nursing, 1975.

*Nursing Quality Assurance Management/Learning System.* Kansas City, MO: American Nurses' Association and Sutherland Learning Associates, 1982.

Office of Planning, Evaluation and Legislation. *PSRO: An Initial Evaluation of the Professional Standards Review Organization.* Washington, D.C.: U.S. Department of Health, Education and Welfare, Health Services Administration, 1977.

### Journals

Carter, Joan H., and Sweeney, Jeanne. "Patient Focus in Multidisciplinary Review." *Quality Review Bulletin* 2 (1976): 21.

Donabedian, Avedis. "Some Issues in Evaluating the Quality of Nursing Care: Part II." *American Journal of Public Health* 59 (1969): 1833–1836.

Eddy, Lyndall, and Westbrook, Linda. "Multidisciplinary Retrospective Patient Care Audit." *American Journal of Nursing* 75 (1975): 961–963.

Garcia, Dianne; Gaines, Mary; and Lowe, Wayne. "Hospital Devises Department to Expedite Patient Care Review." *Hospitals* 51 (1977): 67–69.

Gordon, Marjory. "Determining Study Topics." *Nursing Reseach* 29 (1980): 83–87.

Hover, Julie, and Zimmer, Marie. "Nursing Quality Assurance: The Wisconsin System." *Nursing Outlook* 26, April 1978, pp. 242–248.

"HPR Roundup: Multidisciplinary Audit." *Hospital Peer Review* 3 (1978): 5–7.

Johnson, Arlene. "Communication as the Key to Effective Joint Practice Audit." *Quality Review Bulletin* 2 (1976): 6–8.

Kahn, Kenneth; Hines, William; Woodson, Arlene; and Burkham-Armstrong, Gabrielle. "A Multidisciplinary Approach to Assessing the Quality of Care in Long Term Care Facilities." *The Gerontologist* 17 (1977): 61–65.

Knudson, Maureen. "Teamwork: The Crux of Multidisciplinary Audit." *Quality Review Bulletin* 2 (1976): 22–23.

Kulpa, Judith. "Interdisciplinary Review in Long Term Care." *Quality Review Bulletin* 4 (1978): 15–21.

Mohr, Barbara. "The Action Step in Combined Medical-Nursing Audits." *Quality Review Bulletin* 3 (1977): 3.

"Multidisciplinary Audit." *Quality Review Bulletin* (Special Edition). Chicago: Joint Commission on Accreditation of Hospitals, 1978.

Phaneuf, Maria C., and Wandelt, Mabel A. "Obstacles to and Potentials for Nursing Quality Appraisal." *Quality Review Bulletin* 7 (1981): 2–5.

Ruff, Youna. "Balking at Multidisciplinary Audits." *Hospital Peer Review* 3 (1978): 37.

Sandrick, Karen. "The Whole Is Not Equal to the Sum of Its Parts." *Quality Review Bulletin* 2 (1976): 9–18.

Sell, Heiner, and Goldstein, W. Zacharius. "Evolution, Not Revolution." *Quality Review Bulletin* 4 (1978): 31–32.

Tan, Marva West. "Problem Areas in Multidisciplinary Audit." *Quality Review Bulletin* 4 (1978): 33–35.

Waters, Gloria. "Determining Criteria Responsibility." *Hospital Peer Review* 3 (1978): 51.

Chapter 13

# Program Evaluation: Theory, Method, and Practice

*Cathleen K. Wilson, M.S.N., R.N.*

The evaluation of the quality of nursing care is an essential ingredient in the provision of professional nursing services. Recent trends in health care require, however, that nurses expand their evaluation expertise to include the evaluation of health care programs. These trends include (a) the shift from the traditional illness-centered health care to wellness-centered programs, (b) increasing federal government restraints on reimbursable health care costs, (c) continuing public demands for the accountability of health care professionals, and (d) skyrocketing health care costs.

Health care programs are being carefully scrutinized by consumers, third party payers, and hospital administrators. Does the program influence patients in the way intended? Do patients require *all* the various treatments included in the health care program in order to reach the required health status? Is there a less expensive, but equally effective health care program? What level of professional preparation is required for health care workers providing services? Such questions can be answered only through the systematic development and evaluation of health care programs.

New programs are prompted by technological changes with concomitant changes in practice and by demands for cost containment. Today's nurse-managers are increasingly involved in the development of more efficient and less expensive health care programs. If such programs are to result in quality health care, a systematic process of program development must be used. A nursing quality assurance program can provide feedback to be used by clinicians and decision makers in improving patient care and hospital services to patients. Therefore, nurse-managers require a working knowledge of program evaluation.

## DEFINITION OF EVALUATION

Evaluation has been defined as a process of delineating and providing useful information for decision making, as a systematic process of data collection and analysis, or as a research process in which a social science methodology is used to assess programs in order to obtain useful feedback for decision making (including cost-benefit decisions).[1-3] The terms *evaluation, evaluation research, assessment,* and *nursing research* have been used interchangeably in the nursing literature, creating considerable confusion. In order to develop useful evaluations, it is necessary to differentiate between research and evaluation.

Research methodology is a compilation of many nursing research strategies that have been tested and accepted by nurse-scientists. Each method is based on a set of assumptions. For example, the experimental research method is based on the assumption that the nurse-researcher is able to manipulate the independent or treatment variable being studied. Research methodology can be incorporated into an evaluation study at any point in time; furthermore, its inclusion facilitates the systematic collection of reliable data.

## Evaluation versus Research

Evaluation differs from research in several ways (Table 13–1). First, the goal of the evaluation process is very different; evaluation data are collected for the purpose of making a decision about nursing practice.[4] Evaluation may be initiated by nurses who are providing direct patient care or by managers of health care programs. For example, the head nurse of a psychiatric unit who suspects that the

**Table 13–1** A Comparison of Evaluation and Research

| | *Evaluation* | *Research* |
|---|---|---|
| Purpose | To make a DECISION about nursing standards or nursing practice | To study a hypothesis of the RELATIONSHIP between two or more variables |
| Measurement | Sometimes | Always |
| Values | Value-laden, determines the value or worth of goods and services provided | Strives to be free of bias |
| Applicability | Usually, only to the system or organization doing the evaluation | Ideally, highly generalizable |
| Example | Is this treatment program worth what it costs to provide the service? | Is there a difference in the health care outcomes of patients in a diabetes outpatient program and those who are not? |
| | Are all psychiatric patients receiving family counseling in accordance with nursing care standards in psychiatric nursing? | Do patients who receive family therapy have fewer hospitalizations than those who do not? |

patient population is different from what it was when a treatment program was developed may initiate an evaluation of the treatment program to determine if program goals should be changed in accordance with the change in patients.

Research methods may or may not be used to collect data. They can be expensive and time-consuming, and the availability of time and resources may determine their use. In addition, the importance and expense of the decision that must be made affect whether research methodology is included in an evaluation study.

Nursing research methodology is used to collect and analyze data for the purpose of studying a hypothesized relationship between two or more variables. A nursing research question begins with a nurse's observation. For example, a head nurse may notice a decrease in incident reports after the institution of patient care planning meetings. A staff nurse may notice that some patients verbalize less pain when they are touched. Data collected through the systematic study of these variables will advance nursing science, but may or may not lead to a decision.

Evaluation is also value-laden.[5] The evaluator makes a decision about the worth of patient services. Research has a value base in terms of the selection of variables to study or the choice of a conceptual framework, but the nurse-researcher strives to avoid value-laden terms in order to eliminate any experimental bias.

Finally, evaluation data are generally useful only to the organization that conducted the evaluation.[6] No attempt is made to equate the processes studied with those of other hospital units or other patient groups. The nurse-researcher hopes that the data are generalizable to other organizations or patient groups, however, so that the empirically tested principles can be integrated into nursing practice.

## Continuum of Scientific Rigor

Bloch and Lindeman offered further insights into the conceptualization of evaluation and research. Bloch described evaluation and research on a continuum of scientific rigor (Figure 13–1). Rather than thinking in terms of the presence or absence of scientific rigor, she suggested thinking in terms of degrees of rigor.[7]

In an address to a national group of nurse-researchers, Carol Lindeman described research as a concept with many operational definitions.[8] (An operational definition identifies the strategies required to collect data about the concept.) A nursing concept, such as the concept of anxiety, has not only a specific conceptual definition based on theory, but also operational definitions to be used in the research process. In regard to the concept of anxiety, operational definitions, i.e., data collection strategies, could be interviews, physiological changes in the patient, verbal expressions, or psychological tests. Lindeman applied this model to the concept of research. Theory defines research as a scientific process of describing, analyzing, and explaining relationships; data collection strategies

**Figure 13–1** Continuum of Scientific Rigor

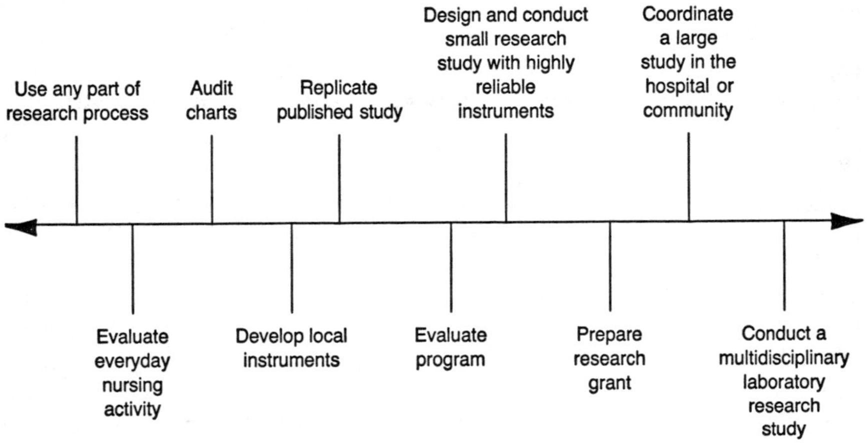


could be the chart audit, a program evaluation method, or a rigorous scientific experiment. Therefore, there is no "best" method of research, but a variety of strategies that can be followed to obtain the needed information. Factors such as the purpose of the research, the nature of the problem, the time frame, and the cost involved must be considered when the appropriate research strategy is selected.

## PROGRAM EVALUATION AND QUALITY ASSURANCE

In terms of level and scope, there are distinct differences between program evaluation and quality assurance. The level of a program evaluation can vary from the complex organizational assessment of many variables to an in-depth evaluation of one health care program within the larger organization. Variables that may be assessed include resource allocation, recruitment of clients, and professional competence.[9] An in-depth evaluation of a particular health care program could be focused on the study of its various components. Quality assurance, on the other hand, is usually concerned with the interactions between patient and nurse.[10] Thus, quality assurance is concerned with only one part of the total program evaluation—the direct nursing care given to patients. In most cases, program evaluation is more system-focused and, consequently, more time-consuming and costly than quality assurance.

Sometimes nursing quality assurance studies can lead to program evaluation. For example, corrective action taken to resolve problems identified in quality assurance studies can lead to the identification of problems in the larger system.

This may result in the evaluation of the organization in its entirety or of a large subunit of the organization, such as the nursing department or the radiology department.

In the systems model of health care, patient care can be considered more than the one-to-one relationship between patient and nurse. Hospital nursing is provided in a complex, interdependent hospital structure that is capable of problem solving, self-regulation, restructuring without a loss of continuity, and adaptation to change.[11] Therefore, program evaluation must be an integral part of any quality assurance program. Figure 13–2 shows the relationship of quality assessment to program evaluation.

## METHODOLOGY OF PROGRAM EVALUATION

Program evaluation in health care has evolved from the social and behavioral sciences as demands for accountability in health, social, and educational programs have increased. Several highly respected educators have developed program evaluation models that can be easily applied to nursing health care programs.

**Figure 13–2** Levels of Evaluation in the Assessment of Quality Care

## CIPP Model

Stuffelbeam developed one of the most comprehensive models of program evaluation, called CIPP for the various stages in the evaluation process: context, input, process, product. The basic assumptions of this model include the following:

- Evaluation is a process of delineating, obtaining, and providing *useful* information for judging decision alternatives.
- Evaluation occurs on a continuum.
- There are four classes of decisions found in evaluation: planning or choosing objectives, structuring or designing projects to achieve objectives, implementing the project design, and recycling decisions.[12]

The evaluation occurs as a program is being developed or changed.

### *Context Evaluation*

In program evaluation, the nurse-manager must examine the context in which decisions must be made, i.e., the health care program. For example, the head nurse of an orthopedic unit may want to develop an intervention program for spinal cord–injured patients and their families. In order to choose the appropriate objectives, the nurse-manager must identify patients' unmet needs and examine the current health program for unused opportunities that might be developed without additional resource or expense. Such information can be collected in a variety of ways. For example, interview guides for use with spinal cord–injured patients and their families can be developed, and orthopedic clinical specialists, nurse-administrators, and physicians can be consulted for their analysis of the needs for intervention programs for these patients.

The head nurse and others then develop objectives for the program that are designed to reduce the difference between the actual intervention that spinal cord–injured patients receive and that which is desired. For each general program objective, a patient outcome objective is developed. A variety of methods, such as questionnaires, interviews, or systematic needs assessment can be used to collect these data. Exhibit 13–1 is an example of a needs assessment form that might be used to collect information about the needs of spinal cord–injured patients.

### *Input Evaluation*

Structure decisions are made during the input evaluation. Information collected by the head nurse during this stage helps to clarify the various strategies for achieving objectives. The nurse-manager addresses questions such as whether the

**Exhibit 13–1** Example of a Needs Assessment

We would like to respond to a list of problems and needs that patients with spinal cord injuries may or may not have so we can improve our current program. Please respond to the needs described below, and write each item according to both frequency and seriousness.

| NEED | FREQUENCY | | | SERIOUSNESS | | |
|---|---|---|---|---|---|---|
| | Seldom | Often | Quite Often | Not Serious | Serious | Very Serious |
| 1. Knowledge of community resources once discharged. | | | | | | |
| 2. Having a nurse or another person to talk to just about my injury. | | | | | | |
| 3. Being able to share my questions and concerns with other patients experiencing the same problems. | | | | | | |
| 4. Having resources for my family to help them cope with my injury. | | | | | | |

*Source:* Adapted from *Research Handbook for Community Planning and Feedback Instruments*, Vol. 1, rev., prepared for Office of Youth Development, Department of Health, Education and Welfare, Behavioral Research Institute, Boulder, Colorado, 1976.

resources are currently available. For example, what does a slide program cost, compared with the cost of an educational booklet in a class? Are small group sessions as costly as individual sessions? Which is the least costly of all the strategies that meet program objectives?

The nurse-manager also consults administrators about personnel resources. Which departments within the hospital are most likely to provide personnel to implement the program? Are new positions required to implement the objectives? In this cost containment era, the nurse-manager may also collect information about which strategies are reimbursable. If there is to be a charge for an educational class, will the fee be reimbursable by private insurance companies and Medicare or Medicaid?

At the end of this stage of program evaluation, the nurse-manager has collected information regarding the effectiveness and costs of a wide variety of strategies to implement the program objectives. This information is the basis on which the appropriate strategies are selected.

The next step is to identify program components and target dates for implementation. The plan for the intervention program for spinal cord–injured patients mentioned earlier is shown in Exhibit 13–2.

*Process Evaluation*

Once the patient education program has been implemented, it must be carefully observed. Data may be collected on the number of patients attending the program; the number of program components each patient attends; patient, family, and nurse satisfaction with the program; identification of physicians who refer patients to the program; and the amount of time personnel spend in providing the program. In addition, each program objective should have specific patient outcomes that can be evaluated. For example, the program for spinal cord–injured patients has a general objective, such as patients' families are involved in the intervention program, and a behavioral outcome for that general objective, such as all families of patients admitted to the orthopedic unit are seen by the psychologist or the clinical nurse specialist within the first seventy-two hours. The nurse-manager implementing the process stage of evaluation determines if these objectives are being met by checking whether the family consultation occurs within seventy-two hours.

Data are collected regularly and used to revise the program as it is being implemented. Perhaps, with the number of admissions and the workload of the clinical nurse specialist or psychologist, seventy-two hours is not a realistic time frame. Data collected at this stage can also be used at the end of the evaluation to explain the reasons that certain objectives were met or not met.

**Exhibit 13–2** Patient Intervention Program for Spinal Cord–Injured Patients

**Program Components**

1. Initial visit by surgical clinical specialist and introduction to group classes
2. Group classes focusing on adjustment, self-care, and community resources conducted in collaboration with the social work department
3. Family education evening for family members of spinal cord–injured patient conducted in collaboration with social work and psychology departments
4. Patient evaluation of the program the day before discharge
5. Follow-up interview one month postdischarge by surgical clinical specialist

**Target Dates**

The program will be implemented for three months and reevaluated continually throughout the pilot study. Data will be collected on patient satisfaction, self-care, patient anxiety, and family satisfaction. Revisions will be made, and the full program should be implemented six months from the date of the pilot. Evaluation will then occur annually.

*Product Evaluation*

The basic program evaluation occurs during the product evaluation. All the information compiled thus far by the nurse-manager is combined. The major question addressed at this point concerns whether the program meets the objectives and why.

## Scriven's Formative versus Summative Model

Scriven's model is useful to the head nurse in deciding at what *point* to begin a program evaluation. This model is based on the following assumptions:

1. There are various roles which evaluators assume depending on the nature of the program being evaluated.
2. Evaluation is simply an assessment of merit.
3. Evaluators must assess the quality of the goals as well as the degree to which the goals are achieved.
4. Evaluations can be conceptualized in two ways: formative and summative evaluation.[13]

Formative evaluation is built into program development. Based on information collected during this kind of evaluation, the processes used to attain the program objectives are modified; for example, program components may be added or deleted. The CIPP model described previously is an example of a formative evaluation. Discrepancies between program goals and patient objectives are carefully analyzed throughout the development of the program. Summative evaluation is initiated by the nurse at the end of a time-defined program. For example, the head nurse of a psychiatric nursing unit has a patient treatment program that recycles itself every eight weeks. At the end of each eight-week cycle, the nurse analyzes discrepancies between program objectives and patient outcomes. Thus, formative evaluation is a process-oriented approach, while summative evaluation is an outcome-oriented strategy.

Scriven's model emphasizes a third approach to evaluation that is designed to eliminate bias. Most professionals are truly committed to the model of practice that they use in their own professional work, and it is sometimes quite difficult for them to evaluate programs objectively. Psychiatric nursing staff, for example, may believe that group therapy is an essential treatment modality for every kind of psychiatric patient; nurses may believe that primary nursing is the only delivery system appropriate for the organization of nursing work. Scriven suggested a goal-free evaluation in which an outsider is asked to evaluate the program's effectiveness without being informed of the goals.[14] Such an evaluator can more readily identify an unanticipated outcome. Furthermore, the amount of evaluator bias would certainly be minimized. This approach might be particularly useful in the evaluation of a highly controversial program.

## EVALUATION OF QUALITY ASSURANCE PROGRAMS

The steps in the evaluation of a nursing quality assurance program closely resemble those of the quality assurance process (see Chapter 5).

### Step 1: State a Purpose

The first step in any evaluation study is to determine its purpose, since the purpose guides the selection of an evaluation method. The time, resources, and evaluation expertise required must be considered. If patients on a particular unit are at risk, problems must be identified and resolved more rapidly than if a major quality assurance program revision is being considered by the nursing department. A longer time period allows for the utilization of consultants in order to develop more in-depth evaluation plans.

The purpose of an evaluation study not only guides the selection of a plan, but also clearly identifies how the data collected will be used in making decisions. The purpose should be stated as clear and concise objectives.

### Step 2: Decide What Is to Be Evaluated

The nurse must use scientifically based knowledge in selecting the evaluation topic. As previously mentioned, the evaluation process can occur at multiple levels (see Figure 13–2), and the variables to be studied change considerably with the level of program evaluation. Not only do the variables change, but also the relationships between the variables change. Table 13–2 shows the differences between the study variables of a quality assurance program at the nurse-patient level and those at a hospitalwide, organizational level.

If the decision has been made to evaluate the quality assurance program at the nurse-patient level, an obvious study variable is the number of quality assurance studies done by the nursing units themselves. These studies might be critically examined with the following questions in mind:

- Are identifiable standards of practice used as guidelines to determine appropriate outcome criteria?
- Are true nursing practice problems being addressed in the problems chosen for study?
- Do the problems reflect an identifiable structure, nursing process, or outcome variable?
- Are appropriate corrective actions being implemented in a reasonable time frame?
- Do quality assurance studies result in identifiable improvement in the quality of nursing care for an identified patient population?

**Table 13–2** Sample of Organizational Variables versus Nurse-Patient Variables

| *Organizational Variables* | *Nurse-Patient Variables* |
|---|---|
| Program objectives | Study objectives |
| Organizational structure (decentralized versus centralized) | Standards of practice |
| - Unit groups | Problem focus (i.e., structure, process, or outcome) |
| Clinical Nurse Specialists facilitators | Corrective actions (e.g., time taken to correct) |
| - Quality Assurance Coordinating Committee | Number and scope of unit-based studies |
| Reporting relationships | Methodologies presently used |
| - Head nurse | Number of studies per nursing unit |
| - Director | |
| - Vice President of Patient Services | |
| - Hospital board | |
| - Hospital administration | |
| Administrative representation | |
| Integration into hospitalwide quality assurance | |
| Relationship with Medical Evaluation Committee | |
| Relationship to hospitalwide quality assurance objectives | |
| Quality assurance resources | |

- Does the methodology (plan) generate the information needed to make changes in nursing practice?

The evaluator may also be interested in examining the nursing quality assurance program at the level of the nursing organization. The questions of interest at this level include the following:

- Is there a difference between what the quality assurance program is meant to accomplish (as described by the objectives) and what is happening in reality?
- What is the organizational structure of the quality assurance program? Is it decentralized like the unit-based model, or is it a central committee? Does the structure support the objectives of the program?

- What are the roles and responsibilities of individuals at various levels of the organization? In relationship to the quality assurance program, do the reporting relationships facilitate or inhibit the quality assurance objectives? What quality assurance expertise is required at what level?
- Are study findings being integrated into management, planning, and educational development?
- How does the nursing quality assurance program relate to the hospitalwide quality assurance program?

### Step 3: Establish Standards or Criteria of Acceptability

Beyond the basic requirements of the Joint Commission on the Accreditation of Hospitals, institutions may have standards regarding the number and type of quality assurance studies conducted each year or standards regarding management's involvement in quality assurance work. Such standards then become the basis of the quality assurance program evaluation.

### Step 4: Select a Plan

There are many models of evaluation. Formative or summative methods may be appropriate, depending on the purpose of the evaluation. A research design may be appropriate. Regardless, it is important that the evaluator select a plan that will provide the kind of data required for the decision-making process.

### Step 5: Adapt and Design the Evaluation Instrumentation

In the St. Michael Hospital study, the variables of study include

- the effectiveness of the unit-based quality assurance studies, including instruments and problem types
- nursing staff knowledge base regarding the nursing quality assurance process
- the relationship of risk management to quality assurance

Questionnaires, interview guides, and checklists have been developed for each question.

### Step 6: Implement an Evaluation Plan

Different models of evaluation suggest different strategies for implementation. In a unit-based quality assurance model, a summative evaluation of the quality assurance program can be conducted at the nurse-patient level. The goal of the evaluation is to measure program accomplishment based on the quality assurance program objectives. For example, one objective of the quality assurance program at St. Michael Hospital is as follows: To serve as a basis for the planning of essential staff development offerings. An evaluation plan may include examining the staff development offerings during a specified time period along with all nursing quality assurance studies done during the same time period to identify any clear relationships between these events.

### Step 7: Implement Plan on a Pilot Basis

After the nursing staff have been informed of the program evaluation objectives and strategies, data can be collected on a pilot unit. This step helps to prevent later errors or misidentification of problems because of faulty instruments. Confusion regarding the questions, potential missing information, and biases in the instruments can be easily identified. Also, the time required for administering the instruments can be examined from a cost-effective perspective.

### Step 8: Implement the Revised Evaluation Plan

The time and resources available, as well as the urgency of problem solution, determine the number of nursing quality assurance groups or quality assurance studies from which data are collected.

### Step 9: Analyze the Data

Data are analyzed and compiled in a way that explains how the quality assurance program is meeting its objectives. A common misperception is that data must be quantifiable and subject to statistical analysis to have true meaning. In program evaluation, data are likely to be qualitative in nature, such as descriptions of knowledge deficits and analyses of interview content. More complex statistical analysis may be indicated, however, if a research design has been chosen as an evaluation strategy.

### Step 10: Decide When and How to Alter the Program

Decisions about future program modification and or development are based on the evaluation conclusions. These conclusions should be summarized and displayed in preparation for the decision-making sessions. Recommendations for planned change should be included in the presentation.

It is important to consider carefully to whom the final evaluation report should be presented and how to present the data. Written reports or formal verbal presentations to a group of decision makers are common methods for sharing evaluation results. At this point, an organizational decision regarding the future and the direction of the quality assurance program can be made.[15]

### Step 11: Develop a Plan to Disseminate Program Changes beyond the Decision-Making Group

The evaluators must develop a plan for sharing changes in the quality assurance program and the rationale for them. In a unit-based quality assurance system, it is critical that all nurses understand and support the direction of the program. Quality assurance committee members may need help in identifying methods of meeting the new program objectives. If the actual organization of the quality assurance program changes, those most directly affected by the change may resist the change effort. Any plan for dissemination of changes must address these and other potential blocks to the change process.[16]

It may be concluded that the rigor of the quality assurance program evaluation should be increased. Plans should be made for educational research to develop nursing staff skills to meet this new objective. In addition, the dissemination plan should address any resistance to learning new researcher evaluation skills.

Clearly, the evaluation of a quality assurance program requires careful thought and planning. Such a program continues to evolve through annual evaluation and subsequent program changes. This process can only improve patient care and quality nursing practice.

## CONCLUSION

As members of the nursing profession, nurses must address current social concerns about the development, organization, and delivery of health care services. Clearly, the complexity of the patient care system requires that nurses develop a wide repertoire of evaluation strategies.

Much of the focus of nursing quality assurance work has been upon evaluating the outcomes of nursing care. Obviously this work is serious and needs to continue in all health care settings. However, nurses are increasingly practicing in multidisciplinary health care systems that require multiple evaluation strategies in order to assure quality care. Methodologies need to be developed for evaluating each component, and the interrelationship of the component.

Nurse-managers can gain access to this wide spectrum of evaluation strategies in a number of ways. First of all, evaluation resources can be developed within the hospital organization by increasing the number of personnel prepared in nursing research, providing monies for education and consultations, and building a library of publications related to evaluation. Nurse-managers can also encourage the dissemination of information among nursing units. Instruments developed by the various nursing units to study nursing problems can be kept in a central collection so that all the nursing units would have access to them. If there is a university nearby, it may be possible to consult nurse-scientists who can provide expertise in more involved evaluation projects. Also, a contract with the university could provide access to more intensive research resources, such as data analysis and computer time.

It is up to the practicing nurse to apply the models borrowed from psychology and education. Without this process, such models will remain outside the realm of nursing practice. As the process of theory application continues, nursing evaluation models will begin to emerge in nursing practice. Although advances have been made in the last decade, nurses must continue to wrestle with evaluation as patient care grows increasingly complex. Developing a wide repertoire of skill in the area of evaluation is a major step in the evaluation process.

**NOTES**

1. W. James Popham, *Educational Evaluation* (Englewood Cliffs, NJ: Prentice-Hall, 1975), p. 34.
2. L. R. Gay, *Educational Evaluation and Measurement* (Columbus, OH: Charles E. Merrill, 1980), p. 6.
3. Janelle C. Krueger, "Establishing Priorities for Evaluation and Research: A Nursing Perspective," *Nursing Research* 29, no. 2 (March-April 1980): 115.
4. Popham, *Educational Evaluation*, p. 34.
5. Walter Borg and Meredith Gall, *Educational Research*, 3rd ed. (New York: Longman Publishing, 1979), p. 601.
6. Ibid.
7. Doris Bloch, "Interrelated Issues in Evaluation and Evaluation Research: A Researcher's Perspective," *Nursing Research* 29, no. 2 (March-April 1980): 69.
8. Carol Lindeman, "Nursing Research for the Advancement of Nursing Practice." Paper presented at Nursing Research, Advancing Clinical Practice for the 80's: A National Symposium, San Francisco, November 18–20, 1982.
9. Avedis Donabedian, *The Definition of Quality and Approaches to Its Assessment* (Ann Arbor, MI: Health Administration Press, 1980), p. 21.
10. Krueger, "Establishing Priorities for Evaluation and Evaluation Research: A Nursing Perspective," p. 115.
11. Basil S. Georgopoulous and F. Mann, *The Community General Hospital* (New York: Macmillan Company, 1962), p. 15.
12. Popham, *Educational Evaluation*, p. 34.
13. Ibid, p. 26.
14. Ibid, p. 27.
15. Joanne Horseley and Joyce Crane, *Using Research to Improve Nursing Practice: A Guide* (New York: Grune & Stratton, 1983), p. 9.
16. Ibid.

## REFERENCES

### Books

Borg, Walter, and Gall, Meredith. *Educational Research,* 3rd ed. New York: Longman Publishing, 1979.

Donabedian, Avedis. *The Definition of Quality and Approaches to Its Assessment.* Ann Arbor, MI: Health Administration Press, 1980.

Gay, L. R. *Educational Evaluation and Measurement.* Columbus, OH: Charles E. Merrill, 1980.

Georgopoulous, Basil S., and Mann, Floyd C. *The Community General Hospital.* New York: Macmillan Company, 1962.

Horseley, Joanne, and Crane, Joyce. *Using Research to Improve Nursing Practice: A Guide.* New York: Grune & Stratton, 1983.

Popham, W. James. *Educational Evaluation.* Englewood Cliffs, NJ: Prentice-Hall, 1975.

### Journals

Bloch, Doris. ''Interrelated Issues in Evaluation and Evaluation Research: A Researcher's Perspective.'' *Nursing Research* 29 (1980): 69–73.

Krueger, Janelle C. ''Establishing Priorities for Evaluation and Research: A Nursing Perspective.'' *Nursing Research* 29 (1980): 115–119.

### Unpublished Works

Lindeman, Carol. ''Nursing Research for the Advancement of Nursing Practice.'' Paper presented at Nursing Research, Advancing Clinical Practice for the 80's: A National Symposium, San Francisco, November 18–20, 1982.

## Chapter 14

# Trends in Quality Assurance: A Vision for the Future

*Patricia S. Schroeder, M.S.N., R.N.*

The world of professional nursing has seen a tremendous evolution in the meaning and the use of quality assurance, and changes continue to occur. Despite the evolution of the concept, however, the process of quality assurance may not have progressed in many hospitals. Nurses may find that their periodic record audit has been the only mechanism to review quality of care over the past ten years. This is very unfortunate, because there is such a long way to go to meet the needs of the present and the challenge of the future.

Several significant trends in nursing and health care affect quality assurance. Some of these trends are happening within the nursing profession; others, outside it. Either way, they must be monitored and occasionally adapted in an effort to maintain and promote care.

### EVOLUTION OF STANDARDS AND CRITERIA

An early step in any quality assurance process model is the identification of standards and criteria. All too often, however, those conducting quality assurance have focused on evaluation and have failed to give sufficient attention to the steps that precede it. It is not unusual for standards and criteria to be developed strictly for the purpose of an audit; in this case, it is not surprising that results often demonstrate deficiency in meeting the standards.

Nursing is at the brink of a "standards explosion." Although various groups have developed standards and criteria in the past, it is now being considered an issue critical to practice. Nurses are finding that, as professionals, they are obliged first to identify standards and then to achieve and evaluate them. Nursing organizations, such as the American Nurses' Association, are continuing to promote and refine their standards. Nurses are beginning to address the ways in which these standards can be incorporated into practice and individualized to reflect given patient populations. Agencies are likewise beginning to assess whether they have sufficient standards for practice and whether those they do have are assessible, pertinent to practice, and appropriately formatted.

Historically, standards and criteria were identified by groups of practicing nurses sitting around a table and brainstorming. This method is no longer sufficient for so important a task. Nursing is becoming increasingly scientific, and the basis for practice cannot be unsystematically identified. Research is necessary for developing standards and criteria, and the process itself is necessary for testing and validating them.

One approach to validating outcome criteria was described by Gallant and McLane.[1] Their study, based on the American Nurses' Association's model for quality assurance[2] and Orem's concept of self-care,[3] involved the use of two instruments that were based on accepted outcome criteria for a given client population. Patients were asked to identify outcomes they achieved on a patient self-rating sheet. These same outcomes were listed on the outcome achievement rating sheet, which was completed by the patient's primary nurse. A comparison was made between those outcomes the patient thought he or she had achieved, and those that the nurse felt he or she had achieved. It was concluded that only five of the ten outcomes were valid. This conclusion was based on feedback related to whether the criteria were measurable, whether they were actually outcomes or processes, whether they reflected the domain of nursing, and the patient and nurse's responses to the achievement of these outcomes. Gallant and McLane felt that, because this process was not complex or time-consuming, it could be used by nurses to test any set of outcome criteria. The trend toward testing of standards and criteria is very important, because practice that demonstrates quality nursing care will be more easily identified.

In the past, many standards have been developed in which medical diagnoses are used as a classification scheme. The progressive refinement of nursing diagnoses may lead the way for the development of such schemes in a nursing framework. Although much work has yet to be done, this trend will greatly affect the evolution of standards and criteria.

## INCREASED ATTENTION TO RESEARCH METHODOLOGY

The controversy is spelled out in the literature as well as in actual practice: Is there a difference between evaluation and research? Bloch suggested that " 'evaluation' and 'evaluation research' be conceptualized as a continuum with varying degrees of scientific rigor. . . . The schema, however, is a continuum rather than a dichotomy and emphasis should be given to degree of rigor rather than absence or presence of rigor."[4] Hegyvary stated from experience in various institutions that, "on the basis of qualitative data, the population of evaluators constitutes its own continuum."[5] At one end of the continuum, evaluators are concerned with the use of research methodology; at the other, they are involved in quality assurance for the express purpose of achieving the standards of accrediting bodies.

The concept of evaluation and research on a continuum of scientific rigor is more widely accepted by nurses than ever before. Perhaps the real issue for discussion is at what point on that continuum should hospital quality assurance programs focus. Obviously, not all evaluations in nursing care can or should be equally rigorous. The trend for the future, however, is to incorporate better research design, thereby yielding more valid results upon which decisions can be based.

Several developments are promoting this evolution. Nurse-researchers are increasingly available to those involved in quality assurance activities in practice settings. This availability can be seen in many forms, such as research positions in nursing departments or liaison roles with researchers in university settings. Consultation services with research centers, expert nurses, and even nonnurse experts in the research process are becoming more common. This trend is greatly improving the quality of evaluation.

Along with researcher availability, many practicing nurses have better education and experience in the use of the research process. The concept of research not only is much less foreign, but also is often incorporated into daily practice activities. This suggests that evaluators more easily understand various important aspects of study methodologies and that nurses are better able to relate to and value the process. This development is happening currently and is likely to continue in view of the incorporation of research courses into undergraduate and graduate curricula. It is also strongly affected by the growing research activity being carried out in practice settings.

More and more tested instruments for use in evaluating nursing care are being published. The value of these instruments is greatly dependent on the standards of practice in the institution considering their use, the conceptual framework around which they were developed, and the objectives of the evaluation. They can provide, however, a head start in the development and execution of a more scientific study.

The increasing emphasis on the use of the quality assurance process for problem resolution and decision making also promotes increased rigor in evaluation activities. In the past, the quality of nursing care was sometimes studied simply to demonstrate that someone had addressed the issue. Standards of accrediting bodies have changed, however, so that problem resolution must now be demonstrated. In order to do this, data from studies must be valid. Because quality assurance activities can be expensive in terms of time and money, both of which are limited resources in many institutions, it behooves those involved to obtain the best possible product for their efforts.

The process of incorporating increased rigor into evaluations in institutions has begun. The aforementioned developments in practice, as well as economics and public policy, suggest that the process will continue.

## CHANGES IN GOVERNMENT AND ACCREDITING BODY REGULATIONS

In *Nursing: A Social Policy Statement,* the American Nurses' Association stated, "It is logical to anticipate that the 1980's will be a decade of increasing regulations with regard to the quantity, costs and quality of health care."[6] It is difficult to dispute this statement. In the 1980s, changes in legislation will dramatically change the health care system. Spiraling health care costs have already precipitated many changes intended to identify a way of providing adequate quality of care at a lower cost.

Health care professionals must seek new ways to provide the highest possible quality of care in the most cost-effective manner. This may require a change in the focus of care, as well as a reevaluation of current methods of care delivery. Mechanisms used in measurement and quality assurance will be increasingly important in evaluating this endeavor.

It is unrealistic to discuss quality assurance in hospitals without acknowledging the impact of the regulations of accrediting bodies, such as the Joint Commission on Accreditation of Hospitals. Recommendations and changes in guidelines made by these accrediting bodies have probably had a greater effect on quality assurance programs in hospitals than any other single factor. This will hold true, particularly in light of the effect of accreditation on health care reimbursement. Therefore, changes introduced through accrediting bodies will play a major part in directing the future path of quality assurance.

## INCREASED NEED FOR AND AVAILABILITY OF COMPUTERS

Increasing accountability and responsibilty in professional nursing today requires the nurse to handle more information than ever before. Because no individual can remember, process, and appropriately channel all those data consistently, computerization has become common. It is unusual today to find hospitals that do not use computers for at least some function.

Recently, nursing departments have begun to use computers to assist the practicing nurse in the day-to-day delivery of care. This phenomenon has taken many forms, based on the type of equipment used, the computer programs developed, and the creativity of the user. Computers may be used to display standards, criteria, policies, procedures, or other guidelines for practice; they may also be used to facilitate documentation, data retrieval, and communication with other departments. Miller and Berry suggested that computers are most helpful in studying quality of care "when a large amount of data of any nature must be handled, when complicated computational analysis is needed or when simple but repetitive computations must be performed."[7]

The possibilities for the use of computers for quality assurance activities in hospitals are incredible. Large numbers of variables can easily be investigated in evaluation studies. For example, patient achievement of outcomes can be related to relevant issues such as staffing, patient census, and acuity of care on the nursing unit. These data may be currently available, but it may be too time-consuming to retrieve them manually. The depth of information, therefore, can be increased.

Obviously, computers do not automatically solve problems; they are only as good as those who use them. Because the initial expense is always significant, they must be carefully selected to meet the needs of the agency. Preparation of the staff is also time-consuming and costly. Most nurses have limited familiarity with computers and their use; therefore, consultants may be needed to direct and assist the nurses at first. These consultants must ensure that the systems promoted have the capacity to meet the increasing needs of quality assurance activities.

## THE EVOLVING ROLE OF THE NURSE

One of the more recent and most powerful influences on the evolution of nursing practice is *Nursing: A Social Policy Statement,* developed by the American Nurses' Association. This statement not only defines nursing, but also addresses the scope of nursing practice and specialization in nursing practice. The initial part of the statement, however, deals with the social context of nursing; here, the American Nurses' Association specifies the terms of nursing's contract with society:

> (1) establishing a code of ethics, (2) establishing standards of practice, (3) fostering development of nursing theory, derived from nursing research into those conditions that are the focus of practice, so as to explain observations and guide nursing actions, (4) establishing educational requirements for entry into practice, (5) developing certification processes for the profession, and (6) other developmental work directed toward making more specific nursing's accountability to society.[8-11]

There is no question that these terms emanate directly from a quality assurance framework. Several are even clearly identified steps in quality assurance models. If nurses, as professionals, continue to respond to this statement with action, it will magnify the importance of quality assurance activities and programming.

Those of us involved in health care carry the responsibility for the future of quality assurance. Through our use of the process and our vision for its future, we are molding the direction that it takes. Change and growth are difficult and sometimes painful, but they can always be seen as a challenge. Our commitment to quality care must clearly direct our energies.

## NOTES

1. Barbara W. Gallant and Audrey M. McLane, "Outcome Criteria: A Process for Validation at the Unit Level," *Journal of Nursing Administration* 9, no. 2 (January 1979): 15–16.
2. American Nurses' Association, Congress for Nursing Practice, *A Plan for Implementation of the Standards of Nursing Practice* (Kansas City, MO: American Nurses' Association, 1975), p. 15.
3. Dorthea E. Orem, *Nursing: Concepts of Practice* (St. Louis, MO: McGraw-Hill, 1971).
4. Doris Bloch, "Interrelated Issues in Evaluation and Evaluation Research: A Researcher's Perspective," *Nursing Research* 29 (March/April 1980): 69.
5. Sue T. Hegyvary, "An Evaluator's Perspective," *Nursing Research* 29 (March/April 1980): 91.
6. American Nurses' Association, *Nursing: A Social Policy Statement* (Kansas City, MO: American Nurses' Association, 1980), p. 5.
7. Perry L. Miller and Theodore J. Berry, "Use of Computers in Studying Quality of Care," *Quality Review Bulletin* 6, no. 5 (May 1980): 25.
8. American Nurses' Association, *Code for Nurses with Interpretative Statements* (Kansas City, MO: American Nurses' Association, 1976).
9. American Nurses' Association, Congress for Nursing Practice, *Standards of Nursing Practice* (Kansas City, MO: American Nurses' Association, 1973).
10. American Nurses' Association, *Educational Preparation for Nurse Practitioners and Assistants to Nurses: A Position Paper* (Kansas City, MO: American Nurses' Association, 1965).
11. American Nurses' Association, *Nursing: A Social Policy Statement,* p. 8.

## REFERENCES

### Books

American Nurses' Association. *Educational Preparation for Nurse Practitioners and Assistants to Nurses: A Position Paper*. Kansas City, MO: American Nurses' Association, 1965.

American Nurses' Association, Congress for Nursing Practice. *Standards of Nursing Practice*. Kansas City, MO: American Nurses' Association, 1973.

American Nurses' Association, Congress for Nursing Practice. *A Plan for Implementation of the Standards of Nursing Practice*. Kansas City, MO: American Nurses' Association, 1975.

American Nurses' Association. *Code for Nurses with Interpretative Statements*. Kansas City, MO: American Nurses' Association, 1976.

American Nurses' Association. *Nursing: A Social Policy Statement*. Kansas City, MO: American Nurses' Association, 1980.

Orem, Dorthea E. *Nursing: Concepts of Practice*. St. Louis, MO: McGraw-Hill, 1971.

**Journals**

Bloch, Doris. "Interrelated Issues in Evaluation and Evaluation Research: A Researcher's Perspective." *Nursing Research* 29 (1980): 69–73.

Cook, Margo. "Selecting the Right Computer System." *Nursing Management* 13 (1982): 26–28.

Gallant, Barbara W., and McLane, Audrey M. "Outcome Criteria: A Process for Validation at the Unit Level." *Journal of Nursing Administration* 9, no. 1 (1979): 14–21.

Hartigan, Evelyn G., and Brown, Jean. "Computers." *Nursing Management* 13 (1982): 29–31.

Hegyvary, Sue T. "An Evaluator's Perspective." *Nursing Research* 29 (1980): 91–93.

Lang, Norma M., and Werley, Harriet H. "Evaluation Research: Assessment of Nursing Care." *Nursing Research* 29 (1980): 25–29.

Miller, Perry L., and Berry, Theodore J. "Use of Computers in Studying Quality of Care." *Quality Review Bulletin* 6, no. 5 (1980): 25–29.

Phaneuf, Maria C. "Future Direction for Evaluation and Evaluation Research in Health Care: The Nursing Perspective." *Nursing Research* 29 , no. 2 (1980): 123–126.

Romano, Carol; McCormack, Kathleen A.; and McNeely, Linda D. "Nursing Documentation: A Model for a Computerized Data Base." *Advances in Nursing Science* 4 (1982): 43–56.

van Maanen, Hanneke M. Th. "Improvement of Quality of Nursing Care: A Goal to Challenge in the Eighties." *Journal of Advanced Nursing* 6 (1981): 3–9.

Appendix A

# Select Evaluation Studies Completed at St. Michael Hospital

---

Table A–1 contains some of the evaluation studies completed at St. Michaei Hospital since January, 1980.

**Table A–1** Evaluation Studies at St. Michael Hospital

| *Topic* | *Objective* | *Comments* |
|---|---|---|
| Discharge instruction in the emergency department | To assess the knowledge of patients regarding wound care 24–48 hours postdischarge from the emergency department<br>To assess the effectiveness of the teaching sheet with reinforcement<br>To enhance community public relations | Joint audit with medical staff. RNs phoned patients 24–48 hours after discharge. Two attempts were made; one on day shift and one on P.M. shift ($N = 63$). |
| Completion of Operating Room assessment record | To determine adherence to four criteria identified as having low compliance on previous audit | Records of all patients treated in OR in one week were examined ($N = 144$). |
| Intraoperative care of patients receiving local anesthesia | To determine recording of blood pressure, pulse, and respiratory rate preoperatively, intraoperatively, and postoperatively, as well as every 15–30 minutes after administration of the medication<br>To set standards of care | Records of patients receiving local anesthesia, excluding those assisted by an anesthesiologist or nurse-anesthetist, were examined ($N = 84$). Recordings of blood pressure, pulse, and respiratory rate preoperatively, intraoperatively and postoperatively were examined. Consistently found more compliant was the one room with an automatic blood pressure monitor machine. Manual measurement cannot reasonably be expected with the timing of cases as is practiced. The information justified ordering more machines. |
| Transportation of patients from Post Anesthesia Recovery Room | To determine preparedness of units to receive surgical patients<br>To determine availability of the unit nurse to assist with transfer of patient from cart to bed and then receive report | The head nurse used the information in planning the next budget. |

**Table A–1** continued

| *Topic* | *Objective* | *Comments* |
|---|---|---|
| | To determine the time spent waiting for the elevator | |
| | To obtain information as basis for changing charges | |
| Administration of quinidine preparations | To determine whether giving quinidine preparations with food decreases diarrhea, nausea, vomiting, and other gastrointestinal symptoms | Two groups of 10 each were examined; Group A received quinidine without special attention to food administration, and Group B received each dose of quinidine with food. As the nurses administered medication, they recorded what was administered to the patient. |
| Patient environment review | To identify whether patient rooms met established criteria for remaining tidy and uncluttered | Thirty-seven patient rooms on nine separate days were evaluated. |
| | To identify whether there is a difference in tidiness and cluttering dependent on the shift | |
| | To introduce quality assurance process to licensed practical nurses and nursing assistants | |
| Knowledge of patients with myocardial infarction regarding illness and therapy | To determine patient's knowledge of myocardial infarction prior to transfer from cardiac care unit | Interviews using a pilot-tested guide were conducted ($N=11$). Studied the evening before or morning of transfer from cardiac care unit. |
| Nursing diagnosis used on a unit | To determine a list of nursing diagnoses used in cardiac care unit | Retrospective review according to six criteria ($N=41$). |
| | To assess statement of each diagnosis with regard to predetermined parameters | |

**Table A–1** continued

| *Topic* | *Objective* | *Comments* |
|---|---|---|
| Revision of Gambro AK–10 checklist | To update sequence and completeness of the checklist used by RNs in preparing machine (hemodialysis) | Subcommittee of a unit Quality Assurance Committee revised and brought the information back to the unit Quality Assurance Committee. |
| Closure of nursing record in case of death of a patient in intensive care unit | To determine whether guidelines for closure of nursing record were being followed consistently | Retrospective audit ($N=9$). |
| Completion of transfer status and discharge summary in intensive care unit | To determine if guidelines for transfer status and discharge summary are documented | The charts of all patients who were discharged and the first 20 patients who were transferred were examined ($N=29$). It was found that guidelines for documenting transfer status and discharge summary differed significantly from the policy on charting. |
| Newborn record used in observation nursery | To evaluate completion of newborn record used in observation nursery<br>To evaluate accuracy of the documentation | A convenience sample was chosen over 3 weeks, included 21 criteria ($N=20$). |
| Oral medications among dialysis patients | To evaluate tools used to document oral medications<br>To determine consistency in use of the form<br>To evaluate documentation of medications given predialysis, intradialysis, and postdialysis | Records of 38 patients receiving 329 medications were examined ($N=38$). All the patients were seen in one month. Physician order sheet, medication record, medication Kardex, and medication cards were examined. |
| Documentation as a reflection of nursing care plan | To determine if charting reflects carrying out of nursing orders<br>To determine if recording reflects an evaluation of nursing orders | Data collected before implementation of Problem Oriented Nursing Records so that a comparison can be done later. |
| Baseline data documentation on children 0–10 years | To determine frequency of measuring admission baseline data, e.g., height, weight, and blood pressure | Convenience sample ($N=30$). Looked at nursing data base and vital sign flow sheet within 24 hours of admission. |

**Table A–1** continued

| *Topic* | *Objective* | *Comments* |
|---|---|---|
| Nursing data base in intensive care unit | To determine if nursing data base is completed<br>To determine what information is most frequently completed and what is not | Looked at all direct admissions to intensive care unit during one month. Tool had 43 items in checklist form ($N=13$). |
| Admission weights | To determine if weights were taken within 24 hours of admission<br>To determine if weight was recorded in appropriate place | Records of successive patients admitted to one unit were examined ($N=50$). |
| Circulation, movement, and sensation checks on patients with long bone fracture admitted to the emergency department | To assess documentation of circulation, movement, and sensation<br>To obtain baseline of practice | Unit clerk recorded hospital number of consecutive patients admitted to the emergency department with long bone fracture ($N=36$). |
| Normal newborn discharge outcomes | To determine documentation of three criteria on normal newborn | Retrospective study ($N=30$). |
| Fever control in children brought to the emergency department | To determine knowledge of parent/guardian bringing children less than 16 years of age<br>To determine correctness of temperature-taking ability of parent/guardian | Concurrent study. Parents interviewed by a structured questionnaire on knowledge of temperature taking. They were asked to demonstrate taking a temperature ($N=21$). As a result of the study, thermometers were made available for purchase. |
| Types of teaching done for child with bronchial asthma | To determine teaching done according to seven parameters | Retrospective chart audit ($N=14$). |
| Use of form, Patient Teaching Record | To determine if Patient Teaching Record is used<br>To identify whether documentation is factual, concise, and measurable | Retrospective audit ($N=25$). |

**Table A–1** continued

| *Topic* | *Objective* | *Comments* |
|---|---|---|
| Newborn bath demonstration | To identify areas of inconsistency in information given to families during a bath demonstration | Concurrent observation of bath demonstration by RNs according to 25 criteria ($N=14$). |
| Patient teaching on postpartum unit | To determine<br>a. number of RNs involved in teaching<br>b. number of days teaching was done<br>c. number of days in hospital<br>d. shift main teacher usually worked<br>e. percentage of teaching done by primary nurse | Retrospective chart audit. Patient Teaching Record was examined ($N=30$). |
| Labeling of IV bags and tubing in intensive care unit | To determine if<br>a. IV bag is labeled according to policy<br>b. IV tubing dated according to policy<br>c. IV fluids are run as scheduled<br>d. alarm and cassette are in proper position<br>e. site care recorded at designated times | Data collected on three different days at the beginning of each shift ($N=20$). Thirty-one IV bags on IMEDs and forty-one minibags, flush systems and keep open IVs. |
| Tracheostomy site care | To determine compliance with procedure for tracheostomy changing times<br><br>To obtain baseline on recording use of Providine iodine solution or Neosporin ointment | Retrospective audit ($N=20$). |
| Process and outcome criteria for children having Harrington rod insertion for treatment of scoliosis | To determine compliance with care parameters outlined in standard nursing care plan, e.g., physical assessment, patient/parent knowledge and psychological well-being | Retrospective audit, ages 1–18 years ($N=9$). |

**Table A–1** continued

| *Topic* | *Objective* | *Comments* |
|---|---|---|
| Interpretation of EKG rhythm strips | To determine presence of rhythm strips for each shift<br>To determine accuracy of measurements of rate, PR interval and QRS interval | Retrospective audit (*N*=5) with 35 strips. Strips from last 48 hours analyzed by members of Quality Assurance Committee. |
| Neurological assessment in the emergency department | To determine whether neurological flow sheet is being used to assess patients with neurological deficits<br>To determine whether a parameter is defined on the neurological flow sheet are being documented | Retrospective audit (*N*=34). Clinical coordinator nurse determined which patients had possible neurological deficits. |
| Marking of lead placement for 12–lead EKG | To determine compliance with policy of marking chest with surgical marker<br>To enhance standardization for subsequent 12–lead EKG | Observation type study (*N*=59). Nurse performing A.M. EKG responded to three questions regarding presence, visibility, and accuracy of the markings. |
| Documentation of intravenous and intramuscular medication for hemodialysis patients | To evaluate forms used for documentation of medication before, during, and after dialysis | Accurate recording is important to ensure safety of patient. Forms can facilitate documentation. |
| Dialysate bottle labeling | To document that dialysate bottles are labeled correctly, e.g., patient name, date and time started, name of bottle, and RN's initials | Observation at specific times on both shifts by two data collectors. |
| EKG strips in intensive care unit | To determine if EKG strips are done according to policy<br>To determine accuracy of measurements and interpretation | Concurrent records of seven patients for the last 48 hours were examined. |

**Table A–1** continued

| *Topic* | *Objective* | *Comments* |
|---|---|---|
| Alarm validation on telemetry unit before and after placement of telemetry technicians | To determine the efficiency of monitor technicians with alarm validation | Alarm histories were collected from the computer for three days on three shifts prior to use of the technician. One month later alarm histories were again collected for the same length of time. Found significant increase in the number of alarms validated. |
| Patients extubated in Post Anesthesia Recovery Unit | To determine compliance with five criteria prior to extubation | Retrospective chart review ($N=34$). |
| EKG | To determine if electrodes are placed correctly<br>To determine if lead placement is identified on the rhythm strip | Concurrent observation. Data collected on evening shift and documentation reviewed from previous shift. |
| Eye-injured patients seen in the emergency department | To determine if visual acuity test done<br>To determine if patient was instructed in follow-up care | Retrospective audit ($N=58$). Admission clerk listed 65 consecutive admissions of eye-injured patients. |
| Temperature monitoring of postoperative major surgical patients | To determine compliance with temperature-taking policy for 36 hours postoperatively | Retrospective audit ($N=20$). |
| Estimating gestational age | To determine accuracy in assessing hair, ears, nipple, breast tissue, genitalia, and sole creases | Observation of RNs by clinical nurse specialist and committee member |
| Intake and output | To assess current practice in monitoring intake and output<br>To refine the categories of patients whom RNs judge require intake and output measurement | Retrospective review on three consecutive Wednesdays. Six data collectors looked at nine patients each to make determinations. ($N = 54$) |

# Index


A

Abdellah, F.G., 5-6, 7
Accountability, 38, 40, 45, 46, 71-76
  decentralization of, 92
Adams, D.L., 124
Ager, J.W., 10
American Hospital Association, 17, 159-160
American Nurses' Association (ANA), 6, 18, 72, 82, 225
  Committee on Nursing Service, 16
  Congress for Nursing Practice, 17, 45, 55, 90
American Society of Superintendents of Training Schools for Nurses, 4
Anderson, B.E., 9, 96
Anonymity, 137, 147, 174, 200
Assessing, 5-6
Attendance at meetings, 62, 63, 65
Attitudes, 138, 142, 143-144
Audit
  definition of, 95
  focus of, 192
  joint, 192
  parallel, 192
  system, 8-10, 16, 18, 175
  *See also* Multidisciplinary audit; Retrospective chart audit
Autonomy, 46, 191

B

Bailey, J.T., 51-52
Bain, R.J., 95-96
Bath demonstration, 165, *166*
Beliefs, 143
Berry, T.J., 225
Blair, E.M., 178
Bloch, D., 207, 222

C

Caldwell, G.B., 144
Cardiac rehabilitation, knowledge of, 138, *139*


*Note:* Pages appearing in italics indicate entries found in artwork.

Cardiopulmonary resuscitation (CPR), 138, *140-141*
Carnevali, D.L., 6
Carrieri, V., 6
Carter, J.H., 193
Causal relationships, 122
Chavasse, J., 144
Christensen, P.J., 6
Claus, K.E., 51-52
Climate, 74-75
Commitment, 42, 62, 64, 65
Compliance. *See* Standards, compliance with
Computerization, 224-225
Concealment, 159, 160, 162
Concurrent document review, 111-120
  advantages of, 117, 119
  disadvantages of, 117, 119
  examples of, 111-117
Confidentiality, 137, 160
Controlling, 72
Convalescence, perception of, 164
Corrective action, 72, 73, 87, 90-91
Cost-effectiveness, 40, 46, 74, 89, 119, 211, 224
Criteria, 221-222
  formulation of, 81, 97-98
  identification of, 86
  lack of, 87
  limited number of, 200
  for multidisciplinary audit, 195-198
  outcome, 17, 79-80, 98, 222
  patient-centered, 196, 197, 200
  process, 17, 79, 98
  refinement of, 89
  sets, 96-97, 125
  structure, 4, 16, 79, 98
  validity of, 7

**D**

Daeffler, R.J., 176
Data analysis, 90, 100, 152, 217
Data collection, 77-220
  accuracy of, 121
  combined techniques in, 171-189
  concurrent, 88
  retrospective, 88
Data summary sheet, 32, *35*, *36*
Decision to change, 52-53
Delphi technique, 144
Demographic data, 143
Diary method, 148-149
Direct questioning, 124
Discharge instructions, 128, 130, *131*
Discriminating, 6
Dock, L.L., 4
Documentation, 88
  aids to, 102, 107
  flow sheets for, 113
  knowledge as determinant of, 102, 107
  presence of, 183, 184
  systems, 74
Donabedian, A., 9, 42, 97
Dunn, M.A., 162

**E**

Eddy, L., 200
Eldridge, A., 5
Electrocardiogram (ECG), 115
Elms, R.R., 164
Encoding, 157
Evaluation, 5-16
  definition of, 205-208
  empirical, 6
  instruments, 6-16
  in nursing process, 5-6
  research, 206-207
  research-based, 6-16
  study, 18
Evaluation study report, 32-34

**F**

Feedback, 51, *52*, 63, 67-68, 117, 137, 152, 195

Feelings, 144-145
Fever control in children, 178, *179*
Finer, H., 7
Flanagan, L., 4
Flow sheets, 102, 113
Frankel, M., 143
Froebe, D.J., 95-96

## G

Gallant, B.W., 222
Gibson, J.R., 71
Goal, 71
Goldstein, W.Z., 192
Gortner, S.R., 40
Griffith, J.W., 6
Groenjes-Finke, J.M., 125-126, *128*

## H

Halo effect, 147
Hansen, M., 144
Harmon, C.A., 144
Harrington rod insertion. *See* Scoliosis
Havighurst, R.J., 124
Hawthorne effect, 158, 175, 184
Health care practices, 146
Hegedus, K.S., 177
Hegyvary, S.T., 222
Horn, B.J., 12-14
Hover, J., 125, 144
Hungler, B., 157, 158, 159

## I

Implementing, 5-6
In-dwelling catheters, 166-167
Incident reports, 143
Information systems, 72, 74
Input, 51, *52*
  evaluation, 210-212
Intake and output, 112, 113, 178-179, *180*
Interobserver reliability, 14
InterQual, 17
Intervention, 159
Interview, 121-135, 161, 174
  biased data and, 122, 123, 174
  cost of, 123, 174
  definition of, 121
  limitations of, 121-123, 174
  and memory, 122
  semistructured, 124, 125
  strengths of, 121-123
  structured, 124, 125, 174
  by telephone, 125-126, *128*, 130
  training for, 122, 123
  types of, 124, 174
  unstructured, 124
Iowa Nurse Utilization Study, 7-8
Ivancevich, J.M., 71

## J

Jackson, B.S., 159
Job descriptions, 74
Johnson, A., 195
Johnson, J., 143
Joint Commission on Accreditation of Hospitals (JCAH), 17, 85, 95, 96

## K

Kakosh, M., 7, 8
Kent, L.A., 177
Knowledge, testing of, 137-138, 144, 146
Knowles, L.N., 5
Knudson, M., 191, 193, 196
Kovner, A.R., 181
Kulpa, J., 197

## L

Lambertsen, E., 16
Lang, N.M., 4, 16-17, 55, 57, 79
Langford, T., 39

Larson, E., 177
Lavandero, R., 144
Leadership style, 62-63
Legislation, 224
Lesnik, M.J., 9, 96
Life Satisfaction Index, 124
Lindeman, C., 207
Little, D.E., 6
Loftland, J., 121

## M

McCarthy, D., 182
McClure, M.L., 40
McGuire, R.L., 16
McLane, A.M., 222
Management, process of, 71-72
Marram, G., 176, 183
Marriner, A., 6
Mayers, M.G., 79, 80, 82, 97
Medication knowledge test, 125, *126-127*
Miller, P., 124
Miller, P.L., 225
Mission, 71
Motivation, 62, 63, 65
Multiple choice questions, 150
Multidisciplinary audit, 191-203
  advantages of, 200
  committee, 194-195
  criteria, 195-198
  definition of, 191
  disadvantages of, 200
  follow-up on, 199
  purpose of, 192-193
  staff support for, 103
Munley, M.J., 161-162
Myocardial infarction, knowledge of, 130, *132-133*

## N

Needs assessment, 210, *211*
Negentropy, 51
Neugarten, B.L., 124
Neurological assessments in emergency department, 102, *103-104*
Nightingale, F., 3-4
Norby, R.B., 79
Nurse observation, 10
Nurse Practice Acts, 9
Nurse, role of, 34, 36-37, 225
Nursing, as a profession, 5
Nursing care
  evaluation of, 16-18, 161-162
  monitoring of, 40
Nursing care plan, 111
  criteria for evaluation of, 111, *112*
Nursing diagnoses, 115, 185-186
Nursing management, 181
Nursing Practice Council, 29, 37, 38
Nursing procedures. *See* Professional Practitioner Rating Tool
Nursing process, 5-6
Nursing resources, utilization of, 181
Nursing schools, 4
Nursing standards of American Nurses' Association, 6
Nursing supervisors, 67, 181

## O

Objectives, 71-72
  weighting of, 14
Observation, 157-169, 174-175
  biases of observer, 158
  definition of, 157, 158
  length of, 158
  limitations of, 158-159, 175
  of patient, 16
  strengths of, 157-158, 174
Observer
  biases, 158
  presence of, 158
  role of, 159-160
Operational definition, 207
Opinion survey, 144
Orem, D.E., 12-13, 222
Organizing, 72

Output, 51, *52*

## P

Pachano, A., 143
Pardee, G., 41
Patient care
  evaluation, 177-179
  trends, 107
Patient census, 15
Patient dependency, 123
Patient history, 122
Patient observation, 16
Patient records, 9, 11
Patient satisfaction, 143-144
Patient teaching record, 113-115, *116*
Patient welfare, 8
Pearsall, M., 181
Peer review, 198, 199
Peripheral intravenous site care, 163
Personal facts. *See* Demographic data
Phaneuf Audit, 8-9, 17, 96
Pilot test, 89, 150, 183, 197-198, 217
Planning, 5-6, 71-72
Polit, D., 157, 158, 159
Postoperative convalescence, 164
Practice-related problems, 31
Preoperative teaching, 100-102, 127-128, *129-130*
Primary nursing, 15, 176-177, 181-186
  definition of, 183
  evaluation tool, 182, *188-189*
Prioritization, 85-86, 144
Privacy, 160
Problem identification, 32, 61, 65, 85
Problem-oriented record, 6, 115, 117, *118*
Problem-solving process, 5, 51-52
Process evaluation, 212
Professional Practitioner Rating Tool, 162-163
Professional Standards Review Organization (PSRO), 15, 16, 17, 18
Professionalism, 17
Program evaluation, 205-220
  CIPP model of, 210, 213
  context, 210
  dissemination of changes, 218-219
  formative model, 213
  levels of study variables, 214-216
  methodology of, 209-213
  plan implementation, 216-217
  purpose of, 214
  and quality assurance, 208-209
  summative model, 213
Provocation, 157

## Q

Quality, 41-42
Quality assurance
  American Nurses' Association model of, 29, 79-80, 222
  definition of, 42-43
  evolution of, 3-28
  in industry, 43-45
  and management functions, 72-74
  models, 17, 79-82
  process, 79-93
  and program evaluation, 208-209, 214-218
  responsibility for, 45-46
  trends in, 221-227
  unit-based. *See* Unit-based quality assurance system
Quality Assurance Committee (QAC), 29, 31-37, 41
  activity development, *60*
  chairperson of, 34, 59
  head nurse's role in, 34, 36
  project development, 53-59
  reports, 67-68
  responsibilities of, 59
  staff nurse's role in, 36-37
  structure of, 31
Quality Assurance Coordinating Committee (QACC), 29, 37-38
Quality circles, 43-45
Quality of care, 10

Quality Patient Care Scale (Qual PACs), 10-12, 15, 17, 160-161
  and Slater Scale, *11*
Questionnaires, 137-155, 174
  close-ended (fixed alternative), 147-148
  construction of, 147-151, 174
  cost of, 146, 174
  as data collection tool, 146-147
  distribution of, 152
  nonrespondent impact, 142-146, 152
  objective, 124, 174
  open-ended, 124-125, 148-149
  program evaluation by, 144, *145*
  rate of return, 147
  respondent impact, 137-142, 152
  revision of, 150

## R

Reactivity, 158, 160, 162
Recall, 157
Recording, 157
Recovery room behavior, 164
Reevaluation, 82, 91
Regulations, 224
Reiter, F., 7, 8
Reliability, 150, *151*
  inter-rater, 159, 198, 200
  intrarater, 159
Reports, 91-92
Research process, 61, 73, 223
Research techniques, *172-173*, 222-224
Retrospective chart audit, 38, 67, 95-109
  clinical examples of, 100-107
  problems in, 104, 107
  sample, *99*
Reviewer bias, 117, 147
Rhode, M.A., 125-126, *128*
Routhier, R.W., 177
Rush Medicus Nursing Process Methodology, 14-16
Russell, D.A., 124

## S

Sample size, 88, 117, 146, 161
Sansam, P.G., 181
Schifalacqua, M., 182
Schmadl, J.C., 42-43
Scientific method, 6
Scientific rigor, 207-208, 223
Scoliosis, 102, 104, *105-106*, 107
Selected Attribute Variable Evaluation (SAVE), 12
Selection, 157
Self-care, 12-13, 222
Sell, H., 192
Shadowing technique, 10
Sinclair, C., 143
Sitzman, J., 6
Skocir, M.A., 182
Slater Scale, 10, 15, 17, 160-161
  and Qual Pacs, *11*
Sniff, D., 115
Social-psychological variables, 123
Spinal-cord injured patients, 210-212
Staffing, 15
  increased, 7-8
Standards, 72, 74, 82-84, 216, 221-222
  compliance with, 61-62, 64, 98
  definition of, 82
  evolution of, 3-5
  lack of, 87
  nursing, 3-5
Stewart, D.S., 161
Strand, N., 117
Stress, 66, 125, 138, 142
Structure criteria. *See* Criteria, structure
Study development, 87-89
Swain, M.A., 12-14
Sweeney, J., 193
Systems approach, 51-69

## T

Tan, M.W., 195, 196-197, 198, 200
Taylor, P., 143-144

Technical competence, 41
Throughput, 51, 52
Timeliness, 88
Tobin, S.S., 124
Trussel, P., 117
Trust, 85

## U

Unit-based quality assurance system
  activities of committee, 63, 65-66
  benefits of, 39-40
  v. centralized system, 39-41
  checklist for implementation, *54-55*
  committees, 62-66
  effectiveness of, 62-65
  implementation of, 51-69
  limitations of, 40-41
  model, 29, *30*, 38-39
  nursing department and, 64-65, 66
  organizational flow chart, 55, 57
  relationship to committee, 63-66
  systems model for, 51-69, 82-92
  time line for implementation, *56*
Unit size, 15
Utilization review, 192, 194

## V

Validity, 150, *151*
Values, identification of, 79
Vanagunas, A., 85

## W

Walsh, M.B., 5
Wandelt, M.A., 10, 15, 161
Watson, A.B., 79
Weed, L.L., 6
Weick, K., 157, 158
Westbook, L., 100
Wisconsin Regional Medical Program (WRMP), 17
Wound care, knowledge of, 128, 130, *131*

## Y

Yura, H., 5

## Z

Zimmer, M.J., 16-17, 125, 144

# About the Editors

Patricia S. Schroeder, M.S.N., R.N., is a clinical nurse specialist in oncology nursing at St. Michael Hospital in Milwaukee, Wisconsin. Currently, she chairs the Quality Assurance Coordinating Committee. She played an active role in the development and implementation of the unit-based concept for nursing quality assurance in 1980, and she has chaired several Unit Quality Assurance Committees. Ms. Schroeder has served in a leadership capacity in quality assurance at several area hospitals. She has spoken on monitoring the quality of nursing care and has acted as a consultant on the topic in various parts of the United States.

Regina M. Maibusch, S.S.S.F., M.S., R.N., is a clinical nurse specialist in respiratory care at St. Michael Hospital in Milwaukee, Wisconsin. Sr. Maibusch currently chairs two Unit Quality Assurance Committees and is active on the Quality Assurance Coordinating Committee. Sr. Maibusch's interest in quality assurance dates back to 1973 when she participated in a workshop on quality assurance and outcome criteria that was sponsored by the Wisconsin Nurses' Association. When she took her position at St. Michael Hospital in 1975, she was appointed chairperson of the Quality Assurance Steering Committee of the Nursing Department. Sr. Maibusch also served as a group facilitator for the regional workshops on quality assurance sponsored by the American Nurses' Association in 1976.

# About the Contributors

MARY A. BRUSKEWITZ, M.S., R.N., is a clinical nurse specialist in diabetes nursing at St. Michael Hospital in Milwaukee, Wisconsin.

NANCY MANSHEIM FORMELLA, M.S.N., R.N., is Director of Nursing Research and Education at St. Mary's Hospital in Rochester, Minnesota.

MICHELE M. MALIN, M.S.N., R.N., is a maternal-child clinical nurse specialist at St. Michael Hospital in Milwaukee, Wisconsin.

ROBIN READING MOSLETH, M.S., R.N., is a former clinical nurse specialist in mental health at St. Michael Hospital in Milwaukee, Wisconsin, and is currently in private practice in the Milwaukee area.

SUEELLEN PINKERTON, PH.D., R.N., is Vice President of Patient Services at St. Michael Hospital in Milwaukee, Wisconsin, and Clinical Associate Professor of Nursing at the University of Wisconsin-Milwaukee School of Nursing.

MARGARET A. SKOCIR, M.S.N., R.N., is Director of Nursing of the medical/critical care units at St. Michael Hospital in Milwaukee, Wisconsin.

MARGARET A. SMERLINSKI, M.S., R.N., is a clinical nurse specialist in gerontology at St. Michael Hospital in Milwaukee, Wisconsin.

PEGGY L. WAGNER, M.S.N., R.N., is a clinical nurse specialist in cardiovascular nursing at St. Michael Hospital in Milwaukee, Wisconsin.

CATHLEEN K. WILSON, M.S.N., R.N., Ph.D. Candidate, Marquette University, is Director of Nursing of Specialty Practice and Evaluation at St. Michael Hospital in Milwaukee, Wisconsin.